'The Oracle. The Ceefax. The undisputed King (Rollo) of TV knowledge.'

RAE EARL

'*The Golden Age of Children's TV* is The Golden Book of Children's TV: lovingly researched and beautifully written. If you love kids TV, you'll love this beautifully researched book. And the gossip . . . from *Rainbow* beef to how the Clangers lost their tails to Jimi Hendrix and the Test Card . . . Golden stuff. Take a year off because this golden book will make you want to watch all your favourite TV shows again. And again. So much delicious TV gossip!'

BIBI LYNCH

'Tim Worthington has forgotten more about children's television than you or I will ever know. Fortunately, he's taken the time to share what he remembers with us . . .'

MITCH BENN

'The wisdom of Florence, the mystery of Dylan and the fun of Zebedee are combined in Tim Worthington's hugely entertaining and charming book. Sincere love, detailed memory and deep knowledge make this dive into children's TV history truly joyful and satisfying.'

SAMIRA AHMED

'I love this book. It's important, invaluable and oddly emotional. Our favourites are there, of course, *Bagpuss*, *Swap Shop*, *Play School*, but Tim Worthington, with unabashed obsession, picks apart three decades of the nation's teatimes, Saturday mornings and long summer breaks. I gasped at every paragraph over some forgotten cartoon or madcap quiz show he'd unearthed. Worthington's approach is never plain cosy nostalgia; he thinks deeply about why some ideas sparked joy, some fell flat and where they sat in the social landscape. His encyclopaedic knowledge of Britain in the '70s, '80s and '90s – as seen in his books and wonderful podcast – always leaves me worrying a freak thunderbolt might strike him down, as his brain alone stores so many obscure memories of our collective youth. More than a national treasure, he's a human pop-culture database.'

GRACE DENT

'Tim Worthington is the acknowledged master of this kind of entertaining but authoritative media scholarship. He goes beyond the clip show cliches to plot a line through the arched window from *Zokko* to *Swap Shop*, taking in Supermarionation, folk horror for tinies and *Junior Showtime*, all with verve and readability.'

STUART MACONIE

'Featuring trillions of kids telly shows like an infinite *Radio Times*, this is a fabulous deep dive into an Atlantis of nostalgia.'

DAVID QUANTICK

Endpaper Picture Credits: Fremantle Media/Shutterstock (George, Bungle, Zippy and Geoffrey Hayes);
ITV/Shutterstock (Emu, Hartley Hare);
Pictorial Press Ltd / Alamy Stock Photo (Roobarb and Custard);
Hugh Threlfall / Alamy Stock Photo (The Clangers);
Pictorial Press Ltd / Alamy Stock Photo (Grange Hill, Captain Scarlet);
Moviestore Collection Ltd / Alamy Stock Photo (The Magic Roundabout, Captain Pugwash, Andy Pandy);
Allstar Picture Library Limited / Alamy Stock Photo (Thunderbirds);
Science Museum Group (Play School)

THE GOLDEN AGE OF CHILDREN'S TV

THE GOLDEN AGE OF CHILDREN'S TV

A Nostalgic Look at Brilliant British Telly!

TIM WORTHINGTON

Black&White

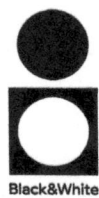
Black&White

First published in the UK in 2024 by
Black & White Publishing Ltd
Nautical House, 104 Commercial Street, Edinburgh, EH6 6NF

A division of Bonnier Books UK
4th Floor, Victoria House, Bloomsbury Square, London, WC1B 4DA
Owned by Bonnier Books
Sveavägen 56, Stockholm, Sweden

Copyright © Tim Worthington 2024

All rights reserved.
No part of this publication may be reproduced,
stored or transmitted in any form by any means, electronic,
mechanical, photocopying or otherwise, without the
prior written permission of the publisher.

The right of Tim Worthington to be identified as Author of this
work has been asserted by him in accordance with the
Copyright, Designs and Patents Act, 1988.

The publisher has made every reasonable effort to contact copyright holders
of images in the picture section. Any errors are inadvertent and anyone who
for any reason has not been contacted is invited to write to the publisher so
that a full acknowledgement can be made in subsequent editions of this work.

A CIP catalogue record for this book is available from the British Library.

ISBN: 978 1 78530 640 2

1 3 5 7 9 10 8 6 4 2

Typeset by Data Connection
Printed and bound in Great Britain by Clays Ltd, Elcograf S.p.A.

www.blackandwhitepublishing.com

For Sylvia Anderson, and the better world
she showed us how to believe in.

'Home, Milady?' – *'Home, Parker.'*

Contents

'Once Upon a Time, Not So Long Ago . . .'   xi
'Now We Return You to the Test Card and Some Music . . .'   xv

1	Saturday (and Sunday) Mornings	1
2	Supermarionation	27
3	Pre-school and Storytelling	55
4	Smallfilms	85
Interlude 1	Watch It!	109
5	Lunchtime Shows	111
6	Comedy	153
7	Factual Shows	183
8	Variety and Game Shows	213
Interlude 2	Look Out for Look-In	235
9	Drama	237
10	Imports	273
11	That's Not a Children's Programme	299
12	The Pre-news Slot	325

Acknowledgements   343

'Once Upon a Time, Not So Long Ago...'

Do you live in a town? Was it Bill or was it Ben? Who is the Phantom Flan Flinger? Can you guess what is in it today? Why don't you just switch off your television set and go out and do something less boring instead?

These are questions that will be familiar to anyone who grew up during the golden age of children's television – from the launch of ITV in the mid-fifties through to ITV and the BBC reorganising their output with an eye on the future in the mid-eighties . . . which itself gave the next generation a whole new golden age of their own. There is something magical about those early years, though – and it's a story that never seems to get told properly. It's 'remember this' and 'laugh at that', but you'll rarely find any conversation about the background to the best-loved shows, or how they evolved and took the rest of television along with them as everything literally went from black and white into colour. You won't find anyone musing on *why* we remember some shows and not others, and how that might or might not relate to what was going on in our everyday lives – all the way from the rise of Margaret Thatcher to the ongoing dispute over the best Cornetto flavour – or, more importantly, what it was actually like to watch them at the time.

THE GOLDEN AGE OF CHILDREN'S TV

It's a time that saw the messy rise of Saturday morning television, a craze for near-the-knuckle spooky serials that often rivalled the X-certificate horror and crime thrillers of the day, the mind-bending influence of pop art and psychedelia, and the Tracy Brothers jetting off in a blast of visual effects that had Hollywood producers seething with envy. It gave the world characters such as Bagpuss, Cheggers, Hamble, Metal Mickey, Marmalade Atkins and Zebedee – and throughout it all, the *Blue Peter* team kept on painting over brand labels on washing-up-liquid bottles as though they hadn't noticed a single thing.

This isn't a definitive history because . . . well, how could it be? The stories of some shows, timeslots and genres need to be simplified in order to be interesting or readable. Some of them start and end at wildly different times and even in wildly different decades, whether due to changing tastes or abruptly changed schedules. There are certain individuals we can't really mention now – although the fact that leaving them out of a history of children's television appears to make little to no difference whatsoever is perhaps comment enough in itself. There are also a great many programmes that can't be mentioned for more innocent, practical and straightforward reasons – there just isn't that much interesting to say about them, and there just isn't the room. I am more than aware that some readers might feel a little put out at a long-forgotten favourite not even being namechecked, but you have to draw the line somewhere and if that line falls this side of *The Country Boy* (BBC, 1989), then frankly, that's just how it has to be. If it helps, you have no idea of how much of a wrench it was to leave out *Spider-Man and His Amazing Friends* (NBC, 1981–83). You can also take it as read that if I haven't mentioned widely shared rumours about, say, obscene innuendo character names or coded symbolism for drug use, then that's because they aren't true, and even affording a passing mention to them would take up valuable space better spent on *Hey, It's My Birthday Too!* (ITV, 1981).

As for the idea of a 'golden age', well, that's just convenient shorthand for a time when television was established enough to know what it was doing but still new enough to be changing and evolving all the time, and children's television generally happened to be where they tried those experiments first. Despite what below-the-line commenters on newspaper features might have to say, children's television did not stop being any good after you stopped watching; you only have to look at *The Demon Headmaster* (BBC, 1996–98), *Dick & Dom in da Bungalow* (BBC, 2002–06), *The Sarah Jane Adventures* (BBC, 2007–11), *Dani's House* (BBC, 2008–12), *Horrible Histories* (2009–14), *Knight School* (ITV, 1997–98), *Miami 7* (BBC, 1999), *Harry's Mad* (ITV, 1993–96), *The Ink Thief* (ITV, 1994), *Archer's Goon* (BBC, 1991) or *Bob the Builder* (BBC, 1999–2004), or ask any of your friends with young children or grandchildren how often *Justin's House* (BBC, 2011–) gets mentioned in a single day for evidence enough of that. There's always, however, a show that seems to start off something, and another that marks a transition to something else, and what happens between those points always produces a story worth telling.

There's something exciting and compelling about the early years of children's television, which is why the shows keep on getting remembered – well, apart from *Oscar the Rabbit in Rubbidge* (ITV, 1978) – and why in so many cases the characters keep coming back. So join me for the story of the shows that we all still quote from even now. It may be baggy, and a bit loose at the seams, but hopefully Emily will love it. THIS IS WHAT THEY WANT!!!!!!!

'Now We Return You to the Test Card, and Some Music...'

In 1967, BBC engineer George Hersee was asked to design the new Test Card. A regular sight in a long-lost world, the Test Card went out when a television transmitter was active but no programmes were being shown, and the point of it was to allow broadcast technicians to check that everything was working correctly and that the picture wasn't bending off slightly towards the top left. The BBC's very first Test Card in 1937 was essentially not much more than a circle; they got a little more sophisticated as television itself also did. With the launch of a full colour service fast approaching in the late sixties, however, something a little different was called for.

With the luminance signal covered by the mysterious grids and shades around the outside of the Test Card, something was needed to represent the chrominance – or in other words, the colour – and George set about devising a suitable photographic central image. Feeling that an adult model would quickly begin to look dated as fashions changed, he instead called on the services of his nine-year-old daughter Carole and her homemade gaudy toy clown, Bubbles. Depicting the unlikely duo as combatants locked in a motionless game of noughts and crosses, with an 'X' handily marking the centre of the broadcast image, BBC Test Card F was first seen on BBC2 on the BBC's very first day of colour broadcasting – 2 July 1967.

With its notorious accompaniment consisting either of wonkily saxophoned – and, crucially, not commercially available – big band music or a continuous 440Hz tone, BBC Test Card F was seen on both channels for hours on end every single day; even conservative estimates put its total screentime in excess of sixty thousand hours. Although its usage decreased as technology advanced and broadcasting hours expanded until it was quietly retired in 1997, Test Card F became an important and much-loved visual icon and later a valuable branding symbol for the BBC, and it continues to appear in new incarnations even today. Its hapless ITV counterpart, the decidedly less visually arresting IBA Colour Bars, could only look on in envy. More importantly, for viewers Test Card F was a literal if inadvertent everyday part of their television watching, especially when they were waiting for children's programmes to start at lunchtimes, in the afternoons or on a Saturday morning. Whether you were excitedly trying to see if you could spot them 'move', marching up and down the lounge to that uncalled for jazzed-up version of 'Michael (Row the Boat Ashore)', or hiding behind the door and refusing to come into the room until that girl who looked like she knew something you didn't and her sinister accomplice had gone, you just didn't get children's television without BBC Test Card F. Well, on the BBC at least. Nobody's ever confessed to having been frightened of the Colour Bars, but let's face it, someone almost certainly was.

Test Card F wasn't actual children's television, though. That was made up of hundreds upon thousands of programmes, some memorable and others... not so memorable; some as unchanging as Carole's fashions, and some more with-it and up to the minute than a Milan catwalk; some silly and some serious; some funny and some

'NOW WE RETURN YOU TO THE TEST CARD, AND SOME MUSIC'

factual; and a huge number that were both of those at once – and so much more besides. So if you want to come with us – yes, we will be calling at Chigley – for a look back at the best, the worst, the most terrifying and the ones where you neither knew nor cared what was going on but still watched them anyway, then switch on your set and let's go. As long as The Test Card Girl isn't still on . . .

1

Saturday (and Sunday) Mornings

'Today Is Saturday: Watch And Smile'

There might well have been no school on Saturdays, unless you were *very* unlucky, but for a long time there was nothing to do in the mornings apart from help your parents – as if you had any other option – with the big shop. Even as you struggled across the multi-storey car park with the plastic bag handles digging harder and harder into your hands, at least you knew that you weren't missing much on television.

Sundays were much the same only without the plastic bags, as you were ushered to and from church – or your own chosen place of worship, although there was scant acknowledgement of any other faiths back then – with the usual round of gossip in the name of the Lord thrown in for good measure. Then it was a case of sitting around waiting to be told to 'help' set the table, and usually being told off for your efforts too, and the idea of being allowed to watch anything – if there was anything on at all – was so sacrilegious as to be almost amusing. Television might have shouted 'The weekend starts here!' at teenagers, but anyone younger was still expected to act like smaller versions of their parents, and if they weren't having any fun first thing in the morning then why should you? Then they *did* start to broadcast children's programmes on Saturday and

Sunday mornings, and a generation began to hope against hope that the sermon would finish or the automated barrier would lift just those crucial couple of minutes earlier.

Saturday may well have later become Tiswas Day, but for many years, all that you'd find first thing on either ITV or the BBC were a handful of cartoons and repeats of old imported Western serials. Saturday morning cinema clubs with their combination of fun and games and rowdy mass singalongs were still a popular tradition well into the sixties, and there seemed little point in mounting any small-screen challenge to their popularity. That all changed, however, thanks to a young BBC producer with a love of studio trickery, a knack for finding unusual bits of film and a deft way with knockabout humour. Following an experiment with *Whoosh!* (BBC, 1968) – a mid-morning Saturday show devised by *Play School* directors Cynthia Felgate and Peter Ridsdale Scott which set presenters Rick Jones, Jonathan Collins and Dawn MacDonald (a ballet dancer who had landed the job after sending in a photo of herself pulling a daft face) riddles to solve in a wacky studio set full of mechanical props and physical puzzles – their *Play School* colleague Paul Ciani was encouraged to make use of his offbeat ideas for a new show with more of a magazine or, to be more accurate, comic format. Driven by huge splurges of psychedelic graphics and bleeping cosmic sounds courtesy of the BBC Radiophonic Workshop, the result was way wilder than anything that you might have seen at your local ABC cinema.

Presented by a talking pinball machine, the jaw-dropping *Zokko!* (BBC, 1968–70) featured animated lolly-stick gags, surreal short films set to current pop hits, live acrobats, illusionists and variety acts, pop songs 'performed' by a psychedelic steampunk organ made out of bubbling test tubes and the gripping weekly comic strip serials 'Skayn and the Moon People' and 'Susan Starr of the Circus'. Deeply strange even by the standards of the late sixties, it's perhaps telling that *Zokko!* was considered worthy of parody by the BBC's absurdist *Monty Python's Flying Circus*. Undeterred at having out-weirded Michael Palin and company, Paul Ciani would go on to continue his Saturday morning experiments with the studio-based show *Ed and Zed!* (BBC, 1970), presented by Radio 1 DJ Ed Stewart and a pop-crazy Brummie-accented robot, and *Outa-Space!* (BBC, 1973), 'hosted' by the control panel of a sentient space probe studying life on Earth, with added scientific profiles of dinosaurs and the cliffhanging adventures of 'Vidar and the Ice Monster'. Somewhere between BBC2's late-night abstract arts shows and the jarring cut-up style of painters like Peter Blake and Pauline Boty, Ciani's 'electronic comics', as *Radio Times* routinely described them, were essentially television for children who'd enjoyed *Sgt. Pepper's Lonely Hearts Club Band* less for the music than for the funny cut-out Beatle figures on the inner sleeve.

What was missing from all of these efforts, however, was the sense of excitement and vibrancy that comes from live broadcasting with an element of viewer interactivity. Both of these arrived with *Tiswas* (ITV, 1974–82) and Noel Edmonds' *Multi-Coloured Swap Shop* (BBC, 1976–82), but their respective rivalry-fuelled successes were something that both broadcasters struggled to repeat. Despite boasting modishly New Wave synthpop-styled theme songs by chart stars Hazel O'Connor and Yazoo, *Get Set for Summer* (BBC, 1981–83) – later shortened to *Get Set* – had precious little in the way of post-punk energy and placed far too much emphasis on improving outdoor activities and painstakingly intricate hobbies, and while presenter Mark Curry had some of Noel Edmonds' affinity with the format, co-host Peter Powell, recruited from BBC Radio 1's afternoon show, never seemed quite at home. Joined by *Swap Shop*'s Maggie Philbin and later by Bucks Fizz vocalist Cheryl Baker, Mark stayed on board for *The Saturday Picture Show* (BBC, 1984–86), which was more or less exactly the same programme.

Although even *Swap Shop* itself was scarcely ever wild and anarchic, the BBC seemed oddly determined to play it as safely as possible with all of its putative successors, although one genuine oddity from this era deserves particular mention. 'Presented' by the BBC's Teletext service Ceefax, *Buzzfax* (BBC, 1981) linked episodes of *Battle of the Planets*, *The Monkees*, the Edgar Kennedy short *The Big Beef* and *Dinky Dog* with a set of quizzes and puzzles that interacted with that week's issue of *Radio Times*, in an up-to-the-minute experiment that must have felt every bit as exciting and futuristic to the audience as their first ever go on a Commodore VIC-20. Although it was never considered worthy of further development, *Buzzfax* certainly proved to be more of a talking point with the few who actually saw it than *Get Set for Summer* ever managed. Rarely has a programme seemed more ahead of its time while also being – at least technologically – very much of its time.

Over on ITV, the other regional broadcasters understandably wanted in on the ATV *Tiswas* action, but all too often made the mistake of just trying to borrow the format outright without allowing their own take on it to develop organically, and in what were often turbulent times dominated by domestic financial and social unrest, mass industrial action and mainland terrorism campaigns, they just couldn't capture that same feeling of escapism. London Weekend Television (LWT) weighed in with *Our Show* (ITV, 1977–78), presented by a team of stage school children which included sitcom-star-in-waiting Nicholas Lyndhurst and future *Grange Hill* regulars Susan Tully and Melissa Wilkes, with the latter's unfortunate mispronunciation of 'Grand Prix' becoming much beloved of 'blooper' shows and providing the show's only moment of lasting infamy. *Our Show*'s adult-hosted replacement, *The Saturday Morning Show* (ITV, 1979), had little to distinguish it, and the same went for Yorkshire's *Saturday Scene* (ITV, 1977), Grampian's *Scene On Saturday* (ITV, 1977) and Tyne Tees' remarkably impact-free trilogy of little-remembered efforts, *Saturday Morning* (ITV, 1977), *Lynn's Look-In* (ITV, 1978) and *Saturday Shake Up* (ITV, 1979–80). In retrospect, it's little wonder that so many children were clamouring for the much talked-about exploits of Chris Tarrant and company to find their way to their region too.

Southern would score more of a success with *The Saturday Banana* (ITV, 1978–89), an intentionally different take on the *Tiswas* setup energetically hosted by Bill Oddie of comedy troupe The Goodies – who inevitably contributed one of his funked-up compositions as a theme song – with assistance from Susan Tully and a jovial boogieing robot called Metal Mickey. The rowdy studio audience members were treated as active co-conspirators in the comic mayhem rather than just cheering bystanders, while guests were obliged to arrive on the set via a huge banana-shaped slide. A measure of *The Saturday Banana*'s popularity can arguably be found in the fact that Metal Mickey went on to star in his own primetime ITV sitcom; a luxury that was never afforded to the chair from Steve Jones' links in *The Saturday Morning Show*.

Meanwhile, Granada literally pushed the boat out with *The Mersey Pirate* (ITV, 1979), a technically ambitious and arguably ill-advised effort relayed live from the deck of Mersey-crossing ferry the *Royal Iris*, ostensibly crewed by local comic talent including Duggie Brown and Billy Butler. It featured a barrage of one-liners from a buccaneering Frank Carson and, posing as a pair of stowaways forever scheming to get their faces on television, Andrew Schofield and Ray Kingsley as Franny Scully and his hard-of-thinking associate Mooey, a pair of scouse teenage tearaways recently introduced to BBC viewers in Alan Bleasdale's 'Play for Today', *Scully's New Year's Eve*. Unpredictable weather conditions inevitably made *The Mersey Pirate*'s voyage a turbulent one, and although it had the good fortune to coincide with the emergence of a new crop of much-vaunted chart-bound Merseyside bands such as Echo and the Bunnymen and The Teardrop Explodes – many of whom performed on the show, and with whom it shared a good deal of an attitude of the North 'fighting back' with fun and creativity during tight economic times – it was with no small irony eventually washed overboard by a huge strike which took ITV off air for several months in 1979.

Not to be deterred, Granada returned the following year very much on dry land with *Fun Factory* (ITV, 1980), set in a gag-manufacturing plant with Billy Butler back on board as the factory manager, assisted by a then little-known Jeremy Beadle and yet another robot – Kurt Knobbler, the creation of inveterate eccentric inventor Wilf Lunn. *Fun Factory* was also notable for using Billy Joel's instrumental 'Root Beer Rag' as its theme music; inspired by this, Butler used it to introduce his BBC Radio Merseyside game show *Hold Your Plums* for decades to come.

While *The Mersey Pirate* and *The Saturday Banana* were arguably the most distinguished of the legions of *Swap Shop* and *Tiswas* imitators, the others were never without their merits – even *Saturday Shake Up* – but they all lacked one common factor. They were attempts to emulate two shows that had independently started with minimal resources and even less available budget almost while nobody was looking, revelled in a low-tech approach to the high-tech equipment around them, and were driven by hosts who were every bit as much personalities as presenters and visibly excited at the prospect of doing a fun and entertaining show where anything could happen and they would just have to deal with it. The rivals, on the other hand, were essentially copying what they were doing, even with all of the pop music and cartoons in the same places, only in a more polite and restrained manner that was never going to convince the audience. Younger viewers wanted fun on a Saturday morning, and in a rapidly changing age when pocket calculators and synthesisers were bringing the future into the pop charts and even the otherwise stuffy confines of school, the actual type of fun they were looking for was itself changing. Poor old *Lynn's Look-In* would never really have a look in.

Sundays, on the other hand, were for quiet contemplation and anything but entertainment. Everybody knew it and nobody dared challenge it, and with a legal requirement to carry a specific number of hours of religiously inclined programming on the seventh day — the 'God Slot' remained rigorously in force right through to the late nineties — television on a Sunday was devoid enough of laughs and action as it was. The early mornings, however, were more or less a biblical desert, especially for any younger viewers who had somehow been allowed to tune in. The BBC's sole concession to any children who had very quietly got up before church was showing one of the gentler and more cerebral 'Watch with Mother' shows, such as *Camberwick Green* or *Mary, Mungo and Midge*, before it devoted time to the more important business of adult education and minority-audience magazine shows.

Over on ITV, most of the morning was taken up with live broadcasts of church services in *Morning Worship* — with the odd crackly and washed-out imported educational cartoon like *The Wonderful Stories of Professor Kitzel* or *Max, the 2000-Year-Old Mouse* or 'look at life' documentary series like *Land of the Lapps* – before the more heavyweight business of rural affairs and topical discussion got underway, and putting out the cutlery for the Sunday roast suddenly began to look like a more entertaining use of your time, after all. In a decade that saw the Church under increasing pressure to wrestle with difficult social and cultural questions in rapidly changing times, at least some things about the Lord's Day stayed the same. That was until August 1976, when BBC1 introduced younger viewers to the sparky and irreverent teenagers collectively known as *The Sunday Gang* (BBC, 1976–81).

With the debatable assistance of a wonky-looking, tape-spool-faced homemade computer and a screeching 'Scottish' puppet mouse called Mackintosh, *The Sunday Gang* met in their book- and gadget-festooned clubhouse hidden away somewhere in BBC Television Centre each week to retell Bible stories in a manner that might actually conceivably entertain and hold some everyday resonance for children, unlike boring old church. Fresh-faced, outdoorsy, go-getter type J.D. (John Dryden), gobby inquisitive loudmouth Teena (Tina Heath), hard-of-thinking but public-spirited country girl Dodo (Jill Shakespeare) and wacky cap-askew inventor Boff (Glen Stuart) were usually to be found, as the rowdy theme song had it, knocking on doors, opening windows and taking a trip through God's creation declaring to all and sundry that they were The! Sun! Day! Gang! with a close harmony invitation to come with them today. Which may not sound like much now but in its original context, for anyone who had otherwise spent the Sabbath being expected to be seen and not heard, it was pretty much as revolutionary as *Tiswas*. Unlike *Tiswas*, however, *The Sunday Gang* was also very much seen as wholesome and improving – if cacophonous – fun, and won awards by the collection plateful, with Tina Heath eventually being nabbed as a new *Blue Peter* presenter; she was replaced for the final series by Alison Christie-Murray as the more artily romantic Ally.

The BBC did make a couple of attempts at repeating the success of *The Sunday Gang*, although none of them ever proved quite as popular as Teena's demands to know why nobody 'elped that poor geezer until the Samaritan come along. Presented by Dana, who had become a familiar face on the BBC's religiously inclined output after winning the Eurovision Song Contest aged eighteen in 1970, the appropriately titled *Wake Up Sunday* (BBC, 1979–82) put the singing and clapping very much to the fore, with musical assistance from chart-troubling St. Winifred's School Choir and acoustic duo The Brown Brothers. Comic relief was provided by inserts featuring tales of stranded alien Wizzy, as written, drawn and narrated by humourist Willie Rushton, but for those who were not fully in tune with the exuberant exhortations to sing along, it could prove something of an exhausting experience.

Less successfully, *Knock Knock* (BBC, 1982–85) employed a rotating cast of singers and storytellers, including Chris Serle, Christopher Lillicrap, Lesley Judd, Janet Ellis, Adrian Hedley and David Yip, to take their own individual look at 'God's wide world' courtesy of a slightly too straight-faced electronic theme tune and a wall crammed with visual effects-derived doors. Perhaps reflecting the fact that times were changing even for the most sacred time of the week, *Knock Knock*'s replacement, *Umbrella* (BBC, 1986–90), adopted a more daytime television-styled approach complete with a chirpy synth-samba theme and multi-faith umbrella-hoisting animated titles, as Bryan Murray and Susan Leong ran off-the-wall features on Sikh schoolgirl five-a-side football teams and Christian volunteer groups entertaining the crowds in Manchester's shopping centres.

Despite the sort of stories that *Umbrella* covered being more or less a staple of their early remit to represent minority audiences, Channel 4 did not really bother with Sunday – or indeed Saturday – mornings at first; in fact, they did not show *anything* before midday on weekends until late in 1986. Fellow new kid on the television block TV-am, however, was only too keen to catch the eye of early risers, many of whom were still high on the excitement of the launch of a brand-new television service and were pretty much a guaranteed captive audience. Ostensibly presented by the animated – and occasionally scattered around the set in in static plastic form – 'Breakfast Beans', *Rub-A-Dub-Tub* (ITV, 1983–84) was very much aimed at much younger viewers and made up of imported animations, such as Poland's *Teddy Drop Ear* and Canada's *Curious George*, and nature rambles with Dick King-Smith, all linked by stories and songs provided by conveniently available TV-am presenters including Anne Diamond, Nick Owen and Lizzie Webb, as well as the more unexpected likes of humourist Ivor Cutler and disco dancing champion Downtown Julie Brown. Its chirpier replacement, *Are You Awake Yet?* (ITV, 1983–86), took place in a corner of the regular TV-am set and paired assorted presenters with voluble red-haired 'naughty boy' puppet Terry and animated stories from *Wimpole Village*, introduced by a naggingly cloying and extremely long theme song urging viewers to 'Open up those AY-AY eyes!' No doubt to the relief of parents who were in no mood to comply with the jauntily sung request, whether in the alternating versions performed by a female session singer or by Terry, the format was eventually reworked as *Cue George!* (ITV, 1986–89), with hugely likeable weather presenter Georgey Spanswick promoted to introducing stories and reading out viewers' letters with only a short instrumental 'sting' to leak through the walls while everyone else was still in bed.

SATURDAY (AND SUNDAY) MORNINGS

TV-am's undisputed if self-proclaimed 'superstar', Roland Rat, was perhaps wisely never let loose on Sunday mornings, although he was never really sighted on Saturdays either. He was, though, the 'superstar' of the school holidays. TV-am did, however, try its hand at a couple of Saturday morning shows aimed at slightly older and more fashion- and technology-conscious viewers, which ironically came closer to recapturing the spirit of *Tiswas* and *Swap Shop* than any of the shows intended as direct replacements for them had. Introduced by yet another Yazoo theme song, 'Electronic' *Data Run* (ITV, 1983–84) uploaded Edwina Lawrie and her all-knowing computer sidekick Edwin into a silicon chip-era world of entertainment news presented as 'Files' and blocks of 'Data'. With an emphasis on pop videos and accompanying interviews rather than performances, the fact that very few actual big names were prepared to get up that early in the morning lent *Data Run* a more 'alternative' sheen, and indeed it is probably best remembered now for an unlikely but enthusiastic appearance by melancholy indie sensations The Smiths. Such was *Data Run*'s popularity that over the school holidays in 1983 it jumped into a weekday slot to become *Summer Run*, introduced by Timmy Mallett superimposed in front of a blurry cartoonish rendition of a seaside pier, with the theme music replaced by an opportunistically summery rewrite of Junior's 1982 hit, 'Mama Used to Say'.

Hosted by the quite possibly Max Headroom-inspired television-dwelling everyman 'A. Wally' – in other words comedian Adam Wide – *S.P.L.A.T.* (ITV, 1984) acronymically promised 'soap, puzzles, laughter and talent'. With his often abstract and satirical links providing the laughter, soap was catered for by 'No Adults Allowed', a running serial written and performed by its exclusively juvenile cast, which allowed for hefty snooks to be cocked at the popular adult drama stylings of the day. Puzzles came in the form of 'Crack It!', a relatively highbrow quiz show presented by James Baker, while talent primarily involved 'Charlie's Bus', a segment in which a double-decker full of children on their way to a fun day out were joined at a bus stop by a mystery pop star. Astonishingly, this once again included The Smiths, who accompanied a gang of kids to Kew Gardens – with Morrissey replying to one youngster's query over where they were headed for with, 'We're going mad!' – where they met up with Sandie Shaw for an impromptu rendition of 'Jeane'. Possibly a little too esoteric for its audience, *S.P.L.A.T.* only lasted for a couple of months, and while 'Charlie's Bus' may have claimed to be headed where there was no fuss as long as the sun is shining, it was very quickly called back to the depot.

TV-am's big Saturday morning success came with *S.P.L.A.T.*'s replacement. It was presented from a small but stylishly designed purpose-built set with modish graphics and – much like two other shows from not that long ago – incorporated both audience contributions and a lack of resources into the structure of the show itself. Variously hosted by Arabella Warner, James Baker, Tommy Boyd, Michaela Strachan and Timmy Mallet, its contents ranged from spelling competition 'Bonk'n'Boob' and talent contests incorporating a very early form of karaoke to rational assessments of popular spooky folk stories in the 'Ghosts, Monsters and Legends' slot, with live music from the often-surprising likes of Depeche Mode and The Housemartins. Driven by witty enthusiasm and a way with silly static caption cards, it proved so popular that it quickly inspired a spin-off for school holiday weekdays, invariably hosted by the seemingly indefatigable Mallett. It was called *Wide Awake Club* (ITV, 1984–89), or indeed *Wacaday* (ITV, 1985–92), and – much like *Zokko!* way back when – it pointed the way forwards for Saturday morning television. Although it still couldn't get you out of helping with the big shop.

'I Wanna Be a Winner'

Even if you didn't watch The News — and even if you just watched *John Craven's Newsround* — the seventies could be a very grim time to be growing up. In fact, you could very deliberately leave the actual news to the actual grown-ups but still find yourself all too aware of the clashes over rising oil prices, the waves of industrial disputes and the threats of factory and pit closures and mass redundancies, because there was simply no avoiding them when they led to power outages. Which they did, a lot. In the middle of the decade, however, two new shows began on Saturday mornings that offered two different yet similar kinds of escapism and fun, and they very quickly became close rivals — and what's more, both shows frequently involved fun and high jinks with the sort of technicians and behind-the-scenes workers that you might otherwise only have seen standing on picket lines on The News.

As with most of the other ITV regional broadcasters late in 1973, ATV Midlands' Saturday morning schedules were taken up by a formless assortment of Supermarionation repeats, Merrie Melodies shorts and old Tarzan movies. Some regions, like HTV and its spaceship-set *Orbit* (ITV, 1973–75) with scarcely convincing astro-technician Alan Taylor and squonking alien caterpillar puppet Chester, had their own in-vision presenters, but most plain didn't bother. The continuity announcer tasked with linking these disparate shows for the Birmingham area was Peter Tomlinson, already well known to viewers for on-air antics such as following late-night horror movies by clambering out from under his desk with a 'terrified' expression. One weekend, suspecting that the children watching were as bored by his links as he was, he began to experiment with incorporating off-the-wall competitions and prepared running jokes. What had started as a bit of fun quickly became a very serious prospect indeed; the interactivity and levity quickly caught on with an audience who were not used to seeing this kind of irreverence on a Saturday morning, and competition entries arrived by the sackful. The response was so overwhelming that, from the first Saturday of the new year, the timeslot was billed as a programme in its own right under the banner 'Today Is Saturday: Watch And Smile' – or *Tiswas*, for short.

A hit with its small but devoted audience from the off, *Tiswas* very soon began to demand more time and effort, and Tomlinson brought in two colleagues with a similar love of mischief and willingness to be sprayed with a soda siphon, John Asher and Chris Tarrant. Although the resources they had to hand could generously be described as less than minimal – Tarrant has often recalled that for more than one show they literally only had a chair to work with – the trio, soon expanded by the arrival of sports reporter Trevor East, were more than capable of creating comedy out of the most unlikely items and, crucially, knew enough about how the studio worked to indulge in a good amount of technical tomfoolery too, frequently opening the show by playing the ATV 'In Colour' ident in reverse. As *Tiswas* built up a loyal following, the presenters also built up spontaneously created in-jokes and running gags, the majority involving buckets of water and shaving-foam 'custard pies' in some capacity – and however the 'higher ups' at ATV may have felt about it, it was obvious that neither the show nor Tarrant's sense of comic invention in particular could be contained for long. *Tiswas* was clearly destined for bigger and better things. The only

SATURDAY (AND SUNDAY) MORNINGS

problem was that it was only seen in one ITV region – and it soon had competition.

Despite the earlier experiments with *Zokko!* and company, the BBC had mostly continued to fill Saturday mornings with repeats of Hanna-Barbera cartoons, silent movie shorts and black-and-white serials like *Champion the Wonder Horse*, which may have been moderately more highbrow than what could be found over on the various ITV regions but was hardly an alternative. In 1976, however, producer Rosemary Gill was tasked with devising a live magazine show to run for three hours on Saturday mornings. Astutely noting the potential in a huge untapped audience of children who wanted to exchange unwanted toys, books or other items that they had finished with in a pre-Internet world, Gill concluded that if carefully coordinated and combined with pop music, news and hobby items, outside broadcast segments and animated inserts, phone-in swapping could form the basis of an exciting and innovatively interactive show. It would, however, need a safe and capable pair of hands to anchor the show – and fortunately there was one close at hand and only too eager to get on board.

Noel Edmonds had arrived at BBC Radio 1 in 1969 and quickly became one of the station's most popular DJs, known as much for his inventive on-air pranks as for his keen interest in the pop charts and broadcast technology. In 1973 he had been promoted to the *Breakfast Show* – the station's undisputed star slot – and also won over a wider family audience with his quick-witted stints presenting *Top of the Pops* and, perhaps less expectedly, ballroom-based toe-tapping contest *Come Dancing*. It was another arguably even less expected engagement in 1975 that suggested there might well be more to Noel as a broadcaster. Broadcast live on Wednesday afternoons, *Z-Shed* (BBC, 1975) invited children to call in to discuss their concerns about homework, family disputes and current news events, with Noel on hand to offer advice and support with just the right balance of sympathy and wit. Finding the format as thrilling as it was dauntingly ambitious, Noel – himself a keen helicopter pilot and racing driver – was an ideal choice for a show that must have initially felt more like piloting a plane than talking to a camera.

The plans for the new Saturday morning show involved phoned-in swaps in the studio, along with live link-ups to in-person 'Swaporamas' at a different outdoor location each week, which meant a second similarly adept presenter was needed – and the perfect candidate came to the production team's attention entirely by chance. Already a popular teenage actor, the immensely likeable Keith Chegwin had written speculatively to the BBC Children's department to let them know that he had lots of ideas and would be happy to come in and discuss them; Rosemary Gill astutely deduced that this kind of cheek would make him ideal for marshalling large crowds of largely unsupervised children live on air. He also quickly established a dynamic rapport with Noel, who dubbed him 'Cheggers' and adopted a mutually lightly teasing older-brother role. Fresh from university, drama student Maggie Philbin had auditioned after seeing an advert in *The Stage* and was enlisted to help to navigate the telephone directory's worth of phone calls, and again brought a note of sibling rivalry to the presenter interactions, which eventually developed into a closer off-camera relationship with one colleague in particular; during a later live link-up, Cheggers proposed to her. The BBC's resident children's newsreader John Craven was ostensibly brought in to handle serious and factual segments, although his unflappable straight-man persona made him an inadvertent comic foil to Noel. There was even a non-existent fifth presenter, 'Eric', an unseen crewman who cued effects and lowered items onto the set at Noel's request, leading to a steady stream of letters from viewers who were convinced that they had spotted him. Even just as a team of presenters they were quite unlike anything that viewers were used to.

Shaking unsuspecting viewers awake with a rousing rocked-up theme tune from Mike Batt – the mastermind behind The Wombles' unlikely run of chart smashes – *Multi-Coloured Swap Shop* opened for business on 2 October 1976. It quickly proved itself to be worth getting up early for and began to attract big-name guests from the pop charts, the movie world, the comedy scene and beyond, with even huge and incredibly cool bands like Blondie more than happy to join in with the fun and bring along their own competition prizes. The excitement of swapping bright and gaudy toys live on television added a dash of colour, or indeed multi-colour, to what were often fairly drab days; and at a time when many households did not have much money to be splashing out on new toys and games when there were perfectly good ones sitting around unplayed with, it brought a glimmer of variety and freshness directly into the viewers' lives too. Edmonds' quick wit, easy manner with the young callers, willingness to bring the studio staff in on the action and show audiences around the 'workings' of television kept up the energy throughout each three-hour broadcast. He even gained a mechanical sidekick in the form of Posh Paws, an anagrammatically named purple dinosaur who sat at the edge of the desk and roared his approval and disapproval – it was difficult to tell – during the phone calls. Knowing that they would get a decent chance to promote their wares in front of an eager audience, celebrities from movie and pop stars to authors and illustrators queued up to chat with Noel and take viewers' calls, and *Swap Shop* was quickly given its own annual end-of-year awards show, wittily dubbed 'The Erics'. More like a day out than a morning spent sat at home watching television, *Swap Shop* — as it was routinely shortened to — was an immediate success and it was soon obvious that *Tiswas* would have to rise to this unanticipated challenge.

In September 1977, and much to Chris Tarrant's initial unease, it was all change at *Tiswas*. John Asher and Peter Tomlinson had left and Trevor East would also leave by the end of the year, and in their place came the equal parts glamorous and boisterous Sally James. Formerly the host of LWT's *Saturday Scene*, a not dissimilar strand to the earliest incarnation of *Tiswas* which mixed cartoons and serials with glamtastic pop interviews and performances, Sally immediately mucked in (literally) with Chris and established a double-act that was almost the antithesis of Noel and Cheggers' sense of confident control — while Sally and Chris were around, anything could happen, and if it didn't then they'd probably try to make it happen. They were joined by a suitably eccentric cast of comic talent who certainly knew what it was like to be on the receiving end of a custard pie. Formerly of sixties pop satirists The Scaffold, John Gorman introduced a series of idiosyncratic characters to liven up proceedings, including the officious yet lovelorn PC Plod and bath-dwelling chip-scoffer Smello. Ventriloquist Bob Carolgees introduced audiences to his uncouth sidekicks Charlie Monkey, Spit the Dog and Cough the Cat, as well as the intrepid Tarrant-underwhelming illusionist Houdi Elbow. Sylvester McCoy, an experienced children's television presenter and a member of situationist stage troupe The Ken Campbell Roadshow, flung himself around with a set-demolishing abandon that might well trouble today's health and safety guidelines.

The most significant discovery, however, was a teenage comic and impressionist named Lenny Henry. Tipped off about his potential

SATURDAY (AND SUNDAY) MORNINGS

by regular *Tiswas* guest Frank Carson, Chris Tarrant hired Lenny on the spot after seeing him slip down a staircase while making his entrance in a stage revue and get a huge laugh from the audience with his improvised reaction. Although his act initially consisted only of impressions, almost causing Tarrant to quietly drop him from the show after a couple of weeks, encouragement from the rest of the team saw Lenny refine his approach and concentrate on his more outlandish and adaptable caricatures who could become 'characters' in their own right, including botanist David Bellamy and his challenges with the letter 'r', newsreader Trevor McDonald – as 'Trevor McDoughnut' – who remained stonily unflappable while reading out dreadful pun headlines while being pelted with water and sporting ridiculously oversized glasses, and Benny Hawkins, the hapless woolly-hatted mechanic played by Paul Henry on the ITV soap opera *Crossroads*. Inevitably, he was frequently surprised live on air by the subjects of his impressions, who always seemed to take it – and the inevitable ensuing custard pie – in incredibly good humour. Lenny also introduced a few of his own comic creations including, most famously, Algernon Razzmatazz, an over-earnest Rastafarian with a hankering for condensed milk sandwiches and whose extremely elongated shout of 'ooo-kaaaaay' reverberated around an increasing number of playgrounds each Monday.

With rumours getting around that something was happening in the ATV region, HTV, Anglia, Granada, Border and Scottish Television amongst others began to show *Tiswas*, which was becoming so big that Chris had been persuaded to withdraw from his more sober broadcasting duties, as reading out a serious news story shortly before being seen with a bucket on his head was hardly good form. This elevated profile also had the good fortune to coincide with the rise of a strand of anarchic punk and ska bands who were only too happy to be pelted with Wunda Gloo in the name of plugging their latest single – although big conventional rock stars like Phil Collins were also clamouring to be invited on the show – and groups of tax inspectors, traffic wardens, Heavy Metal musicians and other public bêtes noires queued up to stand in a cage for no other purpose than to be repeatedly drenched with buckets of water.

An otherwise fairly disastrous attempt at a talent contest did nonetheless discover Matthew Butler, a five-year-old who sang an off-key rendition of 'Bright Eyes' in an oversized rabbit costume to inexplicably hilarious effect, and everyone in the studio was always on the lookout for the Phantom Flan Flinger, a mysterious hooded figure who regularly sneaked on set and delivered a surprise custard pie before making his – or her – getaway. It wasn't just punk rock's sounds that *Tiswas* embraced; the show increasingly took on a cheekily irreverent attitude towards public figures, the establishment and topical events, with teachers and civil servants willingly gunged for the entertainment of the hysterical audience, and Tarrant trying to stage a serious *Panorama*-style political interview with the Phantom Flan Flinger only to meet with the all too predictable 'aggressive response'. The hugely popular 'Compost Corner' segment seemed to have been devised purely as a means of seeing how many times Chris could be interrupted by the camera crew shouting the title back at him – and how much gunge could be flung – in four minutes of television. Meanwhile, having previously used suitably rowdy library music tracks, *Tiswas* also gained its own punchy theme song which boisterously declared that, 'Saturday is *Tiswas*, never a day to miss, 'cause Saturday is Tiswas Day!'

As the seventies drew on, more and more ITV regions began to show *Tiswas*, until it became a genuine national talking point. It's fair to say that Chris Tarrant's concerns about the new direction may have been slightly misplaced. And although most viewers at home probably just flipped between *Tiswas* and *Swap Shop* as and when the 'boring' bits arose, this marked the beginning of a long-standing rivalry between the two shows that frequently spilled out into – mostly – good-natured digs at each other across the airwaves. In a sense, if *Tiswas* was punk rock, then *Swap Shop* was more closely aligned to the sharper and more melodically and lyrically astute New Wave bands that had followed in their wake; something that was arguably only underlined by which acts tended to turn up singing their latest hit on which show. The difference between the two shows and their respective presenters could not have been more marked – while the cast of *Swap Shop* were frequently entrusted with more prestigious projects, including Bank Holiday variety spectacular *Rock Garden Party* (BBC, 1978), team quiz *Hobby Horse* (BBC, 1978) and early evening phone-in game show *Noel Edmonds' Lucky Numbers* (BBC, 1977–78), as well as Maggie and Keith co-hosting Radio 1's early Saturday morning programme *Playground*, the far wilder and messier *Tiswas* frequently found itself criticised by the Independent Broadcasting Authority (IBA), castigated by the tabloid press and even on one occasion berated by a group of GPs for a running joke that involved pretending to pull youngsters up by their ears. They even, in a sense, had rival 'mystery' figures, although who would win in a fight between the Phantom Flan Flinger and 'Eric' is a question that there is no real answer to.

Swap Shop and *Tiswas* both had their own distinct style and character; if you wanted quirky features about Noel test-driving a racing milk float or finding out how Ceefax worked, interspersed with the chance to call in and put your questions to Tom Baker or Kate Bush, you stayed with the BBC; if you wanted comic mayhem and pop stars with too much theatrical gunk in their faces to be able to answer questions properly then ITV was the one for you. There was one area, however, where *Swap Shop* unquestionably had the edge. *Tiswas* had originally developed around classic cartoon shorts and even as the show got bigger, this aspect barely changed, with the occasional Warner Bros. short or clip from a big budget blockbuster movie crammed often awkwardly into the chaos, and more of a big deal being made of the commercial breaks – or, as *Tiswas* had it, 'Telly Selly Time'. *Swap Shop* on the other hand – and as the *Radio Times* handily reminded potential viewers – was built around a regular schedule of inserts that appeared to have been carefully chosen to match the tone of the show, and which were introduced by Noel in a manner that at least suggested he was watching them as well. These included fondly remembered offbeat Hanna-Barbera efforts like *Hong Kong Phooey* and *Valley of the Dinosaurs*, while Trumptonshire creator Gordon Murray contributed a couple of comic shorts aimed at the slightly older audience – punning brother and sister double-act *Skip and Fuffy*, and the tongue-in-cheek musical folk tales of mythical people *The Gublins*. Some of these, it has to be said, were almost as popular with viewers as *Swap Shop* itself.

Staggeringly, the cross-channel rivalry even spilled into the pop charts. There had already been a number of *Tiswas*-related singles, including Algernon Razzmatazz's reggae-tinged 'The OK Song' and Sal, Chris and Trev cashing in on the popularity of fictitious dance craze 'The Dying Fly' – which basically involved lying on your back and waving your arms around in time to Leroy Anderson's 'The Typewriter' – when John Gorman came up with 'The Bucket of Water Song'. Credited to The Four Bucketeers and with an ode to the odour of 'Smello (The Incredible Stinking Man)' on the B-side, it climbed to number twenty-six in the charts in 1980. It led to the album *Tiswas Presents The Four Bucketeers* – which mixed sketch material with Matthew Butler singing 'Bright Eyes', Lenny Henry's David Bellamy singing 'Wuwal Wetweats' and Spit the Dog spitting 'Funky Spittin' Punk Dog' – and a full national tour of what was effectively an edition of *Tiswas* in front of a live audience.

Not to be outdone, and perhaps stung by The Four Bucketeers' appearance on *Top of the Pops* – where owing to safety concerns they were obliged to throw buckets of glitter rather than water – Noel set about engineering a hit of his own. Roping in New Wave singer-songwriter and regular *Swap Shop* guest B.A. Robertson, the presenters piled into a studio and 'I Wanna Be A Winner' was released under the moniker Brown Sauce in 1981, eventually reaching number fifteen. The title possibly revealed more about Noel's intentions than he may have envisaged.

The B-side of 'I Wanna Be A Winner' was 'Hello Hello', Robertson's *Swap Shop* theme that debuted in 1981, but the following year everything changed on both channels. Inspired by the reaction from the tour audiences and by the IBA's increasing pressure over what they could get away with in the timeslot, Chris Tarrant, Bob Carolgees, Lenny Henry and John Gorman all left *Tiswas* to present *O.T.T.* (ITV, 1982), a ramshackle late-night adult counterpart which gave early exposure to 'alternative' comedians such as Alexei Sayle while also featuring some notably less enlightened material. Adult viewers were not impressed, and their existing *Tiswas* audience weren't allowed to stay up for it, with the result that it returned as the more conventional *Saturday Stayback* (ITV, 1983) before disappearing completely. Sally James remained with *Tiswas* for one further series, joined by popular Independent Local Radio DJ Gordon Astley, comedian Fogwell Flax, diminutive actor David Rappaport and Den Hegarty, previously the bass vocalist in comedy doo-wop hitmakers Darts, but it was never quite the same and the show was cancelled at the end of the run, with the final edition going out on 3 April 1982.

Meanwhile, Noel Edmonds, who had kept up his Radio 1 show throughout *Swap Shop*'s run, had been offered a very different kind of 'adult' show by BBC1 – Saturday early evening live light entertainment primetime miscellany *The Late Late Breakfast Show* – and *Swap Shop* bowed out on a high on 27 March, just seven days before *Tiswas*. Their rivalry had even seen them vie to finish first, although arguably *Tiswas* should probably have concluded that bit sooner.

Both shows inevitably proved difficult to replace. The BBC just about managed to land on their feet with *Saturday Superstore* (BBC, 1982–87), which retained Maggie Philbin, Keith Chegwin, John Craven and B.A. Robertson and most of *Swap Shop*'s structure, stylings and contests, only with yet another zany Radio 1 presenter – Mike Read – as the nominal manager of a never entirely clearly defined 'department store' conceit.

ITV's massively hyped new flagship programme from Central (ATV's successor) was *The Saturday Show* (ITV, 1982–84), but the odds were stacked against it from the outset. Initially, presenters Tommy Boyd and Isla St Clair were to have been joined by the enormously popular professional wrestler Big Daddy, who pulled out very shortly ahead of the first broadcast; the hastily re-recorded theme song had very clearly been originally built around his catchphrase 'EA-SY!' The real problem, however, was that, presumably with the constant controversy surrounding *Tiswas* in mind, it was by some distance the blandest show to have appeared in the slot so far. Far from being punk or new wave, this was a middle-of-the-road rock band with one eye on selling a million albums on the brand-new Compact Disc format. An alarming amount of screentime was devoted to 'talented' children and unexciting wishes being granted, and it is telling that the only really widely remembered edition – aside from a brief attempt by Roland Rat to hijack 'The Raturday Show' – was one in which the puppets from Gerry Anderson's *Terrahawks* (ITV, 1983–86) visited the studio. This may even have had some bearing on what happened next; in a desperate bid to liven matters up, Tommy was paired with Bonnie Langford for a revamped version under the title *Saturday Starship* (ITV, 1984–85). Despite some decent sci-fi stylings and Bonnie's tireless attempts to get the audience up and dancing, it still failed to blast off into the stratosphere.

With a theme tune noticeably 'inspired' by Harold Faltermeyer's recent hit, 'Axel F', Granada's *TX* (ITV, 1985) purported to invite viewers 'inside' the transmission process, with relatively highbrow hosts Tony Slattery, Sue Robbie and Alison Dowling, and suitably esoteric guests including eccentric comics Stanley Unwin and Frank Sidebottom. It was possibly a little too sophisticated for its own good, and resident game show 'Knock Your Block Off' would spin off as a show in its own right and actually outlast *TX*. Meanwhile, viewers in the TVS region had been enjoying their own opt-out for several years already in the form of *Number 73* (ITV, 1982–88). Cleverly structured as a sitcom with Sandi Toksvig acting as the de facto matriarch of a boarding house full of young and enthusiastic – and usually not especially bright – tenants, and intentionally given a catchy and easily imitable rapid-fire theme song, it effortlessly succeeded where all of the other putative *Tiswas* replacements had failed, and eventually graduated to the entire ITV network and ensuing enormous popularity. However, the fact that it is now best remembered for inciting controversy with an ill-advised performance by Iggy Pop suggests that some of the lingering concerns over *Tiswas* still hadn't quite gone away.

Some producers were clearly keeping note of what didn't work as much as what did, though. Tyne Tees' *Get Fresh* (ITV, 1986–88) paired fashionable and down-to-earth presenters Gareth 'Gaz Top' Jones and Charlotte Hindle with slime-flinging alien puppet Gilbert and a chart-credible theme from Big Audio Dynamite, while *Saturday Superstore*'s replacement, *Going Live!* (BBC, 1987–93), which essentially updated the basic *Swap Shop* structure for what was to all intents and purposes a new technological era, debuted the following year. Both built successfully on elements of many of the above shows – and, with the literal dark times that had often formed an unwitting backdrop to *Tiswas* and *Swap Shop* now happily a distant memory, these new shows gave a whole new generation a Saturday morning rivalry of their own.

2
Supermarionation

'Stand by for action!'

On Wednesday 12 September 1962, John F. Kennedy – the thirty-fifth president of the United States of America – took to the stage at Rice Stadium in Houston, Texas, and told the world that before the decade was out, America would have put a man on the Moon. That same day, over in a small film studio in Slough, a husband-and-wife team of filmmakers were planning to put a man – or rather a puppet – underwater.

Kennedy's 'We choose to go to the Moon' speech was a decisive moment in the Space Race, and it defined geopolitical relations and scientific ambition for decades to come. More importantly, it also inspired a generation to wedge cardboard boxes on their heads and demand to be taken to your leader, dreaming of literally rocketing off and boldly going where no man has gone before. Gerry and Sylvia Anderson didn't just inspire a generation to dream of going into space – they also made them want to explore the ocean depths, rescue disaster victims, repel alien terror attacks and outwit spies in a quiet rural village. With a string of hits boasting special effects and model work that were the envy of the movie industry, Gerry and Sylvia aimed higher, further and faster than anyone else in children's television – and took an eager audience with them.

Active in the film industry since the early fifties, it wasn't until – fittingly – a couple of days after Russia had launched both the first artificial satellite, *Sputnik 1*, and the hapless first four-legged cosmonaut, Laika, into space that Gerry Anderson's career blast-off began. AP Films, a production company he had formed with Arthur Provis, had been engaged by writer Roberta Leigh to make a puppet series based on one of her characters, and *The Adventures of Twizzle* (ITV, 1957) made its debut on 13 November 1957; poor old Laika was purportedly still in orbit at the time. A discarded toy with extendable limbs, Twizzle and his odd-pawed cat Footso formed a community of do-gooders with an assortment of similarly unwanted playthings. The series was a success with its intended audience, but arguably had a more important legacy in terms of who it introduced Gerry to. Barry Gray, Vera Lynn's regular accompanist who had previously arranged some of Roberta's songs for her, was brought in as the musical director, while to help navigate the increased workload, AP Films had hired a secretary – Sylvia Thamm.

Following the success of *The Adventures of Twizzle*, AP Films again collaborated with Roberta Leigh on *Torchy the Battery Boy* (ITV, 1959), a not entirely dissimilar show about a lamp-headed poseable boy action figure created by toymaker Mr Bumbledrop, who uses his battery-powered luminant functionality to travel to Topsy Turvy Land, a psychedelic planet inhabited by toys confiscated from 'naughty' children. Although Gerry, as he later frequently recounted with no hint of diminishing disdain, was less than happy about having become a puppet filmmaker by default when he held loftier artistic ambitions, it was obvious even at this stage that he was determined to improve and innovate regardless of what he was working with. Although you would scarcely know it from the tinkly songs and cutesy puppets, *Torchy the Battery Boy* was a huge technological and creative leap forwards with more elaborate sets, more sophisticated puppets with less visible strings – Twizzle's had looked like they could support a suspension bridge – and even an early attempt at pyrotechnic effects. It may only have been a couple of carefully angled sparklers creating the illusion of Torchy's rocket taking off, but it was one small step in the right direction.

But Gerry and Sylvia still very much had their foot on some particularly sawdust-strewn ground for their next step. Following a difference of creative opinion with Roberta Leigh, AP Films had decided to go it alone in the exciting new world of puppet serials, and with Westerns still in vogue as the big pre-Space Race craze, they turned their attention to a certain frontier town where, as one of his frontier days-evoking songs made abundantly clear, anything can happen. Sherriff Tex Tucker kept a sharp-shootin' eye on law and order in *Four Feather Falls* (ITV, 1960); a task made slightly easier by the four magic feathers on his hat. A gift from Native American chief Kalamakooya as a reward for rescuing his son in the desert, the feathers allowed Two-Gun Tex – 'the smartest guy in town', according to the theme song – to fire his six-shooters just by thinking about it and afforded meaningful communication with his horse Rocky and dog Dusty. With the assistance of good ol' locals Ma Jones, Granpa Twink and Little Jake, Tex invariably won the day against the mine-looting and bank-robbing schemes of seemingly undissuadable local bandits Pedro and Fernando.

Unlike the earlier more or less entirely independent shows, *Four Feather Falls* – based on an idea by Barry Gray – was made for ITV in association with Granada, and it's fair to say that the additional budget was used more wisely than how Pedro and Fernando might have spent it. AP Films moved from their ad-hoc studios in residential manor Islet Park House to a converted warehouse on Slough

Trading Estate, and Sylvia, who had become increasingly involved on the production side, graduated to supervising on-set continuity. Barry Gray composed a set of songs very much in the country-tinged rock'n'roll style that was all over the hit parade at the time, and he enlisted real-life chart star Michael Holliday to provide Tex Tucker's singing voice; Tex's speaking voice was provided by a real-life television star, Nicholas Parsons, whose wife Denise Bryer had been a regular member of the voice cast since *The Adventures of Twizzle*. Perhaps most significantly, Gerry and his team had developed a system using practically invisible tungsten steel strings and an electromagnet concealed in the puppets that allowed them to appear to 'speak' in time to the pre-recorded dialogue. *Four Feather Falls* was a massive hit and inspired a huge volume of tie-in merchandise, to which Granada's puzzling response was that they did not see the need to make any more of it. They weren't alone in exercising caution about its success; increasingly concerned about the risky expenditure, Arthur Provis had withdrawn from the partnership before work on the series was complete.

Instead, Gerry and Sylvia – now promoted to co-producer – took their new idea to Lew Grade at ATV, and with the driven, ambitious and ingenious filmmaker and the glamorous and sociable aspirant writer and director with a keen sense of style and character forming an effective creative partnership, they were literally looking to take to the skies. *Supercar* (ITV, 1961–62) followed the jet-age escapades of the titular land, sea and air-traversing rescue vehicle that the theme song dubbed 'the marvel of the age', created by the eccentric Professor Popkiss and Doctor Beaker and piloted by square-jawed adventurer Mike Mercury, his juvenile sidekick Jimmy Gibson and their comic relief chimpanzee Mitch, as they embarked on daring edge-of-the-seat rescue missions and bids to foil the plots of their arch enemy Masterspy. Everything about *Supercar* pointed towards it being bigger and better than anything seen on television before, and perhaps this optimism and ambition was reflected in the fact that Gerry and Sylvia, who had grown increasingly close over the previous couple of years, took a day out from the filming schedule to get married.

As much as viewers might have thrilled to the frontier town exploits of Two Gun Tex of Texas, *Supercar* – launched just as Mitch's kindred spirit, Ham the Astrochimp, was conquering the stars for apekind – was a bold and exciting glimpse of a possible near future that did not seem too far removed from reality. With Reg Hill's stunning design for Supercar itself and the first of Barry Gray's naggingly catchy space-age theme songs combining beat boom sounds, a full soundtrack orchestra and early electronic instruments, it looked and sounded exciting too. Lew Grade's flair for an international distribution deal through ATV's subsidiary company ITC made it an even bigger success than anyone had hoped for, particularly with Mike Mercury becoming the first of many of their lead characters to deploy a deliberately transatlantic accent, and they even had a memorably impressive-sounding name for their innovative puppeteering process – *Supercar* was the very first show to be introduced as being 'Filmed in SUPERMARIONATION'.

Even as Mike Mercury and company raced to the rescue, huge events were happening up in the stars way beyond the limits of even Supercar's capabilities. On 12 April 1961, the USSR had rocketed into the lead in the Space Race as *Vostok 1* carried Yuri Gagarin towards orbital velocity to become the first human in space; Alan Shepard could only haplessly follow on the first manned American space mission on 5 May. Doubtless both were very much on Gerry and Sylvia's minds when they came up with Steve Zodiac, the intrepid pilot of *Fireball XL5* (ITV, 1962). Bolstered by Space Doctor Venus, Professor Matthew Matic and Robert the Robot – and occasionally Venus' unsteadily voiced pet, Lazoon Zoonie – the World Space Patrol's interplanetary vehicle Fireball XL5 set off on missions from the secret South Pacific headquarters of Space City, generally involving encounters with aliens who looked very much of their time without – mostly – looking comical or embarrassing.

Inspired by reports that the Soviets were experimenting with horizontal rocket launch systems, the slickly designed Fireball XL5 and its detachable front section, Fireball Junior, inspired a fleet of tie-in toys and opened each episode with a startling ninety-second take-off sequence which certainly left poor old Torchy's rocket on the launch pad. Those opening titles were accompanied by Barry Gray's suitably cosmic beat instrumental 'Zero G', but it was the closing credits where *Fireball XL5* really took flight, with a catchy pop song in which aspirant teen idol Don Spencer wistfully recounted his wish to be a spaceman and win the heart of a woman with starry eyes; not surprisingly, 'Fireball' became an actual hit late in 1962. Possibly its most significant legacy, however, was Venus, the first of a line of strong, independent and scientifically minded female characters introduced and often voiced by Sylvia; the resemblance that several of the puppets bore to her was almost certainly not a coincidence. On 14 December 1962, just over a month after *Fireball XL5*'s own launch, America's *Mariner 2* accomplished the first ever successful planetary flyby mission. You probably won't need to guess *which* planet.

Meanwhile, although their respective departures had been amicable, Arthur Provis and Roberta Leigh couldn't resist the temptation to try dragging their former associates into a Space Race of their own. Forming Wonderama Productions, they employed a suspiciously familiar style of puppetry for *Sara and Hoppity* (ITV, 1962), based on Leigh's storybooks about Sara Brown and her odd-legged mischievous toy doll who had been brought to life by a 'goblin ring'. ITV was never particularly happy about a series that dealt so matter-of-factly with naughty behaviour and insisted on some of the episodes being refilmed, so their next series, *Space Patrol* (ITV, 1963), was made very much with international distribution in mind.

Intentionally based on recent space-travel technology developments, and with atonal electronic music created by Roberta herself, *Space Patrol* depicted the quirky short-haul near-future escapades of Captain Larry Dart of the United Galactic Organisation and his associates Slim the Venusian and Husky the Martian as they maintained law and order across the habitable solar system. *Space Patrol* was enough of a hit that it must have given Gerry and Sylvia cause for concern, but Arthur and Roberta seemed to have difficulty following it up. *Send for Dithers* (ITV, 1966), about a clumsy handyman and his penguin co-worker, and the Esso Petrol co-funded *Wonder Boy and Tiger* (ITV, 1967), who orbited the Earth on a magic carpet looking for people to rescue, were only taken by a handful of ITV regions and some did not show them until the early seventies. Meanwhile, the more sophisticated space escapades of *Paul Starr* (1964) and *The Solarnauts* (1967) – a glossy live-action pilot starring Derek Fowlds and Martine Beswick – were not picked up at all. Looking back now, it isn't difficult to see why – Wonderama's designs and storylines were still stuck in an earlier age of comic strip fun which left them sitting at Mission Control while the Supermarionation shows were rocketing beyond the stratosphere.

In any case, with their previous genre-switching success very much in mind, Gerry and Sylvia were already looking in a different – and much wetter – direction. *Stingray* (ITV, 1964) was the space-age flagship submarine of the World Aquanaut Security Patrol – or W.A.S.P., for short – and patrolled the ocean depths under the command of dashing heartthrob Captain Troy Tempest and his trusty co-pilot 'Phones' Sheridan as they strove to defeat the latest plot by sub-aquatic despot Titan and his surface agent X-20 and fleet of 'Terror Fish', as well as assorted pirates, malevolent pond life and other watery ne'er-do-wells. Overseen by Commander Sam Shore from his hoverchair, W.A.S.P.'s Marineville headquarters could literally disappear beneath the ground in a clamour of sirens and dramatic percussion-led music if circumstances called for it, but even there Troy couldn't find much relaxation. Cultured and sharply dressed communications supervisor Lieutenant Atlanta Shore and W.A.S.P.'s mute and mysterious mermaid associate Marina both had designs on him and an only moderately friendly rivalry with each other, but they were also more than capable of confronting *Stingray*'s various challenges entirely by themselves – or sometimes slightly reluctantly together – with the nominal hero of the show often shown up by their emotional maturity and ingenuity.

Opening with Commander Shore's warning to 'Stand by for action!' and a dynamic opening song that put many a James Bond theme to shame, it wasn't just the format that marked *Stingray* out. At Lew Grade's urging and with a view towards longer term sales to American networks, *Stingray* became the first British television series to be made entirely in colour, although viewers in the UK had to wait until the very end of the decade to find out that Marina's hair was green. The puppets, effects work and the dynamic editing – particularly effective with *Stingray*'s constant switching between underwater and surface-level action – were all getting more and more sophisticated, and Barry Gray scored another hit with the closing theme, a plaintive ballad sung 'by' Troy Tempest by way of popular crooner Gary Miller in praise of 'Aqua Marina', which played over images of the puppet love triangle gazing longingly at each other from afar. Gary unwittingly had competition in the form of Duke Dexter, the first of several Supermarionation puppet pop stars, who ran up against Titan in one episode, and *Stingray* also introduced yet another tradition for the shows – the Christmas special in which a very healthy-looking 'sick' puppet child accidentally causes a crisis and then saves the day.

By the mid-sixties, Gerry and Sylvia were literally amongst the stars. The massive success of *Thunderbirds* (ITV, 1965–66) had taken them onto the big screen and into the world of glitzy premieres and allowed them to create an entertainment empire of their own. Promising '21 Minutes of Adventure', Century 21 Records issued a string of story records featuring the characters and music from their shows, while Century 21 Toys filled the high streets with replicas of Thunderbird 5, and the weekly *TV Century 21* presented further adventures of the Tracy Brothers and company in comic form, alongside the slightly darker escapades of some interlopers from the BBC – *Doctor Who*'s recurring adversaries, the Daleks, in an epic saga that delved deep into their mysterious origins and the morality of their quest for universal conquest. AP Films was even correspondingly renamed as Century 21 Films, but from the harsher and more minimalist company logo and Barry Gray's accompanying dramatic 'sting' onwards, it was beginning to look like something had changed.

There had always been a darker Cold War-driven side to the Space Race, and *Captain Scarlet and the Mysterons* (ITV, 1967) – which perhaps tellingly was launched on the same chilly late September evening as Patrick McGoohan's symbolist thriller *The Prisoner* – was very much a reflection of this. Fittingly, it has the most involved format of any Supermarionation series; after a mission by global security organisation Spectrum to investigate the source of mysterious radio waves traced on Mars goes disastrously wrong and results in a misjudged attack on a Martian city, the normally peaceful Mysterons swear to exact revenge on Earth via a terrorism-driven war of attrition. As well as superior technology, the Mysterons – only ever represented by eerily floating circles of light and a deep disembodied voice – have one distinct advantage over their adversaries; they can create an exact replica of a person or an object and place it entirely under their control. While Captain Black, who had led the fateful mission, elects to side with the Mysterons, an attempt to replicate his former colleague Captain Scarlet is thwarted with the result that, thanks to those unique Mysteron properties, he becomes practically indestructible. Operating from Spectrum's skyborne headquarters Cloudbase, the colour-coded Spectrum agents and a squadron of crack female fighter pilots dubbed The Angels found themselves having to consistently contend with intercontinentally threatening sabotage, politically sensitive assassination attempts and other potential crises that might well have had Mike Mercury and Mitch the Monkey counting their blessings.

If these higher stakes adventures sound more violent and explosive then that's because they were – *Captain Scarlet and the Mysterons* is surprisingly bleak and graphic for a children's show, with very little humour to be found anywhere, and some episodes even opened with a warning to viewers not to copy their indestructible hero's antics, although how and where they might be able to get hold of a runaway experimental tank was never entirely clear. This darker tone may well have been a reflection of a growing frustration that Gerry in particular was feeling at still having to work with puppets when he wanted to move into live action work; it is also true that the puppets are much more realistic from this point on, and the occasional quick cuts of actual human hands and feet performing the action that marionettes couldn't, which had occasionally featured from the earliest days, suddenly become much more prevalent. Shortly after completing production, the Andersons began work on their first live-action feature film, the not entirely unrelated sci-fi thriller *Doppelgänger* (1969, released in America as *Journey to the Far Side of the Sun*), a well-reviewed but commercially unsuccessful effort starring Ian Hendry and Roy Thinnes as astronauts who discover a hidden mirror image of Earth on the other side of the solar system.

Despite all this, however, *Captain Scarlet and the Mysterons* was another massive success, inspiring the usual amount of merchandise – reputedly, at one point demand was so great that Dinky had to dedicate their entire manufacturing plant to their die-cast replica of the Spectrum Pursuit Vehicle – but one particular item mysteriously failed to appear. In addition to his spectacularly eerie four-note motif for the Mysterons, Barry Gray also wrote a catchy closing song performed by a hotly tipped pop group coincidentally called The Spectrum. Although the band themselves were well known enough to have their own strip in *Lady Penelope* comic, and the theme song is most people's immediate reaction if you mention *Captain Scarlet and the Mysterons*, it was oddly never released as a single.

The same cannot be said for *Joe 90* (ITV, 1968), whose dynamic Motown-inspired guitar and organ-duet instrumental theme later bizarrely became an in-demand floor filler on the Northern Soul scene, although some might say that the music was the most exciting part of the show. *Joe 90* revolved around nine-year-old Joe McClaine, recruited as an agent by the World Intelligence Network after his inventor father 'Mac' McClaine develops the Brain Impulse Galvanoscope Record And Transfer – or B.I.G.

R.A.T., for short – that allows Joe to access the brain patterns of assorted experts via a pair of customised and famously thick-framed glasses. Although *Joe 90* was a likeable and whimsical series, the format also restricted the amount of peril that the lead character could realistically be placed in, and ultimately it also fell victim to the unfortunate truth that most children do not like watching other children doing well and getting to have adventures. There were some outstanding episodes – not least the Christmas special in which Joe poses as an angel to outsmart forgers who are trying to drive away custom from a church with hokey ghost stories – but, overall, *Joe 90* is remembered as the slightest of the Supermarionation shows.

Barely two months after Neil Armstrong took one small step for man and one giant leap for mankind, *The Secret Service* (ITV, 1969) brought Supermarionation back down to Earth with a very soft bump. Comedian Stanley Unwin starred in both human and puppet form as Father Unwin, a priest who found himself working for British Intelligence Service Headquarters Operation Priest – or B.I.S.H.O.P., for short – after a parishioner entrusted him with the secrets of a miniaturisation device. Joining him on his size-changing, vintage car-led, spy-trouncing escapades were intelligence agent Matthew Harding, posing as the vicarage's thickly accented gardener, and a superior who it has to be said looked suspiciously similar to Captain Scarlet, with Father Unwin giving their adversaries the linguistic slip by diverting into Stanley's celebrated trademark nonsense language 'Unwinese'. Broadcast in a Sunday evening slot and full of outlandish plots and absurd humour, it should have worked but the unusual visual style alienated viewers, the lack of high-tech hardware alienated toy manufacturers and the Unwinese alienated Lew Grade, who felt it would be impossible to sell to America and cancelled the series after only thirteen episodes had been made.

Lew Grade was, however, a little more taken with a proposal for a live-action adult series about a secret military organisation defending Earth from aliens harvesting human organs, and with *UFO* (ITV, 1970) Gerry and Sylvia left Supermarionation – and children's television – behind them. Glamorous Riviera-straddling detective series *The Protectors* (ITV, 1972–74) was followed by *Space: 1999* (ITV, 1975–77), which while it certainly angled to get younger viewers asking to 'stay up' to see its mix of streamlined tech and flashy futuristic uniforms – not to mention the near-ubiquitous toy Eagle Transporters – was still fundamentally aimed at an older audience. *Into Infinity* (BBC, 1975), a *2001: A Space Odyssey*-inspired semi-educational space adventure show starring Brian Blessed and aimed at the American networks – where it was broadcast as *The Day After Tomorrow* – only got as far as a pilot episode. *The Investigator* (1973), which continued *The Secret Service*'s experiments with combining live action and puppetry, could only manage an unbroadcast pilot and a couple of possibly hastily manufactured tie-in toys. By this time, Gerry and Sylvia's personal and professional relationships were over – and so, it seemed, was the story of Supermarionation.

With literally nowhere left to go after the Moon landings, public interest in space travel was starting to wane by the mid-seventies, with news stories slipping down to third or fourth place in the headlines and a general feeling that we'd seen it all before. Elsewhere in the television schedules, however, Destiny Angel, Virgil Tracy and company were taking off again. The ITV regions had found that the Supermarionation shows made for convenient, cost-effective and most importantly hugely popular slot fillers, leading to successive generations discovering their thrills and giving rise to frequent revivals of interest that continue through to this day.

By this time Sylvia had moved on to a successful production career in American television, but following a late seventies full of false starts, Gerry eventually found himself drawn back towards puppetry and children's television. Showcasing the new rod puppet-based 'Supermacromation' system, *Terrahawks* (ITV, 1983–86) followed cloned scientist Dr 'Tiger' Ninestein and his intrepid band of space-age fighter pilots as they sought to defend Earth from Zelda, a sophisticated wizened android exiled from the planet Guk who aimed to turn it into a new home for her similarly aesthetically off-putting kind. Although a planned parallel pop career for singing Terrahawk Kate Kestrel ironically never quite took off, *Terrahawks* was a huge success with an audience already well used to early eighties Supermarionation repeats, with a flashy design aesthetic that fitted perfectly with the early home computer age and a more knowingly ironic form of humour that was never far from the surface. More importantly, the heroic spherical robot Zeroids, led by Windsor Davies as Sergeant Major Zero, sparked a sell-out toy craze to rival even the fervour for Dinky's Thunderbird 2. The name and the technique may have changed, but Gerry Anderson was back, and he went on to delight slightly older audiences with *Dick Spanner, P.I.* (Channel 4, 1987), *Space Precinct* (BBC, 1994–95) and *Lavender Castle* (ITV, 1997).

The fervour surrounding the Space Race, which began before Gerry and Sylvia had so much as tugged a puppet string and wound down before they had even fully moved on to live action work, soon abated and space travel never quite inspired the same degree of hopes, dreams and aspiration again. The shows that they made with one eye on the news coverage of launches and landings, though, just keep on doing exactly that with successive generations. Although we never did actually see any of the puppets successfully take a small step.

'5 . . . 4 . . . 3 . . . 2 . . . 1 – Thunderbirds are GO!'

On 24 October 1963, the Lengede-Broistedt iron mine, near Salzgitter in West Germany, was flooded when a wastewater pond broke through into the tunnels. Seventy-nine of the hundred and twenty-nine mine workers escaped almost immediately and several more would be rescued over the following days. For eleven others trapped deeper in the shaft, however, there seemed to be little hope – but the rescue workers refused to give up. Bringing in specialist drilling and evacuation equipment from surrounding areas, some of which took days to arrive, they managed to bring them to safety on 7 November in an event that was quickly dubbed the 'Lengede Miracle'. It was the first rescue of its kind to receive round-the-clock live international television coverage, and its legacy extended way beyond the news.

Amongst the viewers who had been glued to their television with their fingers crossed were Gerry and Sylvia Anderson, and right at that moment, they were trying to come up with a new idea that could take the success they'd found with *Stingray* to a wider family audience. Gerry in particular had found himself fascinated by the dedicated rescue equipment and the tension of the race to get the machines to the mine in time, and with the sensation of a shared viewing experience almost without precedent very much on their minds, the new idea that they had been looking for began to fall into place. The concept for a series based around a fleet of futuristic multi-purpose rescue vehicles seemed like a winner, and Gerry and Sylvia headed off to their holiday villa in Portugal to write a pilot script for what was then being referred to as 'International Rescue', but that they felt still needed a punchier title to rank with *Supercar* and *Stingray*. It was at this point that Gerry remembered a letter from his beloved elder brother. Flight Lieutenant Lionel Anderson had tragically been killed in action in 1944 aged just twenty-two, but before his death he had regularly written home to the teenage Gerry from the training airbase at Falcon Field, Arizona. One such letter in June 1942 had excitedly told of how the camp had been visited by a number of Hollywood stars, including Gene Tierney and Preston Foster, who were there to make an action film designed to bolster wartime morale. Its name? *Thunder Birds* (1942).

There's little doubt that this deep emotional connection, coupled with a desire to get families watching together, helped to make *Thunderbirds* into the enormous enduring success that it became, but at the same time everyone involved was working at the top of their game and determined to do something a little different and a lot better, and that started with the format itself. Inspired by the success of the NBC Western series *Bonanza* (1959–73), Sylvia had astutely suggested that having more than one lead character would push them into having to come up with new and inventive storylines to incorporate everyone, while there was also an obvious appeal in making the rescue vehicles themselves technically even more stars of the show than their pilots. So it was that International Rescue came to be headed by billionaire former astronaut Jeff Tracy, with the respective Thunderbirds operated by his five sons, each named after the real-life heroes of the Project Mercury manned space missions – Scott (Carpenter), Virgil (Grissom), Alan (Shepard Jr), Gordon (Cooper) and John (Glenn Jr).

SUPERMARIONATION

Taken at face value, *Thunderbirds* seemed straightforward enough. After an initial official rescue attempt had failed, a call would come through from a potential disaster zone to International Rescue, frequently after tests on a revolutionary new transport system or high-tech fuel source had either been sabotaged or otherwise gone awry. From their secret base on their private South Pacific paradise Tracy Island, Jeff would alert whichever of his sons were required, monitoring their efforts via videolinks concealed behind framed portraits with flashing eyes hanging on the wall of his lavishly appointed villa, and the day is invariably saved with seconds to spare. What made *Thunderbirds* anything but formulaic, though, were those five vehicles and their separate skillsets, and the differing combinations in which they had to be deployed to pull off an ingenious and successful rescue misson in risky circumstances. What was more, they were all stunning designs caught somewhere between the jet age and the space age, combining sleek futuristic sophistication with a convincing mission-worn look and amusingly over-involved covert launch sequences that were repeated in every episode.

Scott led the team in Thunderbird 1, a hypersonic rocket plane that took off from a hangar situated beneath Tracy Island's retractable swimming pool. In order to get to it, he stood against a revolving section of fake wall in the villa which carried him onto an extendable gantry. Further along the wall, a huge painting of a rocket flipped over to deposit Virgil onto a chute that dropped down into heavy-duty transport aircraft Thunderbird 2. After selecting the appropriate pod for the mission – variously containing such dedicated specialist equipment as tunnelling deep-drill on wheels The Mole, heat-resistant excavation vehicle Firefly, a selection of adaptable elevator cars and the incredibly specific monorail restraint system The Monobrake – Thunderbird 2 took off from a hangar hidden behind some hydraulically tilting palm trees; its famously aerodynamically challenging front-facing wings, added by the model makers simply because they felt that it looked more exciting that way, never proved a barrier to this. The appropriately named Pod 4 housed Thunderbird 4, a compact utility submarine that could have given Stingray a run for its money; Thunderbird 4 was piloted by former W.A.S.P. aquanaut Gordon, who as a consequence suffered the indignity of having to share Virgil's boarding procedure and never got one of his own. Youngest brother Alan reached short-haul spacecraft Thunderbird 3 via an ascending sofa in the villa, which then took off through the middle of Tracy Island's circular guest house. Alan ostensibly swapped places once a month with John on Thunderbird 5, a space station in permanent orbit directly above Tracy Island, which monitored all available broadcast frequencies for any signs of impending potential emergencies.

The Thunderbird vehicles were designed and maintained by 'Brains', a mysterious scientific genius known only by his nickname, whose shyness and inarticulacy masked a relentlessly inventive technical mind. Amongst his many innovations was a chess opponent slash robot assistant called 'Braiman', who also conveniently carried out physical tasks and undertook feats of calculation that were beyond the capabilities of humans. Also resident on Tracy Island were Jeff's mother 'Grandma' Tracy, who made sure that the Tracy Brothers' culinary needs were met, Brains' teenage tech assistant and Alan's occasional love interest Tin-Tin Kyrano, and her father, Kyrano, who acted as Jeff's de facto butler. Slightly inconveniently, Kyrano was unknowingly under the psychic influence of his half-brother The Hood, a black-market arms dealer determined to steal the secrets of the Thunderbirds, who frequently staged disasters in the hope of getting a closer look at them in action although invariably he met with a comic comeuppance. International Rescue's two biggest stars, however, ended up almost eclipsing even the five Thunderbird vehicles in popularity.

Model, socialite and international celebrity Lady Penelope Creighton-Ward had come to the attention of the intelligence services while at finishing school, and after a successful career as a secret agent accepted Jeff's invitation to supervise International Rescue's efforts across Europe. Aloysius 'Nosey' Parker, on the other hand, was a career safe-cracker with his heart in the right place who was serving time in Parkmoor Scrubs when he was tipped off about a legendary haul in a rigidly secured stately home. This turned out to be a setup by Lady Penelope, who had been observing Parker for some time and who offered him a full pardon if he joined her as a butler, chauffeur and full-time fellow agent. Unswervingly loyal to 'Er Ladyship, Parker accompanied Penny on assignments in FAB1, a customised pink Rolls-Royce kitted out with harpoons, cannons, tyre-slashing wheel trims and other gadgets that would have had James Bond seething with envy. He was also never wary of using his other 'talents' when circumstances called for them, but that wasn't as often as you might assume – from outsmarting captors to daring stunt-driving to deploying chemical agents in hazardous circumstances, Lady Penelope was more than capable of doing it all by herself.

Inspired by the mid-sixties emergence of a wave of well-heeled society women who were nonetheless fiercely talented and independent, including model Jean Shrimpton, actress Jane Asher and designer Mary Quant, Sylvia had developed Lady Penelope as an aspirational figure for any young girls watching who combined, as the tie-in comic strip put it, 'elegance, charm and deadly danger'. Although a number of voice artists were considered, including Fenella

Fielding, ultimately only Sylvia herself was able to give the right sense of poise and depth to her own character – whose likeness, she later discovered, had been intentionally modelled on her by sculptor Mary Turner. Meanwhile, Parker's haughty yet humble cockney tones were based by David Graham – who also voiced Gordon Tracy and Brains – on a waiter called Arthur who Gerry had observed at the Kings Arms in Cookham, Berkshire; reputedly once in service of Elizabeth II at Windsor Castle, Arthur's pursuit of airs and graces had led him to develop an unusual habit of dropping his aitches and then putting them back in the wrong place. In contrast, the Tracys – Peter Dyneley as Jeff, Shane Rimmer as Scott, David Holliday as Virgil, Matt Zimmerman as Alan, and Ray Barrett as John – were all given transatlantic accents to maximise the show's international appeal, and with their flashy blue uniforms and cunningly upbeat callsign 'F-A-B', they looked set to take the world by storm.

A cast that big – and indeed vehicles that were literally that big – needed even bigger production facilities, and filming was divided between two stages so that separate units could shoot material back-to-back. Techniques that had been developed for previous shows, such as the puppets having interchangeable heads to suggest changing emotions and an independently operated conveyor belt and scrolling film roller that gave a convincing illusion of travelling at speed, were refined and perfected as the size of the solenoids in the puppets' heads became ever smaller and the strings became ever less visible, and Derek Meddings and his team created visual effects that outdid anything in any must-see movie blockbuster.

There was only one thing that *Thunderbirds* still needed – a theme tune that captured all of this excitement. Barry Gray had already written a jaunty pop song extolling the virtues of International Rescue in the style of *Fireball XL5* and *Stingray*, and he recorded a couple of potential versions of it with Gary Miller on vocals. This was originally intended to be used as the main theme and, although presumably with the intention of scoring yet another hit single first and foremost in everyone's minds, it was clearly written on one of his off days and did not exactly serve to underline the on-screen action. Then, as legend has it, while unable to sleep one night he found himself plagued by a naggingly rousing military drumbeat and accompanying fanfare, and the majestic *Thunderbirds* theme was born.

Introduced by Jeff Tracy's '5 . . . 4 . . . 3 . . . 2 . . . 1 – Thunderbirds are GO!' countdown and accompanied by images of the Tracy Brothers and their remarkable craft, it was in many people's estimation – not least Gerry's – the final element that pulled all of the others together. Production commenced in September 1964, and in December, with nine episodes in the can and another ten ready to enter production, Gerry took the completed pilot episode, 'Trapped in the Sky', to Lew Grade – and he was about to find out just how huge *Thunderbirds* was going to get.

Accounts of what took place and what was said differ, but there is one crucial detail that everyone involved seems to have agreed on – when the closing titles began to roll, Lew Grade leapt from his chair shouting, 'This isn't a television series, this is a feature film!' and pleaded with Gerry to extend the running time to fill a more profitable hour-long slot while pledging to up the budget by a third. Although this meant going back and filming more material for the already completed episodes at the same time as pressing ahead with the existing production schedule, a team of writers, including Sylvia and newcomer Tony Barwick, managed to find inventive ways of filling out the scripts with more character and comedy moments and – ingeniously – inserting a prior failed rescue bid that necessitated a desperate call to International Rescue.

In fact, there was a drive throughout *Thunderbirds* to avoid falling into any routines of clichés or formulas that would make the show feel the same every week, and while viewers might have known to expect the usual thrills and spills from episodes with titles like 'Operation Crash-Dive' and 'Pit of Peril', there were others that tried and succeeded in doing something a little different. In 'Sun Probe' Alan and Tin-Tin have to rescue astronauts locked on a course headed directly into the sun, while 'Martian Invasion' sees The Hood rig an accident on the set of a sci-fi movie in the hope of catching film of the Thunderbirds in action, and in 'The Uninvited' Scott and two archaeologists stumble across a sinister secret organisation constructing armaments in a pyramid.

'Cry Wolf' features an encounter with two young fans who have built their own Thunderbirds, while 'Ricochet' takes a topical look at the pirate radio boom when a pop DJ's stray signal throws a satellite out of orbit, and 'The Cham-Cham' follows Lady Penelope – posing as cabaret singer Wanda Lamour – into the showbiz set in search of the source of coded messages hidden in pop records. Her Ladyship also takes the lead in the more cliffhanger serial-style 'The Perils of Penelope', while 'Lord Parker's 'Oliday' sees the resourceful chauffeur come to the rescue when a Mediterranean resort town is threatened by its own solar power generator, and 'Vault of Death' brings him up against his old cellmate, Light-Fingered Fred, in a bid to rescue a Bank of England employee trapped inside a maximum-security storage area.

Most atypically of all, 'Attack of the Alligators!' is exactly what the emphatic title suggests, and the making of the episode was almost like a *Thunderbirds* script in itself. An RSPCA inspector arrived on set after receiving a tip-off that the baby crocodiles were being 'persuaded' to move by being prodded with an electrode; but after spotting a puppet and spending the best part of an hour enthusing about the show, which had been on air for barely a month by that point, the inspector volunteered to take annual leave and supervise the reluctant co-stars himself. Further on during production, one of the alligators slipped its leash, reputedly causing Derek Meddings to vacate the set with a single leap, leaving his waders behind; Lady Penelope, however, was not so fortunate and lost a hastily replaced leg to one of the peckish extras.

Filming continued through to December, but *Thunderbirds* made its debut on ITV – doubtless with that RSPCA inspector glued to his set – on 30 September 1965 and was instantly an even bigger hit than possibly anyone bar Lew Grade had bargained for. Although Peter Cook and Dudley Moore got in early with 'Superthunderstingcar' – one of the very few Supermarionation parody sketches about visible strings and faux-American accents that actually has any actual funny jokes in it – *Thunderbirds* was as loved as it was lampooned, and Sylvia in particular was always proud to point out that it was as integral a part of the Swinging Sixties as The Beatles and England's World Cup victory. There must have been a similarly triumphant mood to that of Nobby Stiles as he held the Jules Rimet trophy aloft when they saw the tie-in merchandising deals that were coming their way too.

Although there had been best-selling toy versions of the Supermarionation vehicles going all the way back to *Supercar*, Liverpool-based die-cast toy manufacturer Dinky were quick to spot the potential in *Thunderbirds* and – beginning a long association with Gerry and Sylvia – rushed out two models timed to hit the shops in time for Christmas. With pop-out legs and a detachable Pod 4 containing a miniature Thunderbird 4, the bulky Thunderbird 2 was an instant hit, even if one variant was notoriously coloured light blue rather than green. FAB1, which remained reassuringly pink throughout, came with models of Lady Penelope and Parker, a rocket that fired through the radiator grille and wheel-activated rear-firing harpoons, and is rumoured to have been Dinky's biggest selling toy of all time. In fact, perhaps suggesting that girls had never been properly catered for by tie-in merchandise previously, Lady Penelope really did seem to be outperforming the Tracy Brothers off-screen – and she even got her own ice lolly.

Blasting off in 1963, Lyons Maid's rocket-shaped Zoom lolly had initially been promoted as a tie-in with *Fireball XL5*, complete with specially filmed adverts and a send-away offer for your very own XL5 model kit. Barring diversions while *Stingray* hooked up with the more nautically appropriate Super Sea Jet lolly, and *Captain Scarlet* promoted the suitably more straight-faced Orbit, the association continued right through to *Joe 90* decommissioning a sinister secret laboratory with the aid of a handy Zoom – but in 1967, Penny and Parker switched their flavoured frozen water allegiance to a new contender all of their own. Initially pushed as 'especially for girls', the appropriately named and enduringly popular Fab lolly soon wisely widened its appeal, but it did at least come accompanied by a series of whimsical advertising mini-adventures starring the unlikely duo.

That wasn't their only off-screen secret assignment; Scott and company might well have attracted a huge number of new readers to *TV Century 21*, but it was 'Er Ladyship who got her own comic. While it was very much aimed directly at girls, *Lady Penelope* was in no sense a 'girls' comic', with Penny's adventures bolstered by dynamic action strips featuring Marina and The Angels alongside fellow small-screen favourites *The Beverly Hillbillies*, *Daktari*, *The Girl from U.N.C.L.E.* and *The Monkees*. Well-loved for its high-quality free gifts, including a now much-sought-after spy locket with a hidden mirror and secret compartment, *Lady Penelope* continued delighting readers right through to 1969, when it gave way to the somewhat less enduring *Joe 90 Top Secret*. Meanwhile, arguably slightly less successfully, the *Thunderbirds* vehicles themselves appeared in essentially anthropomorphic form in a strip in *Candy*, a peculiar Century 21 comic led by a photostrip about two unnervingly humanlike dolls who come to life and roam around real-world scenarios. Possibly not altogether surprisingly, Candy and Andy never did get their own television series.

There were also story records and paperback novels featuring brand-new adventures, a theme single with much-loved car-chase-dominated story-song 'Parker, Well Done' on the B-side, and more puppets, models, bagatelle games and dressing-up uniforms than anyone could fit onto their Christmas list. *Thunderbirds* was so huge, in fact, that it even made it onto the big screen barely a year after it had first appeared on the small one. Produced in association with United Artists, *Thunderbirds Are Go* (1966) was filmed between March and June 1966, although it was not without its logistical headaches – two new properties had to be bought on Slough Trading Estate to accommodate the production, and all of the puppets, sets and vehicles had to be remade in larger form to stand a chance of looking acceptable on a massive cinema screen.

Based around a race to rescue the crew of celebrated exploratory space cruiser Zero-X when their return to Earth after a Mars mission runs into difficulties, the film also finds room for a battle with fire-breathing Martian snakes and an extended fantasy showbiz sequence where Lady Penelope and Alan visit the interplanetary Swinging Star nightclub to watch Cliff Richard and The Shadows performing in puppet form. Cliff and The Shadows released an accompanying

EP of soundtrack music, Century 21 toys brought out an elaborate remote control electronic Zero-X toy, Zero-X itself was carefully introduced to *Thunderbirds* fans via its own strip in *TV Century 21*, and all signs pointed towards the film becoming a box-office smash. Following the glamorous premiere at the London Pavilion theatre on 12 December 1966, however, *Thunderbirds Are Go* struggled to attract audiences, and while many theories have been put forward for its failure to perform — from the fact that it had the misfortune to be released in the same week as *Batman* and *Born Free* while established family favourite *The Sound of Music* was still playing to packed houses, to Sylvia's admission that the Swinging Star was poorly realised and looked indulgent — perhaps the simplest explanation is Gerry's: audiences were never really going to get excited about seeing something at the cinema that they had already seen on television.

Work continued on new television episodes in tandem with the movie shoot, until Lew Grade sensed that the distribution deals were running out of steam and persuaded Gerry and Sylvia that it was time to come up with a new idea. Meanwhile, United Artists decided to have another try at conquering the box office with *Thunderbird 6* (1968), but on this occasion its lack of impact was not really as difficult to understand. More of a light comedy than an action movie, the storyline revolves around a plot to highlight Brains' latest invention — an airborne cruise liner called *Skyship One* — and spends more time recreating its exotic destinations than it does on the actual Thunderbird vehicles, which barely feature at all. As if that wasn't disappointing enough for younger audience members, the promised Thunderbird 6 is revealed to be Alan's vintage biplane, in a joke that was possibly funnier to parents than to anyone looking forward to seeing something that *had* to be even better than Thunderbird 2.

SUPERMARIONATION

Although it certainly looks impressive, *Thunderbird 6* doesn't quite come off as a feature-length adventure, and it's perhaps telling that while it was filmed in the autumn of 1967 and awarded a 'U' certificate in January 1968, United Artists delayed its release until July. Not even a bizarre incident that saw Century 21 Productions prosecuted by the Ministry of Transport on a charge of dangerous flying while filming the aerial sequences – the case was ultimately dismissed in court – could do much to drum up publicity. Gerry and Sylvia had been set to arrive at the premiere at Leicester Square Odeon on 29 July 1968 in a lifesize replica of FAB1, but – perhaps with ironic appropriateness – it broke down on the way.

Thunderbirds itself had gone out on a high with 'Give or Take a Million', in which the inevitable very healthy-looking 'sick' child wins the chance to spend Christmas at Tracy Island and inadvertently foils a bank robbery in the process, enjoying pride of place at the head of the evening schedules on 25 December 1966.

But the story of the Tracy Brothers did not end there. While various attempts at reviving and remaking *Thunderbirds* have come and gone, the original series just keeps on coming back and winning over new generations of fans – most famously in 1991, when a repeat run on BBC2 sparked such a huge wave of popularity that a Tracy Island playset sold out well before Christmas, leading to *Blue Peter* showing viewers facing a disappointing Christmas Day how to make their own out of household items; in turn, the response to this was so overwhelming that they very quickly ran out of instruction sheets and so had to repeat the 'make' and release it on video. Perhaps this isn't too surprising, given that *Thunderbirds* was event television inspired by the idea of event television, and the feature films – including the big-budget live-action 2004 version, which Gerry made no attempt to disguise his contempt for – weren't; a trip to the cinema is a very different experience to the whole family crowding around the television.

Thunderbirds was one of the first shows to get the whole family crowding around the television for sheer entertainment, and there are still more shows that do that now than you might be led to believe. Much like Gerry and Sylvia back in 1963, however, there are still rescue attempts that keep everyone glued to their sets for less fun reasons, and they frequently involve equipment that could have filled several of Thunderbird 2's pods, often assisted by volunteers from the real-life *Thunderbirds*-inspired organisation, the International Rescue Corps. Brains would have been proud.

3
Pre-school and Storytelling

'Through the arched window'

Had everything gone to plan, BBC2 would have launched on 20 April 1964 with an evening of cultured and highbrow entertainment. Absurdist comedy troupe The Alberts at large in Television Centre with an elephant were to be followed a production of *Kiss Me, Kate*, starring Howard Keel and Patricia Morison, a performance from Soviet comedian Arkady Raikin and an elaborate fireworks display. The new minority-interest channel was setting out its stall in fairly blunt terms. Then, just as the introductory fanfare rolled onto the screen, a massive power cut took the channel off the air and BBC2 instead had to launch the following morning with Virginia Stride and Gordon Rollings pretending to be farmyard animals.

Play School (BBC, 1964–88) wasn't quite as trivial as that bizarre turn of events might make it sound. It wasn't the first programme aimed at pre-school viewers – a number of ITV regions had presented their own adaptations of long-running American show *Romper Room* – but more often than not these were little different to what you would have got if you just stuck a camera in a corner of an actual nursery school. By the early sixties, however, attitudes were changing, and new free-thinking ideas were coming in thick and fast – even the word 'nursery' was falling out of favour – and the progressive, forward-thinking BBC2 needed a very different kind of show for its youngest viewers. It may not have been able to protect you from elder siblings' tales of the terrors that awaited you in 'big school', but at least it would keep you entertained and educated while they were trying and failing to work out one end of a set-square from the other.

Play School arrived at a time of change and new ideas within the BBC itself. The Children's department had recently been subsumed into Families and Serials, and newly installed head Doreen Stephens brought with her a fresh perspective and a determination to shake up what she saw as a tired and out-of-touch approach. Doreen installed Joy Whitby as series editor and Cynthia Felgate as producer, with a brief to develop a daily format involving a single small and sparsely appointed studio, two presenters and what amounted to around £2,000 per week in today's money. As much as it may have arisen from the sheer lack of available resources, this setup also reflected the new European-influenced kindergartens starting to spring up around the UK. This particularly suited Cynthia; formerly a member of a touring theatrical troupe specialising in shows for primary schools, she felt she knew and understood the actual viewers that these shows had been trying to reach, and that the usual prim talking-down approach would never have cut it in an echoing school hall full of council-estate children rebutting all appeals for quiet and attention.

Play School's format was a simple and rigid one, but it also packed an incredible amount into a twenty-five-minute programme and had enough flexibility to allow for different content each day. Opening with the invitation 'Here is a house. Here is a door. Windows: one, two, three, four. Ready to knock? Turn the lock. It's *Play School*!' and a modish animated self-drawing house, the presenters introduced

PRE-SCHOOL AND STORYTELLING

themselves and demonstrated everyday objects, played games, sang songs with accompanying actions, and challenged you to tell the time from the position of the big hand and little hand of the *Play School* clock and its clarinet-led tick-tocking rhythm, underneath which was an object related to what the day's guest storyteller had in store. A further guessing game involved predicting whether a short documentary film would appear through the arched, round or square window; as impossibly and unpredictably random as this may have appeared to viewers at home, the windows were actually selected on the basis of the predominant shape seen in the films. Then it was back to the presenters for a cheery sign-off, and the animated house closed its door for another day. Not all of the earliest innovations lasted the course – initially each section was introduced by its own rhyming couplet, while for several years the week was divided up into Useful Box Day on Mondays, Dressing Up Day on Tuesdays, Pets Day on Wednesdays, Ideas Day on Thursdays and Science Day on Fridays – but otherwise *Play School* remained largely unchanged for most of its twenty-four-year run.

Similarly enduring, despite in a couple of cases looking very much of their time, the *Play School* toys helped and more often than not hindered with all of the above. Humpty was a modish stuffed re-interpretation of his nursery rhyme namesake, while Jemima was a polka dot-bowed and extremely sixties rag doll, and Hamble had a cautionary backstory all of her own.

The ungainly and cheap-looking plastic doll was actually plucked from a range mass-produced by Woolworths, with the intention that any of the children watching with their own personal Hamble would feel an extra sense of involvement. Unfortunately, the majority of viewers disagreed, along with the presenters – many of whom later gleefully admitted to on-set maltreatment of their loathed co-star — and, ultimately, the consumer market; the 'Hamble' was eventually withdrawn from sale due to a lack of demand and very quickly faded from public view to the extent where 'she' was only really known and ultimately remembered on account of the *Play School* association. It's difficult to think of a more concise statement on the transitory risks of rampant consumerism than the historical ignominy of this unloved doll.

Replacing an earlier one-size-fits-all Teddy, who was stolen from the studio during a recording break, varyingly statured stuffed bears Big Ted and Little Ted were usually called on to perform the more robust roles as, frankly, they stood a much better chance of being able to stand upright for more than three continuous seconds. Antique rocking horse Dapple was less frequently sighted, possibly on account of taking up a considerable proportion of the available studio space, and others such as the obviously named Tiger would come and go without making much of an impression, but those five main iconic toys arguably became the most recognisable feature of *Play School*. Which in Hamble's case was admittedly recognition for all the wrong reasons, but that will have mattered little to any youngster who got to sing along to 'Well Jemima, Let's Go Shopping' on *Play School*'s *Play On* album or record their thoughts in Little Ted's Jotter. Unless they'd been unfortunate enough to be given Hamble's Day Book instead, of course.

Although they had to jostle for star status with the toys, *Play School*'s presenters were a similarly eclectic assortment, drawn initially from the worlds of fringe theatre and folk music, along with trendy teachers with a taste for performing; one early introduction who remained with *Play School* throughout its existence, Brian Cant, frequently recounted how his audition simply consisted of being thrown a box by Joy Whitby and told to row out to sea. Other fondly remembered names from the early days included actress

PRE-SCHOOL AND STORYTELLING

Julie Stevens, singer-songwriter Rick Jones, comedian Johnny Ball, and husband and wife theatrical partnership Eric Thompson and Phyllida Law. Even from its earliest days, *Play School* strove to be as diverse and inclusive as possible; Italian model Marla Landi and folk musician Johnny Silvo, who was the London-born son of an African American soldier, were familiar faces, while actor Paul Danquah was not only Black but – although viewers would not necessarily have been aware of this – openly gay.

This degree of diversity, laudable for the time, may well have been part of the reason why the popular press initially treated *Play School* with a degree of suspicion, although in fairness they and others like them were wary of clever BBC2 mocking them with its plays and books in general; BBC Director of Television Kenneth Adam confided to *Radio Times* in April 1964 that he had received protests from religious and community leaders concerned that the addition of a third television channel would do little bar encourage further physical and mental slovenliness in the population. The hordes of mind-numbed hermits never quite materialised, though, and Adam's assertion that BBC2 was intended to provoke the opposite response from viewers was arguably borne out by the success of *Play School*. Despite the fact that a significant proportion of the audience lacked the higher definition sets required to receive BBC2, the show, the clock and the toys quickly became an influential reference point that in turn informed real-life pre-school education.

In response, ITV quickly weighed in with a direct lift of its format; *Play Time* (ITV, 1966–68), presented by Gwyneth Surdival and ship-jumping *Play School* presenter Jennifer Naden, with Nana the Bear, Spot the Dog, Snod the Kitten and Katy the Doll. *Play Time* found itself levered out of the nearest randomly shaped window soon enough, but its appearance probably hastened the decision to afford *Play School* an afternoon repeat on BBC1, where it became a permanent fixture from 1968 – and the innovations didn't stop there. Along with the rest of BBC2, *Play School* switched to colour in 1968. As the sixties rolled into the seventies, new faces like Chloe Ashcroft, Carol Leader and Carole Chell were joined by a gaggle of struggling singer-songwriters, including Toni Arthur, Derek Griffiths and Lionel Morton, whose lost would-be acid folk classics were often retooled for the show with new lyrics about Little Ted queueing at the grocer's – many of them later collected on the now highly collectable *Play School* album *Bang on a Drum*.

For many, however, the most significant addition was the infectiously energetic Floella Benjamin. Born in Trinidad and Tobago, Floella had emigrated to the UK with her family aged ten and had triumphed in the face of hostility, abandoning her ambition to be Britain's first Black woman bank manager for an acting career in West End musicals, including the original UK production of taboo-breaking countercultural musical *Hair*. Floella was soon spotted by the *Play School* production team, and her enthusiastic fusion of white and Black British culture did much to inspire thoughts of acceptance and integration in a generation who loved her too much to ever think otherwise.

Play School was also mildly revolutionary in the way that it was marketed abroad; too parochial for actual episodes to air overseas, it was simply sold in 'kit' form with scripts, films and props provided for broadcasters to adapt as they saw fit. The Australian version, whose presenters have included many familiar faces from *Home and Away* and *Neighbours*, continues to run to this day, while many broadcasters conveniently 'forgot' to include Hamble, and the Swiss reputedly contrived to nail Humpty down. The surplus revenue from this arrangement was sufficient to fund a series of spin-off shows aimed at slightly older viewers, including improv comedy free-for-all *Play Away* (BBC, 1971–84) and Johnny Ball's historical panto romp with Julie Stevens and Derek Griffiths, *Cabbages and Kings* (BBC, 1972–74), but by this time, *Play School* itself had competition.

In October 1972, ITV had been granted permission to expand its broadcasting hours to run a full afternoon service, and one of the IBA's conditions was that a proper structured line-up of educational broadcasting for the under-fives should form part of it. The various ITV regional broadcasters were invited to submit programme ideas, and Yorkshire Television weighed in with *Mister Trimble* (ITV, 1973–77), presented by Tony Boden in the guise of an eccentric inventor who watched short educational filmed inserts through his magic telescope, aided and abetted by talking goldfish Glug and a boy band-style pop group who lived downstairs. Introduced by a sprightly flutey theme and the Granada logo redrawing itself into the titular smiling-doored abode, *Hickory House* (ITV, 1973–77) variously featured Amanda Barrie, Louise Hall-Taylor, Nicolette Chaffey and Julie North as the custodians of a house full of talking household implements led by grouchy Dusty Mop and indolent Humphrey Cushion, with Alan Rothwell as their resolutely unchanging hand-lending neighbour. True anarchy, however, could only be found in a very different house full of puppets further down the M6.

ATV's *Pipkins* (ITV, 1973–81) began as *Inigo Pipkin*, with George Woodbridge as the oddly monikered puppet maker whose creations – intentionally if child-unnervingly made out of scraps and leftovers with a deliberately unpolished look – had a habit of attaining sentience with unpredictable personalities. Lugubrious treasurer Tortoise, food-fixated Brummie inventor Pig, highly strung diva ostrich Octavia, chirpy and eager to learn monkey

Topov, marionette medic Doctor Stethoscope and laconic Irish badger Mooney would all wind up lending a hand around the workshop, but it was Hartley Hare who became the real star of the show. Vain, arrogant, temperamental and as cynical as any pundit on a late-night arts show, Hartley nonetheless had a heart of gold and a desire to please, and was generally both the cause of and the solution to all of everyone's problems.

With a catchy bubblegum pop theme song from 'Rupert' hitmaker Jackie Lee, the show was a hit from the outset; *Inigo Pipkin* had been in production for less than a year when George Woodbridge sadly died, however, and from 1974 the series was known as *Pipkins*. In Inigo's absence – which was actually noted on screen – the puppets formed a charitable organisation named The Help People, with the aid of Wayne Laryea as Mr Pipkin's former assistant, Johnny; when he eventually had to leave, the puppets took to the streets with banners reading 'WE NEED ANOTHER JOHNNY!' and somehow ended up recruiting Jonathan Kydd as Tom, who in turn was replaced by Paddy O'Hagan as Peter, with Sue Nicholls as next-door neighbour Mrs Muddle.

As the unusual recruitment methods might suggest, *Pipkins* was anything but a run-of-the-mill lunchtime children's programme. The storylines may always have had an educational intent or a moral to relate – invariably underlined in no uncertain terms by a loud psychedelic animation of chiming clocks that it was 'TIME ... for a story' – but they were frequently absurdist and lightly satirical, often involving madcap outdoor sequences with bewildered onlookers in the background, and everyone involved seemed to actually be aware that they were in a television programme. Indeed, when *Pipkins* finally concluded after ATV lost its ITV franchise in 1981, Hartley simply informed viewers that next week there would be 'a new programme with new people'. *Let's Pretend* (ITV, 1982–88) may have been introduced by a funnel-nosed caterpillar puppet making inquisitive synthesiser noises at the episode's key prop – although the earliest instalments had the props being scoffed by a cardboard whale at the end of a conveyor belt – and a huge cast of prop-wielding presenters telling entertaining stories, but somehow it was just never quite the same.

The real success story, however, was Thames' *Rainbow*, which was first seen on 16 October 1972. Despite also being set in a 'house' that bore a suspicious resemblance to a sparsely furnished television studio with guest storytellers and documentary films, *Rainbow* set out to be as distinct from *Play School* as possible, deploying vaguely fashionable designs, animation and music, and built around comic interaction with scarcely describable puppets, although it looked a little different at first.

Rainbow was originally presented by David Cook and two hand puppets – cheery Sunshine and melancholy Moony – with music from seven-piece psych-folk band Telltale, who also composed and recorded the celebrated *Rainbow* theme, complete with prog-styled hallucinogenic interludes in the rarely heard full version. As the series progressed, however, two background characters began to become more popular with viewers – a well-meaning but naive human-sized bear named Bungle and a loudmouthed naughty boy-type creature with a zip fastener for a mouth, Zippy. Sunshine and Moony were gradually phased out and replaced by Bungle and Zippy and the latter's newly introduced friend, a shy pink hippo named George, while Telltale initially handed over to Charlie Dore, Karl Johnson and Julian Littman – who also provided the theme song for BBC schools' show *You and Me* (BBC, 1974–92) – and then the first iteration of a trio who for many would come to define *Rainbow*.

Rod Burton, Jane Tucker and Matthew Corbett joined the show in 1974, as did a new presenter who, it would turn out, had some unfortunate history with one of the band. In his repertory theatre days, Geoffrey Hayes had appeared in a play alongside Matthew, who had to leave suddenly to help his father, Harry – handler of Sooty – with a stage show. An aghast Geoffrey had reputedly expressed a disbelief that anyone could ever sell their artistic soul and work with puppets; reportedly, the two somehow managed to avoid ever raising the orange bear in the room with each other. Matthew left to take over full-time Sooty-handling duties in 1976, upon which Rod, Jane and Matt became Rod, Jane and Roger, with the addition of Roger Walker, who in turn left in 1980 to be replaced by Freddy Marks. A drama school contemporary of Peter Davison, and cast as Brad in one of the earliest productions of *The Rocky Horror Show*, Freddy seemed to bring an extra spark to the triple-act, and most people have now forgotten that there was any other iteration of Rod, Jane and . . . Increasingly incorporated into the actual storylines of *Rainbow* rather than just appearing in their musical segments, Rod, Jane and Freddy became so popular that they were given their own spin-off series casting them in self-written surreal fairytale-like scenarios; *Rod, Jane and Freddy* (ITV, 1981–91) eventually clocked up a staggering 120 episodes.

This wasn't the only spin-off from *Rainbow*. Cosgrove Hall Films, which contributed various animations, including the opening titles and the scraping and squiggling-accompanied 'lines and shapes' sequences, also came up with several stop-motion inserts that graduated to a series in their own right. Introduced by a jaunty folk-pop song written by former Herman's Hermits guitarist Keith Hopwood, brother and sister *Sally and Jake* (ITV, 1973–74) were always keen to help out the adults in their hometown Dimbledale, with the debatable assistance of their spectacularly indolent and aptly named pet cat Sly. Public-spirited old dear *Grandma Bricks of Swallow Street* (ITV, 1977) was forever encouraging her ethnically diverse assortment of neighbours to get together and have a grand old day out, while Robin and Rosie Cockle's family had moved from the heart of the city to *Cockleshell Bay* (ITV, 1980–86), where in a neat inversion of *Sally and Jake*'s day-to-day situation, they were always having to look for something to do in their more sedate surroundings. More often than not, that 'something' was precipitated by the activities of pasty-nabbing seagull menace Ben Gunn.

Rainbow was the show that endured, but other storytelling shows included Yorkshire's Valerie Pitts-fronted animated Edwardian bathing frog-introduced *Gammon and Spinach* (ITV, 1977–83) and the only marginally higher concept lake-skipping *Stepping Stones* (ITV, 1976), with Elisabeth Sladen and Keith Barron. There was also Granada's magnetic-shapes-on-tree-stump-based *Once Upon a Time* (ITV, 1979–82), as variously hosted by Peter Davison and sixties pop star Mark Wynter, and mop-free *Hickory House* replacement *Daisy, Daisy* (ITV, 1978), with Alan Rothwell and Jan Harvey. Meanwhile, viewers in Wales had their time-honoured 'own programmes', including HTV's cave-set collection of oddball characters in oddball costumes, *Miri Mawr* (ITV, 1972–78), and the jubilantly introduced *Ffalabalam* (ITV, 1980–89), set in a model village towered over by the human presenters, which would case much consternation to non-Welsh speaking viewers when they had to be parachuted into their region due to a transmitter fault.

None of them ever quite came close to rivalling *Rainbow*, or for that matter *Play School*, which had a timely overhaul in the late seventies with an updated house, a host of new younger presenters alongside old favourites, and possibly the only memorable *Play*

School pet – foul-tempered cockatiel Kattoo, whose impatient shriek is surely indelibly burned into the subconscious of a generation.

By the early eighties, though, matters were beginning to change – not least because of the Education Act 1981, which gave local authorities the power to establish their own nursery schools and completely overhauled the treatment of children with what were now termed special educational needs – and no matter how much of a treat it might have been to see *Rainbow* on one of the big televisions in the school hall, the shows themselves were becoming increasingly detached from the classroom experience they were intended to emulate. Thankfully, the newly launched Channel 4 was effectively run by the broadcasting equivalent of trendy teachers who were only too happy to adapt to evolving educational needs with a series of socially aware and increasingly odd programmes.

Chips' Comic (Channel 4, 1983–85) was set in a newspaper office where gaudily boiler-suited editor Elsa O'Toole, technician Gordon 'Inky' Griffin and canine roving reporter Rover – Andrew Secombe in an unwashable-looking shaggy dog costume – put together each issue of their chirpy educational magazine with the help of bulky yellow computer slash printing press Chips, which was then available to buy in your local newsagent's the following Thursday. With puppets designed by *Spitting Image* creators Peter Fluck and Roger Law, *Helping Henry* (Channel 4, 1988) featured a Jeremy Hardy-voiced alien named N-3 – or Henry – who had inconspicuously disguised himself as a dining room chair as he observed the everyday activities of the 'two-legs', with the assistance of remarkably tolerant young associate Stephen. Written, produced and presented by Floella Benjamin, *Treehouse* (Channel 4, 1987–89) featured songs, games and stories in a set that looked more like an adventure playground than a schoolroom, built around an animatronic talking tree which, unfortunately, a handful of the children who appeared on the show were visibly unnerved by.

Perhaps the strongest indication that Jemima and the gang were not so much through the square window as over the hill, however, came with *Pob's Programme* (Channel 4, 1985–87). A gaudy orange and pink clattery puppet with a long stripy jumper and a barely intelligible dialect, Pob ostensibly lived 'inside' your television, notoriously introducing himself by misting up the screen with his breath and writing his name in the condensation, ensuring a steady stream of letters to Channel 4's viewer response show *Right to Reply* from people who considered this tantamount to encouragement to spit. Pob presided over an assortment of abstract animations, interactive puzzles and games and educational 'makes', while a celebrity guest followed a strand from Pob's jumper around a walled garden in search of the story they had ostensibly come to read. Closer to the rest of Channel 4's early programming – and in particular their similarly television-dwelling pop show host Max Headroom – than any of the other efforts, *Pob's Programme* quickly caught on by virtue of its sheer oddness. Anna Wood's Ragdoll Productions went on to create some of the most popular and enduring children's shows of the nineties, including *Rosie and Jim* (ITV, 1990–2000), *Tots TV* (ITV, 1993–98) and *Teletubbies* (BBC, 1997–2001), of whom Pob was presumably some form of distant evolutionary ancestor.

Perhaps realising that the big hand was pointing somewhere they hadn't expected, *Play School* 'moved house' to BBC1 – complete with an animated removal lorry-based trailer – in September 1983 and embarked on an ambitious and, in retrospect, ill-advised revamp. With more of an emphasis on wacky humour, a jazzier theme tune and a new logo that resembled the cover of a home design store catalogue, this wasn't the *Play School* anyone was used to, not least with the controversial installation of an additional triangular window. New younger presenters with one foot in fringe theatre were brought in alongside zany sock puppet dog Bingo and an unpredictable kamikaze cuckoo now living in the unfathomable Heath Robinson-esque contraption standing in for the clock. Hamble was replaced by the more ethnically diverse and, more importantly, less terrifying Poppy, while the BBC's newly launched early-morning *Breakfast Time* was parodied in puppet-led inserts as 'Tea Time Television' – or TTV, for short.

Although TTV was popular enough to spin off into *TTV: Tea Time Television* (BBC, 1985–88), anchored by bin-reclining unkempt puppet moggy Scragtag, *Play School* itself was very hastily rowed back. But it proved too little too late, and it had already lost too many friends. In 1985 the afternoon repeat was quietly dropped – although a compilation of highlights from each week's shows did air on BBC2 on Sunday mornings for a time – and, to a chorus of wailing and gnashing of teeth from the newspapers who had once frowned at it, *Play School* closed its door for the last time on 11 March 1988. In its place came *Playbus* – later *Playdays* (BBC, 1988–97) – created by Cynthia Felgate and featuring a weekly set of rotating 'stops' that very much reflected the experiences of modern working parents trying to entertain and educate their children on the move. Rumours that Humpty tried to work his way into the programme by wearing a bus driver's hat sadly cannot be confirmed.

Even a generous observer would say that *Rainbow* was starting to look a little out of step by this time too, but it ploughed relentlessly on, and not without good reason. The generation that had grown up watching Geoffrey and company were now teenagers and students, and had come to embrace the show with irony-laden nostalgia, more often than not accompanied by distinctly off-colour jokes about the cast and settings. The show itself had barely changed in over a decade – even the original theme and the by now crumbly-looking animated titles were still in place – and this not only arguably neglected its intended audience while pandering to another one altogether, it also made it more vulnerable to the whims of the 'top brass'. When Thames lost the weekday franchise for the London ITV region in 1991, its successor, Carlton, was not interested in *Rainbow*, and the final edition abruptly went out on 6 March 1992. A million student unions promptly organised petitions but to little avail – an independently produced reboot, with the original puppets and newcomer blue rabbit Cleo now working in a toy shop, came and went in 1993 without anyone really noticing – and the tabloids took vindictive delight in reporting that poor old Geoffrey had been spotted working in a supermarket.

Rainbow, *Play School*, *Pipkins*, *Hickory House* and all of the others – possibly even *Daisy, Daisy* – had delighted a generation who clapped and sang and laughed and learned along with them, not least because they got to do so at home rather than at nursery school, but once again, attitudes were changing and their approach was starting to feel as out of date as 'Peter and Jane' books and erasers with an 'ink' side. Computers were beginning to find their way into classrooms, and craft lessons were less about making desk tidies than they were about putting together your own newspaper, albeit without Inky and Elsa's assistance. It was time for pre-school television to finally put on its uniform and head for big school.

'And I'll tell you . . . tomorrow'

On 31 July 1964, the Public Libraries and Museums Act 1964 – which made it a statutory requirement for all local authorities in

England and Wales to maintain a comprehensive library service accessible to all – gained royal assent. A lot of new libraries built in the same concrete, minimalist style suddenly sprang up all over the UK, new books in glossy laminated dustjackets flooded in to fill them, and a weekly visit to get a couple of books out became a family ritual for decades to come. It wasn't always as much of a thrill as that might make it sound, though – even aside from the fact that after choosing your books, you would have to make your way through the maze-like and eerily silent adult section to locate your parent or guardian, tiptoeing trepidatiously past shelves full of thrillers with scarily stark covers, you might still find that your local library didn't have the book everyone was talking about at school in stock. Fortunately, a much bigger and much more esoterically stocked library had also just opened on television – and it would stay open for decades.

It was the popularity of the storytelling slot in *Play School* – then itself only a couple of months old – that led to a suggestion that a longer dedicated programme aimed at a slightly older audience would be ideal for BBC1's main afternoon children's slot. *Play School* editor Joy Whitby assigned her colleagues Anna Home and Molly Cox to develop the new project, and while they soon worked up a format that could encompass all forms of stories ancient and modern, comic and serious, fantastic and realistic, what they still didn't have was a suitably catchy name. On a short break in the Scottish countryside, Anna remembered a traditional rhyme that began 'I'll tell you a story of Jack A'Nory', and in those pre-internet days had to wait until she returned home to check up on its origins in a library. It was, it turned out, a derivation of a politically motivated slogan, and she was amusedly indignant never to receive a single letter of complaint about this.

PRE-SCHOOL AND STORYTELLING

Introduced by an onomatopoeic theme tune and a rotating kaleidoscope featuring images from the story – an idea that Anna Home borrowed intentionally from 'Watch with Mother' show *Picture Book* (BBC, 1955–63) – *Jackanory* (BBC, 1965–95) essentially involved little other than a storyteller reading a serialised adaptation to the camera, but that description makes it sound a good deal more straightforward than it actually was. Limited production time and presenter availability meant that there was no option other than for them to read from huge rolls of annotated and physically edited autocue paper rather than learning the text, while the show itself was recorded in one take with no edits, somehow managing to combine both the advantages of cutting-edge broadcast technology and the fraught tension of live television at the same time.

Commissioned for an initial six-week run, *Jackanory*'s first week was taken up by a collection of British folk tales read by actor Lee Montague, beginning with 'A Cap of Rushes' on 13 December 1965. Like the other four instalments that week, it featured Lee narrating directly to camera – and indeed directly to the audience; Anna Home's intention was that the presenter would always speak as if addressing each viewer individually – with occasional cutaways to a dancer or an illustration, both to add some variety and to give them an opportunity to catch their breath.

Setting out its stall early as a show that could have anyone from scientists to tugboat captains as storytellers, that initial six-week run also included a selection of Alison Uttley stories read by theatrical legend Wendy Hillier and Hans Christian Andersen tales from her contemporary Enid Lorimer, Christmas stories from educational pioneer Brian Way, African folk tales from calypso musician George 'Young Tiger' Browne and comedy star Hattie Jacques' interpretation of *Mary Poppins*. Before they had even reached Hattie's week, however, *Jackanory* had been commissioned to run all year round, proving such a sensation that it was profiled in March 1966 on the BBC2 arts show *Late Night Line-Up*, with the formidable actress Margaret Rutherford admitting to the presenters that she had found her week of Beatrix Potter stories more daunting than any West End production.

The show was soon attracting very big names indeed – in the first couple of years alone Alan Bennett, Dudley Moore, Jane Asher, Thora Hird, Sheila Hancock, Jon Pertwee, Susannah York, George Melly and Rodney Bewes all made appearances – but the focus was always on matching the correct reader with the correct story, and they could find themselves bookended by everyone from singer-songwriter Julie Felix to historian Wendy Wood. Some readers seemed to strike a particular chord with the audience, though, and two in particular became almost synonymous with *Jackanory*.

Bernard Cribbins first appeared in December 1966 reading a selection of panto-associated fairy stories; across a whopping 111 further appearances, he read everything from *The Wizard of Oz* and *Through the Looking-Glass* to *The Wind in the Willows* and Dalek creator Terry Nation's children's novel *Rebecca's World*, though he was most popularly associated with Joan Aiken's outlandish tales of a girl and her unpredictable pet crow, *Arabel and Mortimer*.

Kenneth Williams was already a star of stage, screen and radio when the idea of using him on *Jackanory* was broached. There were concerns, however, from within the BBC, who considered that his taboo-breakingly outrageous double-act with Hugh Paddick as resting 'theatricals' Julian and Sandy in the Home Service sketch show *Round the Horne* was not necessarily something that should be associated with a children's programme; and indeed concerns from Williams himself, who had somehow come under the impression that he would be required to wear a special *Jackanory* hat. Eventually, without a hat and with a distinct lack of omi-palone to his trollin', he arrived at the studios late in 1968 to read an adaptation of Noel Langley's *The Land of Green Ginger*, beginning an association that continued throughout his career; he made more than sixty appearances and frequently spoke of *Jackanory* with fondness in his otherwise famously waspish diaries.

Although he found himself reading stories by anyone from Roald Dahl to historian Nikolai Tolstoy, Williams came to be most closely associated with two recurring strands that allowed him to fully indulge his talent for facial expressions and outrageous voices – Norman Hunter's absurdist tales of life in and around the fictional kingdom of Incrediblania, including the celebrated tale of *The Dribblesome Teapots*, and Swedish author Nils-Olof Franzén's comic tales of intrepid detective Agaton Sax. Previously little-known in the UK, the Agaton Sax books became hugely popular in the seventies, largely on account of Williams' readings and Quentin Blake's illustrations.

Williams also became enthusiastically involved with the regular *Jackanory* writing competitions, which saw viewers invited to submit stories, plays and poems, with the winning entries read out on air – although, considering that they began in 1968, it is worth noting that ITV had recently staged a similar endeavour with Rediffusion's *Write a Play* (ITV, 1965–67), presented by Jimmy Hanley with a repertory company including Geraldine Newman, Derren Nesbitt, Aubrey Morris and Tim Brooke-Taylor. In 1975, one of the winning entries was a wry comic short about a remarkable antique find, 'The Rag and Bone Man', written by thirteen-year-old David Benson. Although he was initially displeased with the voices that Williams gave to his characters, David eventually became an actor himself and went on to play Kenneth in several productions, including revivals of *Round the Horne*. Quite what anyone who had been wary of the idea of him appearing on *Jackanory* back in 1968 would have made of that is sadly not on record.

Although the earliest editions had mostly featured the readers sitting on a wrought-iron bench with an object related to the story on a table next to them, *Jackanory* quickly expanded its horizons and began to experiment with different styles, settings and locations and even live-action filmed inserts, with silent footage in *The Children of Green Knowe* (1966), *The Bookshop on the Quay* (1968) and *The Warden's Niece* (1968), followed by the arrival of the talkies with *The Witch's Daughter* later that same year.

While the stories would and could come from anywhere and everywhere, some up and coming writers seemed to fit *Jackanory*'s approach especially well, and the show played a significant part in the rising popularity of, amongst others, Helen Cresswell, Nina Bawden, Joan Aiken and Roald Dahl, and Joyce Grenfell's readings of Astrid Lindgren's Pippi Longstocking stories brought the previously obscure and untranslated books to wider attention. Many of the illustrations were provided by in-house BBC graphic artists Mina Martinez, Paul Birkbeck and Graham McCallum, who produced staggeringly detailed and evocative pieces of art that were often only seen on screen for a couple of seconds, and they must have felt somewhat relieved when some of their illustrations later found their way on to the covers of tie-in *Jackanory* storybooks.

The fleeting screentime proved the absolute making of another artist, however. Quentin Blake was a prolific but largely unknown children's illustrator when he was first approached to work on *Jackanory*. But his scratchy, impulsive and energetic style proved ideal for punctuating stories at key moments, notably his designs for *Arabel and Mortimer*, which became so synonymous with the characters that they were even used as the basis for a BBC puppet adaptation in 1993. As well as providing artwork for hundreds of editions, Blake also occasionally presented stories featuring his odd hedgehog-dragon hybrid character Lester, illustrating and embellishing the stories as he went on a huge roll of paper.

Meanwhile, aspirant writer and illustrator John Grant was working as an architect when he sent some of his stories about Littlenose – an ice-age boy who was something of an outcast on account of his remarkably ordinary hooter – into the *Jackanory* production office. Originally written to amuse his children, the stories had been roundly turned down by publishers, but his suspicion that they would find more favour on television proved to be correct. Beginning with *Two-Eyes, the Mammoth* in 1968, Grant wrote, drew and presented more than fifty stories featuring the resourceful cave-dweller, and consequently went on to enjoy a hugely successful literary career. No doubt to the regret of those publishers who hadn't been interested way back when, the Littlenose stories were also subsequently published by BBC Books. Also featured regularly – and read more than once by different presenters – were Joan Eadington's stories of the comic schemes and trivial feuds of Northern schoolboy Jonny Briggs, which would later spin off into their own live action series (BBC, 1985–87).

Surprisingly, ITV's attempts to get in on *Jackanory*'s action were few and far between, although Thames made a fair attempt with *We'll Tell You a Story* (ITV, 1980–82). Eschewing straight readings of books in favour of a more fragmented approach with impressionistic descriptive diversions and shared joke-suggesting asides to camera, it featured a rotating cast of guest readers including Barbara Flynn, Una Stubbs, Patti Boulaye and Julia McKenzie interacting with host Christopher Lillicrap, who also provided the catchy theme song and curious interludes where he 'painted' a wall to reveal an entirely different vista with the aid of nothing more than some cursorily applied visual effects. Lillicrap stuck around for *Flicks* (ITV, 1984–87), an assortment of stories and songs with an early eighties American AOR-styled theme song that sought to encourage a wider interest in literature in all of its varied fictional and non-fictional forms, before being tempted back to the BBC for *Busker* (BBC, 1984–85), a series of self-penned stories about Bully Thompson, Beefy Higgins, Swotty Hardwick and the other 'Back Alley Kids' in the guise of a chirpy guitar-strummer at train-deprived Weybury Junction. ITV never attempted such a direct encroachment on *Jackanory*'s territory again. In any case, *Jackanory* itself had more stories to hand than they appeared to know what to do with.

Attempts had been made at launching spin-off shows, with Creationist-leaning Sunday afternoon Bible story reinterpretations *In the Beginning* (BBC, 1970) and *The New Beginning* (BBC, 1972), but *Jackanory Playhouse* (BBC, 1972–85) succeeded by virtue of actually doing something different with the format. An anthology series of one-off plays mostly performed on a single studio set, they were generally – as was underlined by opening titles featuring renaissance theatrical archetypes swapping costumes in a flip-book style – tales with a humorous or fantastical slant, although there were occasional more serious entries.

The first run in 1972 included 'Lizzie Dripping and the Orphans', written by Helen Cresswell and starring Tina Heath as Penelope Arbuckle, a teenage girl with a reputation as a dreamer who encounters a village witch that nobody else will believe her about. It proved popular enough to inspire a full series of *Lizzie Dripping* (BBC, 1973–75), and a series of novels that, in a pleasingly postmodern note, were later read for *Jackanory* by Patricia Routledge. With a lot of juvenile roles to fill, *Jackanory Playhouse* was also keen to engage up and coming acting talent, and during the final run in 1984, the title role in historical farce 'The Prattling Princess' was taken by Patsy Kensit, very shortly before she went on to find wider fame, fortune and acclaim.

Meanwhile, its parent show gave no indication of slowing down and in October 1979, *Jackanory* marked its three thousandth edition in remarkable style with an ambitious ten-part presentation of J.R.R. Tolkein's *The Hobbit*. Gathered around a blazing campfire in a woodland clearing — or at least an approximation of one in a small BBC studio — Bernard Cribbins, Maurice Denham, Jan Francis and David Wood swapped positions, characters and narrative duties as they thundered through Tolkein's dense descriptions and riddling dialogue, with their delivery and physical repositioning becoming ever more urgent as the cliff-hanger of each instalment loomed. It was a fine way to mark a rarely equalled achievement, and also illustrated just how willing *Jackanory* was to experiment with its format in both small ways and large, if they suited the story being told. Whether it was Judi Dench reading *A Dog So Small* in the company of a gang of surprisingly well-behaved puppies in 1978, Spike Milligan's suitably wild and eccentric delivery of absurdist thriller *Help! I Am a Prisoner in a Toothpaste Factory* in 1979, David Baxt stirring latent emotions with adolescent love rivalry saga *The Cybil War* in 1984, or Tom Baker ominously yet dispassionately intoning the tale of *The Iron Man* to a musique concrète backing in 1986 — slightly different, it has to be said, to Denholm Elliot's more sedate 1972 reading — *Jackanory*'s strength was that you never quite knew what you were going to get, or how you would get it.

Although subtly adapted variants of the kaleidoscope and the theme still occasionally appeared, by the eighties it was more common for stories to be introduced by appropriate showtunes, movie themes or pop songs, and it's possible that many viewers had their first exposure to The Shadows' 'Apache' via *The Indian in the Cupboard* with Martin Jarvis in 1981, or even The Beatles through 'Magical Mystery Tour' introducing Hywel Bennett reading *The Phantom Tollbooth* in 1983. In 1982, they even produced a full-cast dramatisation of Nicholas Fisk's saga of adolescent space pioneers, *Starstormers*, which measured up well against the higher profile sci-fi efforts of the day; and in December 1984, Martin Jarvis read *William at Christmas* from inside a replica of The Browns' family home, complete with period décor and furnishings. *Jackanory* even had a royal visitor in 1984, as the Prince of Wales narrated his children's book *The Old Man of Lochnagar* while standing against a rock on a very chilly-looking Scottish hillside.

A handful of further spin-off shows stayed close to the *Jackanory* format while aiming for a very different tone. Tellingly pushed to the very edge of the children's schedules, and in suitably close proximity to the equally terrifying prospect of The News, *Spine Chillers* (BBC, 1980) featured a series of classic supernatural stories by the likes of M.R. James, John Wyndham and H.G. Wells given suitably ominous voice by such heavyweight theatrical types as Freddie Jones, John Woodvine and Jonathan Pryce in musty Victorian study and laboratory sets. Just in case any stragglers who were too young or of too nervous a disposition to appreciate the subtleties of 'The Stolen Bacillus' were still looking in unaware, it handily opened with distorted clock chimes and wind and animated scratchy drawings of an abandoned house.

Unless you had a fear of accidentally becoming engaged to obnoxious heiresses, there was less disturbing potential to be found

PRE-SCHOOL AND STORYTELLING

in *Welcome to Wodehouse* (BBC, 1982), with John Alderton and Paul Eddington clearly having a whale of a time introducing a new generation to the delights of Bertram Wilberforce Wooster and Blandings Castle. In an indication of how much matters had moved on since *Jackanory*'s earliest days, *Never Kiss Frogs!* (BBC, 1989) ran through a set of quirky romance stories with familiar Children's BBC faces Sophie Aldred and Jonathon Morris. One particular spin-off in 1986, however, showed as much what *Jackanory* was capable of as it did the fact that it might struggle to adapt to changing times.

By 1985, Tony Robinson may have been better known for his appearances in edgy comedy shows like *Who Dares Wins* (BBC, 1983–88) and *The Black Adder* (BBC, 1983), but he had also enjoyed a long early association with Children's BBC, and a rant to his colleagues in the bar about how much he disliked *Jackanory* – after appearing in the *Jackanory Playhouse* production 'Rolf the Stonemason' – in 1984 led to a challenge to do something better himself. With the aid of *Blackadder* writer Richard Curtis, he adapted several Greek myths into 'Theseus the Hero', which was transmitted as part of *Jackanory* in January 1985. Far from classical presentations of the classics, these impressionistic takes were informed by Tony's belief that they were at heart simple stories elaborately told, and in a manner that was not as far removed from hit American adventure series like *The Dukes of Hazzard* and *The A-Team* as scholars might like to think. He delivered them directly to camera while haring around appropriate locations with camerawork inspired by the dynamic handheld approach favoured by BBC youth shows at the time.

Intended to shake matters up, 'Theseus the Hero' attracted so much positive attention that Tony and Richard were invited back for a full-scale standalone series on a similar theme. Delivered in the to-camera manner of an alternative comedian while darting around heritage sites and through crowds of bemused pensioners on shopping trips, 'Odysseus: The Greatest Hero of Them All' (BBC, 1986) was very specifically aimed at the sort of children who might have ordinarily considered the subject wide berth-invitingly boring. The retold Greek myths gleefully concentrated on the inherent absurdity and elements of gross-out humour, and drew a great deal of critical attention before being rapidly repeated in a more prominent slot on BBC2; a tie-in paperback also sold out two successive print runs. Tony returned to *Jackanory* to read Terry Jones' *Nicobobinus* in 1989 and a collection of Old Testament stories under the banner 'Blood and Honey' in 1991, and also joined forces with Toyah Willcox for a musical retelling of the legend of Boudicca in 1988, but even they could not have prepared anyone for *Jackanory*'s single most controversial – and popular – moment.

A leading light of the alternative comedy boom, Rik Mayall was still considered dangerous and outrageous enough to be widely denounced as 'shocking' in 1986, so booking him to read Roald Dahl's *George's Marvellous Medicine* was daring, risky and – for the audience that it was actually made for – absolutely electrifying. Using his full array of wild voices and even wilder facial expressions, Rik turned the tale of a boy who mixes up a supernaturally powerful elixir from household items into a careering, haphazard tour de force that wasn't officially presented in character as Rik from *The Young Ones* but may as well have been. He also carried the whole exercise off with a great deal of style and charm, meaning that those who did not want to simply make fools of themselves by writing in to complain that it was 'vulgar' or 'rubbish' had to resort to expressing concerns that it was encouraging children to experiment with dangerous substances; presumably the considerable comic mileage that he had repeatedly derived from warning against tampering with medicine or cleaning products had

PRE-SCHOOL AND STORYTELLING

completely passed them by. Fondly recalled and regarded by many as *Jackanory*'s finest hour and ten minutes, it's a fair bet that your teacher would have brooked little mention of it while trying to get you all to settle down for another chapter of *Still William* the following day. While indignant parents might have complained, children loved it and more importantly so did veteran *Jackanory* storyteller Bernard Cribbins, who excitedly informed the production team that he had really enjoyed what Rik did with the story.

With its influence obvious everywhere else in the BBC's children's schedules – from Michael Hordern and animator Sheila Graber's acclaimed retellings of Rudyard Kipling's *Just So Stories* (BBC, 1985) to *What's Your Story?* (BBC, 1988–90), featuring Sylvester McCoy introducing an ongoing serial based entirely on suggestions sent in by viewers – in some regards *Jackanory* was approaching the nineties with a new sense of confidence; and although scheduling conflicts saw them miss out on the actual anniversary date, there was no way that the show's twenty-fifth birthday could go by without a fuss. While earlier anniversaries and milestones had often warranted little more than a half-sentence mention in *Radio Times*, *Silver Jackanory* – launched on 2 January 1991 – was a huge event involving a lavish tie-in collection of stories in both book and double-cassette format, promotional events at local libraries and a months-long season of on-screen celebrations.

As well as an assortment of competition winners' stories given readings by the likes of Mel Smith, Jan Francis and Danny John-Jules, *Silver Jackanory* also took in a new interpretation of *Charlie and the Chocolate Factory*, read by Sylvester McCoy; a repeat of Victoria Wood's 1989 telling of *Matilda*; Helena Bonham Carter reading Philippa Pearce's *The Way to Sattin Shore*; new self-penned stories from Tony Robinson, Griff Rhys Jones, and *Going Live!*'s resident comedians Trev Neal and Simon Hickson in the guise of their 'World of the Strange' characters; a Comic Relief Special with Angus Deayton, Clive Anderson and Tony Slattery; and inevitable jubilatory appearances for *Arabel and Mortimer*, *Lizzie Dripping* and *Jonny Briggs*.

In the true tradition of a story with a twist ending, however, this celebratory mood was to prove a little optimistic. Following a huge modernising overhaul of Children's BBC's output, *Jackanory*'s number of episodes per year had been steadily decreasing since 1985, and early in 1994 it was moved back to an earlier timeslot. The difference may only have been ten minutes, but it was a difference that brought it closer to programmes intended for the youngest end of Children's BBC's audience – literally the opposite to *Spine Chillers* – and it was only a matter of time before *Jackanory* ran into trouble.

Accompanied by weird angular and jagged model animations and threatened intonations of chaos and destruction, Janet McTeer and Jonathan Hyde's reading of Ted Hughes' *The Iron Woman* in the week commencing 1 March 1994 provoked a flood of complaints from parents whose sobbing offspring had not exactly been expecting this straight after the arts and crafts jollity of *Bitsa* (BBC, 1991–96). Meanwhile, older viewers who would probably have appreciated the exceptional production more than likely did not even see it. Possibly not entirely coincidentally, BBC1 broadcast its last edition of *Jackanory* on 31 March 1995, after which it was moved to Sunday mornings on BBC2, with entire stories told in one long show.

Longtime *Jackanory* writer and director turned producer Nel Romano had done her best to revive the show's fortunes, introducing a fresh roster of readers including Paul Merton, Kathy Burke, Mike McShane, Sandi Toksvig and Ade Edmondson, as well as bringing back Tony Robinson and Rik Mayall – the latter reading the almost equally memorable *The Fwog Pwince: The Twuth!* – and capitalising on the improv comedy boom by introducing 'Pass the Story', a strand in which a troupe of players including Sylvester McCoy, Jim Sweeney, Richard Vranch, Vicky Licorish and Siobhan Finneran made up a complete tale from scratch.

It was, however, a bold attempt to revive a show with no support or encouragement, and once it was cast away on BBC2 at a time, on a day and in a format it was never intended for, *Jackanory*'s days were numbered. The final run included such prominent storytellers as Alexei Sayle, Floella Benjamin and Diane-Louise Jordan, but it's doubtful that their efforts reached the audience that they deserved. Lost and unloved, *Jackanory* bowed out on 24 March 1996 with a suitably poignant and reflective reading by Alan Bennett of *The House on Pooh Corner*. It was a ceremonious end in unceremonious circumstances.

Like all good books, however, there was no simply putting *Jackanory* back on the shelf. The show was briefly revived by CBBC in 2006, and then by CBeebies as *Jackanory Junior* between 2007 and 2009, eventually evolving into the same channel's enduring *Bedtime Stories* (2009–). Dolly Parton reading *Dog Loves Books* on a digital-only channel may seem a long way from 'A Cap of Rushes', but it's not really that big a distance at all. Especially when you compare it to the long walk past all those Agatha Christie and Frederick Forsyth books to find your dad. There may be fewer libraries now, but you can bet that in whatever one is nearest to you, there's still a waiting list for *Agaton Sax and Lispington's Grandfather Clock*.

4

Smallfilms

'Wake up, be bright, be golden and light'

Once upon a time, not so long ago, children's television was being made by two successive generations of creatives trying to please a third who they were expected to at least encourage to be creative themselves. Some were young, dynamic and thrusting, determined to wrest the best possible entertainment out of new technology and make modern and relatable programming for a new audience in a rapidly changing society. Some came from an earlier age of storytelling pre-dating television and even in some cases radio, who could never quite understand why you might need a story about a street-cleaning lorry when one about a wooden toy soldier would do. Somehow, between them, they usually got it right – but the contrast was not necessarily as jarring as it might appear. Many children watched these new and exciting shows while being looked after by their grandparents, who – coming from that same wartime generation – would spend the rest of the day entertaining them with activities that engaged the hands and mind as much as the eyes and ears, and with tales both of and from the 'old days'. The shows included those made by a pair of animators whose productions took full advantages of the possibilities of television while simultaneously harking back to a time when the men of the northlands sat by their great log fires and told a tale.

Oliver Postgate was working as a stage manager for ITV's London area broadcaster Associated-Rediffusion when, believing he could do better than the meagre and threadbare output that he felt the company was foisting on its youngest viewers, he wrote a six-episode serial entitled *Alexander the Mouse* (ITV, 1958). The story of an unsuspecting rodent who finds himself crowned king in a mouse cathedral underneath the London Docklands, it was immediately commissioned and, to help Oliver realise it, he was paired up with art teacher Peter Firmin and – less happily – a new and exciting animation system. Based around an all too particular arrangement of mirrors and magnets, Vistamotion purportedly allowed animation to be broadcast 'live' by manipulating figures with magnetic poles, but as any child watching would have been all too aware, when two characters were accidentally pushed towards each other the wrong way around, one would inevitably spin around and wind up upside down; and, as the show was broadcast live, there was no option but to reach in and manually right them on camera. Many of Postgate and Firmin's later shows famously unnerved some viewers, but sadly there is no surviving audience response survey recording how many children were traumatised by suddenly seeing a giant hand on-screen.

There was plenty of praise for their efforts, though, and plenty of imagination on display as well; surviving artwork from *Alexander the Mouse* includes an ingenious realisation of a 'mouse choir' made up of what look like close evolutionary relations of certain better-known characters from another of Postgate and Firmin's Smallfilms shows. This mild acclaim was enough to persuade Oliver, suitably repelled by magnetism, to invest in a camera and teach himself to animate on film using cut-outs designed by Peter, making his other equipment himself out of mechanical junk and odds and ends. This display of initiative led to *The Journey of Master Ho* (ITV, 1958), a willow pattern-inspired serial about a boy and a water buffalo aimed at deaf viewers and broadcast with sign language, and they also contributed puppets and films to *Musical Box* (ITV, 1959–64), presented by folk singer Wally Whyton and based around traditional stories and nursery rhymes.

The much more straightforward *Dogwatch* (ITV, 1960–61) saw Oliver as a lighthouse keeper regaled by literal shaggy dog stories from Peter's puppet Fred Barker as they watched short films on a steam-powered television; Fred and his voice artist Ivan Owen subsequently joined forces with owl puppet Ollie Beak for a slot on lunchtime miscellany *Small Time* (ITV, 1955–66). And when a third puppet was needed to join Howard Williams and Scottish hedgehog Spike McPike for a new 'Small Time' show called *The Three Scampies*, Peter came up with a well-heeled fox in a tweed jacket. With the addition of Ivan Owen's boom-booming 'cad'-type voice, Basil Brush was born.

Smallfilms' big break, however, came with a little story about a steam engine from the top lefthand corner of Wales who dreamed of singing with a choir. Heavily influenced by *Under Milk Wood*, Dylan Thomas' landmark 1954 BBC radio drama, *Ivor the Engine* (ITV, 1959–64) told the tale of the apparently sentient, slow but sturdy old locomotive, his patient driver Jones the Steam and the eccentric local residents and employees of the Merioneth and Llantisilly Railway Traction Company Ltd as they helped to realise his coal-fuelled dream, building up to the installation of three church organ pipes in place of Ivor's whistle.

Ivor's 'singing' voice and the charming, shunting theme which slowly but surely picked up speed were the result of Oliver and Peter's first collaboration with a musician who became a major part of the Smallfilms story – Vernon Elliott. A classical bassoonist and longtime member of the Royal Philharmonic Orchestra, Vernon had been recommended to Oliver by popular bandleader Steve Race, who was at that point acting as a musical adviser to Associated-Reduffusion. Working from Oliver's carefully timed, intricate yet comic doodles on the scripts, Vernon was able to create beautifully evocative and character-underlining musical motifs as well as assorted crashes, bangs and wallops for a small ensemble featuring woodwind, brass, piano and percussion. The actual crashes, bangs and wallops – not to mention Ivor's shuffling engine sounds – were provided by Oliver, and more importantly he also provided the narration, in a deep and densely expressive tone that spoke the way that Ivor's cut-out mining valley backgrounds looked. Smallfilms – the production banner that they had adopted for Ivor the Engine – was starting to make a name for itself, and it wasn't long before the other channel started to take an interest too.

Inspired by an exhibition of medieval playing pieces the Lewis Chessmen, the saga of *Noggin the Nog* (BBC, 1959–65) and his fellow blocky Norsemen began with the epic and windswept tale of Noggin's quest to find a bride to avoid his kingdom falling into the hands of his disreputable uncle Nogbad the Bad. Noggin eventually meets and marries the exotic and benevolent – but more than capable of seeing off their adversaries all by herself – Nooka of the North, with a little romantic encouragement courtesy of her peculiar green bird emissary, the Graculus. Subsequent historical chronicles saw the Nogs coming to the aid of the people of Hotwater Valley in their struggle against the Ice Dragon but inevitably finding all was not quite as it seemed: a quest to retrieve Noggin's stolen crown – you'll never guess who it was stolen by – in an otherwise untested Flying Machine; an encounter with the minuscule Omruds; and Nogbad's attempt to hijack the Nogs' brand-new, literally explosive invention, the Firecake, for his own clandestine purposes. Redolent of a lost world of cinema screens full of grand sweeping shots of longboats and stirring yet haunting music, Oliver's voice resonated with friendliness and warmth in the midst of loneliness and isolation, much as it had done with *Ivor the Engine*, and matched beautifully with Peter's similarly friendly and rich yet archaic and austere designs and illustrations. It was a combination that captivated viewers of all ages, helping to make Smallfilms' productions both distinctive and beloved.

It was an aesthetic that appeared across a long series of shows, including some other largely long-forgotten earlier efforts. The penguin-like *Pingwings* (ITV, 1961–65) lived in a corner of a barn on Berrydown Farm, where they enjoyed whimsical adventures intercut with live action scenes featuring the blissfully unaware Mr and Mrs Farmer and Gay the goat. As Smallfilms' ad-hoc studio was situated in a barn adjacent to the converted farmhouse that acted as the Firmin family home, many of the animated sequences were actually shot in the great outdoors, giving the earnest-looking knitted creatures an additional air of believability.

The Seal of Neptune (BBC, 1960) and *The Mermaid's Pearls* (BBC, 1962) may have looked like the adventures of *Noggin the Nog*, but they took place deep beneath the icy storm-lashed waves as Cyrus the Seahorse and Bartholomew, or Shrimp to his friends, the Shrimp – in what became something of a recurrent motif for Smallfilms – sought to reunite mislaid sub-aquatic treasures with their rightful owners. Based on V.H. Drummond's storybooks about an enthusiastically over-imaginative toddler at large in a small town, *Little Laura* (BBC, 1960) was financed by Drummond herself as an independent production with narration from Denise Bryar; it hasn't been seen anywhere since, and it's not impossible that Laura's own peculiar brand of eccentric mischief is somehow responsible for its disappearance.

Sometimes, though, that distinctive artistic aesthetic could prove a little too much for any younger viewers who didn't entirely share it. Shown as part of the magazine show *Clapperboard* (BBC, 1964–65) alongside a profile of Smallfilms, *The Pogles* (BBC, 1965) was a serial so dark and macabre that even Nogbad the Bad might have hidden behind the sofa when it came on. Previously everyday rustic tree-dwelling imp-folk, Mr and Mrs Pogle and their pink and ginger squirrelish house pet Tog found their woodland idyll turned upside down by the arrival of a small child they named Pippin, followed with unnerving haste by the arrival of a witch who wants to abscond with him; this was less surprising once it became apparent that he was actually the son of a Fairy King left with the kindly couple for safekeeping. The Pogles eventually manage to drive the hooded, crooked-eyed sorceress away through a combination of Tog's ingenuity and a haunting existential incantation, but in reality they could really have just as easily got rid of her with paperwork. The BBC liked *The Pogles* enough to want to see more of them in a show aimed at slightly younger viewers, but did not want the witch anywhere near it. The original serial was only shown once, and the nightmarish sorceress was sent packing, broomstick and all, never to be seen again. Their wariness of the witch possibly isn't too hard to understand, as legend has it that some of Oliver's children would not even set foot in the same room as the puppet.

Introduced by Oliver asking, 'Now where shall we find the Pogles?' over a makeshift wooden sign helpfully pointing the way, *Pogles' Wood* (BBC, 1965–67) concentrated instead on the now Wiccan-untroubled family's homespun philosophies and make-do-and-mend sense of home entertainment. Thanks to Pippin's curiosity and Tog's high spirits, the outdoor sequences took them further than any Pingwing ever dared, including out on the water and up in the air, although they were always careful to duck out of sight if an actual human appeared. Friendly flowers and the Pipe Cleaner People, however, provided a much greater reason for sociability.

Without a witch to scare them away, viewers took to *Pogles' Wood* with great enthusiasm – the long-running children's *Pippin* comic, featuring strips based on many of their animated small-screen contemporaries, was originally launched as a direct tie-in with it – and it's a measure of the show's popularity that despite being made in black and white, it was still being shown in the 'Watch with Mother' slot well into the seventies.

Clangers (BBC, 1969–74) was their first colour production, but although it took Smallfilms if not quite into the future then at least into the not-too-distant reaches of space, their future ironically took the production company into the past. Not as far back as Noggin and his longboats had ventured, but somehow more distant, and in sepia too.

In the second run of BBC Schools' primary literacy strand *Words and Pictures* – usurping Gabriel Woolf and his puppet pals Lazybones and General George and their escapades in *Up in the Attic* (BBC, 1970) – *Sam on Boffs' Island* (BBC, 1972) featured Tony Robinson as Sam Samson, a young daydreamer who finds he is able to travel to the land of the Boffs, a race of tiny humanlike figures including What-Boff, Paper-Boff, Sell-Boff and the alphabetically assigned Say-Birds, whose economy and society is based around words and letters. The puppets and artwork for the show were created and animated by Oliver and Peter, and it brought them into contact with two musicians who would play a major role in their next show. *Sam on Boffs' Island* was written by the renowned children's author Michael

Rosen, and to conjure up the skittering jigs and reels he had envisaged to accompany his eccentric inventions, he had recommended two musicians he had previously worked with as part of legendary folk musician Ewen MacColl's Critics Group, multi-instrumentalists John Faulkner and Sandra Kerr. Having impressed Oliver greatly with their contributions, John and Sandra remained on board for *Bagpuss* (BBC, 1974), Smallfilms' most ambitious, most widely remembered and arguably – although this is certainly a closely contested honour – most well-loved work. You could even say it was the most important, the most beautiful and the most magical.

Each episode of *Bagpuss* opened with quaint plucked acoustic tones on archaic instruments and a series of sepia-tinted still images following a young Victorian girl named Emily – in reality Peter's daughter, also called Emily, photographed in and around the family home – as she made her way to her shop which didn't sell anything; instead, it just displayed lost items in the window in the hope that their owner might be passing and spot them. The shop was also home to Emily's stuffed cat Bagpuss – 'the most important, the most beautiful, the most magical, saggy old cloth cat in the whole wide world' – who, possibly out of her awareness, magically came to life when she recited the incantation, 'Bagpuss, dear Bagpuss, old fat furry catpuss, wake up and look at this thing that I bring. Wake up, be bright, be golden and light – Bagpuss, oh hear what I sing,' as the image suddenly shuddered into colour with a spectral shimmer on a dulcimer.

As the pink and white sage stretched and yawned, a number of other characters scattered around the shop also blinked into existence. Williemouse, Jenniemouse, Lizziemouse, Janiemouse, Eddiemouse and little Charliemouse – the ornamental mice on a frieze running around a novelty, bellows-powered, musical magic lantern 'Mouse-Organ' – Madeleine the Rag Doll in her wicker chair, banjo-toting tin-dwelling Gabriel the Toad, and Professor Augustus Barclay Yaffle, a carved wooden bookend in the shape of a woodpecker, who would hop down to a series of descending pizzicato notes from his suitably academic bookshelf — bearing such lost-in-time titles as *Arctic Adventure* and *Where to Look for Wild Flowers* — to join the throng pondering over what Emily had brought them this time. The mice would clean and repair it while singing a shrill-voiced round about their chosen method of restoration before suggesting a wildly fantastical imagined purpose; Yaffle would counter this with a more rational and scientific postulation; and Gabriel and Madeleine — or John and Sandra — would sing a folk song vouchsafing a purported backstory that sat somewhere between the two, accompanied either by pictures and animation dreamed up by a Thinking Cap-sporting Bagpuss, or projected after much huffing, puffing and heaving, onto the wheezing Marvellous Mechanical Mouse-Organ. With everybody more or less satisfied, the object was pushed into the window as Bagpuss gave a big yawn and settled down to sleep — although on a couple of occasions he started to curl up before anyone was ready, leading to a frantic viewer-alarming scramble to get the object and themselves back into position in time — and everyone retreated back into sepia and back into the past. Even Bagpuss himself, once he was asleep, was just a saggy old cloth cat. Baggy, and a bit loose at the seams, but Emily loved him.

In retrospect, it isn't difficult to see why viewers fell for *Bagpuss* in such an emotional and enduring manner. Each episode includes three or four different animated segments in different styles but with all of them driving the narrative, plenty of guessing games and low-level dry humour, and John and Sandra's songs, many of which would not have sounded out of place on a contemporaneous acid-folk album that now changes hands for ridiculous sums of money. Even the actual objects featured in the episodes have become cultural shorthand – whether it's the squawking bagpipe-resembling tartan pincushion creature known as the Hamish; the inside-out cloth homestead of Silly Old Uncle Feedle; the fragmented crown that a bored princess tossed into the sky for her unwanted suitors to follow as they turned into dragonflies; the ballet shoe that a pair of determined mice row, row, rowed towards their promised land of revolting stinking Stilton Cheese; or the ornate cushion favoured by the uncomfortably throned Bony King Of Nowhere.

If there is one particular episode that pretty much everyone remembers, then it's the one where the mice momentarily fool Professor Yaffle into believing that a toy mill is being used for forging chocolate biscuits out of breadcrumbs and butterbeans until – against their suspiciously hasty advice – he ventures round the back and discovers the extent of their ingenious and industrious deceit, followed by Gabriel and Madeleine defusing the situation with a spellbinding number charting the changing of the seasons through the lengthy genesis of a loaf of bread, lightened right at the conclusion by a memorable exhortation to a baker to 'get out of bed, put that silly old hat on your head'.

It's impossible to say for certain, but part of the reason for the enduring popularity of *Bagpuss* may lie in the fact that there were so many happy accidents during the show's production. Bagpuss himself was originally supposed to be a less memorable and more Tog-resembling shade of ginger and white, but a mix-up with the fabric dye meant he came back with pink stripes. Yaffle was originally intended to be a more humanlike academic named Professor Bogwood, who had got as far as concept art before the BBC – perhaps recalling the problems they had met with courtesy of the witch in *The Pogles* – insisted he was changed to a less imposing figure. The need for tight editing to fit everything in even gave rise to a mystery of sorts; during the opening titles, Gabriel inexplicably croaks like an actual toad rather than speaking with his usual rustic accent. It wasn't until the scripts were published many years later that anyone realised that this was because he was supposed to be hiccupping, a revelation that had been cut from the titles for timing reasons.

As it turned out, Smallfilms themselves were just as adept at finding and restoring an object from the past. In response to both public affection and their own enduring love of the series, Oliver and Peter remade the second and third ITV runs of *Ivor the Engine* (BBC, 1976–77) in colour for the BBC, with only very minor modifications required to the scripts and characters. Installed in the pre-news slot, where it formed an effective wind-down after the excitement of *Blue Peter* and hard-hitting drama, it was arguably even more popular, and was still being shown regularly well into the late eighties.

However, as the eighties approached, children's expectations of entertainment were changing and Children's BBC was changing with them, and Smallfilms was at risk of being left behind. Buoyed by the warm reception to the *Ivor the Engine* revival, they commenced work on a similar full-colour remake of *Noggin the Nog* late in 1979, but found that the black rocks were standing guard against the cold sea harder than ever. The new series got as far as a four-part retelling of 1961's 'Noggin and the Ice Dragon' and a two-part adaptation of the 1972 storybook *Noggin and the Pie*, but they met with surprisingly little enthusiasm within the BBC. Although in fairness they were launched with a decent amount of publicity, Noggin's new adventures were deemed to be just that little too much out of step with modern tastes, and were not shown until 1982, and even then only in a late-afternoon slot on BBC2, as a lead-in to teen drama *Maggie* and directly opposite the main evening news bulletin.

Adapted from Frank Muir's children's storybooks about *Prince Amir of Kinjan*, a scruffy and dissolute, calamity-prone Afghan puppy with a yellow duck permanently lodged atop his head, *What-A-Mess* (BBC, 1979) may have boasted narration from the widely beloved droll-voiced author and theme music from Andrew Lloyd-Webber, but it was relegated to a daily mid-morning slot over the Christmas holidays, possibly suggesting that Smallfilms' low-key and gentle approach was starting to be regarded as a little out of touch.

Based on Rumer Godden's 1947 novel *The Dolls' House*, which was sufficiently dark and macabre even on the printed page for both Rumer and Puffin Books editor Kaye Webb to express doubts over its suitability for adaptation as an animated children's series, *Tottie: The Story of a Doll's House* (BBC, 1984) still invokes a shudder amongst a generation who had presumably tuned in expecting nothing stronger than miniature furniture-based fun. Opening with an ominous existential assertion that 'Dolls are not like people – people choose, but dolls can only be chosen', the sinister and nightmarish plot revolves around a quartet of unloved and ungainly dolls – the pet-mauled and scribbled-on Highland soldier long since stripped of his regimental accoutrements Mr Plantagenet, celluloid Christmas cracker gift Birdie, unbalanceable plush baby doll Apple and cheap-joined wooden Tottie – who form themselves, along with wool-scrap dog Darner, into an ad-hoc family while being stored away in a shoebox.

Any hopes for a brighter future they may have had when they found themselves installed in an elaborate doll's house newly inherited by two young girls named Emily and Charlotte are dashed on the arrival of Tottie's old nemesis – a haughty and immaculately appointed porcelain doll named Marchpane. Determined to position herself as both head of the house and the sole recipient of Emily and Charlotte's affections, the vindictive Marchpane wages a cruel and tyrannical war on her terrified housemates, culminating in her tricking the easily flammable Birdie into coming into contact with a candle while attempting to rescue Apple from a staged accident. The serial ends with Marchpane being donated to a museum — where she relishes the prospect of an endless stream of visitors staring at her — along with Tottie's bleak reflection that Birdie had looked beautiful while being consumed by fire, and a shellshocked audience hoping that *Grange Hill* might actually provide some light relief.

With its unsettling atmosphere enhanced by the fact that the humans only appear in still images while the dolls move throughout, and an affecting turn from Una Stubbs as Birdie, *Tottie* felt tonally slightly at odds with the new direction a modernising Children's BBC was taking, and it is telling that the more upbeat sequel, *Tottie: The Doll's Wish* (BBC, 1986), in which a humbled Marchpane gets her comeuppance at the hands of loud and go-getting American action doll Melinda Shakespeare, is not nearly as well remembered.

The cloak-and-dagger soap opera shenanigans of the *Tottie* saga could not have been further removed from what turned out to be the very last Smallfilms production. Looking not unlike a story from the Marvellous Mechanical Mouse-Organ, *Pinny's House* (BBC, 1986) was a whimsical tale about the inquisitive exploits of a thimble-sized doll who lived in an altogether more cordial and sedate doll's house with her nautical friend Sam from the wooden ship next door, which were generally brought about by the eccentric play scenarios of their human owner Jo. With narration from actress Matilda Thorpe and music from Welsh neo-traditional folk outfit Ar Log, it somehow managed to feel fresh and contemporary while still retaining the established Smallfilms style, although most of those who had thrilled to the exploits of Major Clanger and Gabriel the Toad had by then grown up and moved on and mostly did not see it. Despite being repeated as many times as

Bagpuss and in the same much-loved timeslot, *Pinny's House* always seems to fall off the edge of Smallfilms retrospectives as casually as Pinny herself fell off the edges of work surfaces.

Perhaps it *was* all a little out of touch by that point. Oliver and Peter later diversified into other pursuits, and for a time even their most-loved creations had all disappeared from our television screens and were at risk of being forgotten. But when Bagpuss went to sleep, his friends most certainly did not go to sleep too. As the generation who had grown up watching their shows reached adulthood, Smallfilms' work came to be regarded with fresh nostalgic affection and critical adulation, proving once again that there's nothing wrong with telling old-fashioned stories in an old-fashioned way. Pushed into a corner of a curiosity shop, they had been given a quick once-over and come out more vibrant and complete than ever. Because – just like Emily – we loved them.

'Stranger stars by far than ever shone in our night sky'

As the Apollo 11 mission prepared to enter lunar orbit in July 1969, it wasn't all that had everyone stuck back on Earth excited about space, the final frontier. The long race to the Moon had generated an associated craze for all things cosmological that was more factual than fictional, and which rocketed on into infinity – or at least into the late eighties, when Space Shuttle launches and satellite signals were still just about considered headline news stories and it was still incredibly exciting to hear a terse, crackly sentence relayed from space with a beep after it, playing over a fuzzy photo of a NASA control room. Space-related books and do-it-yourself science kits – though possibly not MB Games Star Bird or Thomas Salter Toys Starblazer Electronic Space Command Belt – were roundly considered to be 'good' presents with strong educational value, and many a youngster would affect to have seen a comet blazing through the night sky via the low-powered telescope they had been given for their birthday. Teachers were plagued by questions about what would happen 'if' a Black Hole did something cosmologically improbable, invariably leading a classmate to chip in with an unhelpful comment about a *White* Hole, desperately trying not to give the game away that they may well have heard of it but didn't have any idea of what it actually was. For anyone who had found themselves fascinated by comets and nebulae, Patrick Moore leaping about on a beach squinting into the clouds on *The Sky at Night* – or, if you weren't allowed to stay up, John Craven next to a wonky inset picture of some stars – was pretty much appointment viewing.

There was another galaxy beyond even this, though, where fact met fiction and the potential existence of aliens was treated with absolute scientific seriousness, no matter how many arms they purportedly had. Audiences raced to see everything from *The Day the Earth Stood Still* (1951) and *Forbidden Planet* (1956) to *Close Encounters of the Third Kind* (1977) and *E.T. the Extra-Terrestrial* (1982), and if anyone was too young to get in, that didn't stop them from relating lurid and wildly inaccurate versions of their contents on the playground. Bores in the kitchen at parties disclosed unasked-for theories about how 'they' had been 'here' 'all along', and harassed mothers expressed a desperate hope that if aliens *did* exist, they might have the decency to be more civilised than us. Tellingly, when a cosmic voice claiming to be 'Vrillon of Ashtar Galactic Command' broke into ITV's early evening news bulletin after hijacking the Southern region transmitter, a large number of viewers believed 'him' to be all too real.

Jones the Steam and Mrs Pogle probably never had much cause to consider the possibility of life on other planets, but it would come literally crashing into the Land of Nog in the 1967 storybook *Noggin and the Moon Mouse*, in which a spaceship carrying a small pink mouse-like creature makes an unexpected landing in a horse trough. Once Thor Nogson had determined that the unlikely visitor had come in peace, he took him to his leader, and Noggin and Nooka helped the unnamed emissary from another world to collect the substances needed to fuel his return flight – oil, vinegar and soap flakes. Eventually they bade the friendly little pioneer a fond farewell as he blasted off into the night sky, never expecting to see him again.

Eight hundred years into the future, however – or just two years in strict chronological terms – television viewers would be seeing a good deal more of the Clangers. The story of the Moon Mouse's intergalactic voyage to television – although he lost his tail along the way, with Oliver later explaining his species had evolved away from it because it kept falling in their soup – began with a request from the BBC for Smallfilms to produce a new series in anticipation of BBC1's launch as a full-colour service on 15 November 1969. That wasn't the only major technological giant leap on the horizon, as when work began on the series, Neil Armstrong's small step onto the moon was only a feverishly counted-down matter of weeks away. Stanley Kubrick's *2001: A Space Odyssey* was still packing out cinemas after nearly a year on release, and an indefatigable would-be pop star with several years of unsuccessful singles to his name called David Bowie was starting to get radio play with an epic story-song titled 'Space Oddity' – so when Oliver's son Simon told him a bizarre tale of a giant who lived on the Moon sporting armour to protect him from meteorites and subsisting on soup drawn from the satellite's interior, something seemed to align amongst the stars. Although Petula Clark and a midnight broadcast of her Royal Albert Hall concert just beat them into Buzz Aldrin status, the Clangers made their debut on

16 November in one of the first broadcasts that most viewers in the UK would have seen in colour. Not that the Clangers themselves would have been especially impressed by that.

Taking their name from the clattering dustbin lids covering the crater entrances to their sub-surface home, the pink knitted mouse-like Clangers lived on a small blue unnamed planet close to but almost invisible from Earth, where well-meaning but curious Tiny Clanger and her slightly older brother Small Clanger spend their days looking for something interesting to do, more often than not involving an object that has landed on the planet after drifting through space, and frequently requiring the intervention of elder family members Major Clanger, Mother Clanger and Granny Clanger. Shielded from planet-bound projectiles by their homemade armour, they communicate via a series of expressive whistles and live mainly on blue string pudding and soup doled out from subterranean wells by the genial but exacting Soup Dragon. Also resident on the planet, in a vertical pond running up a cave wall, are the Froglets, small orange creatures with huge blinking eyes who teleport around in a magical top hat, along with the cave-illuminating Glow Buzzers and their hive of glow honey, and the ravenous flying Sky Moos. The technically ingenious Iron Chicken lives on a nest of scrap metal just above the planet, and there are frequent visits from helpful bugle-like neighbours The Hoots. Dotted around the surface are Music Trees bearing notes that power the Clangers' flying Music Boat, and a sentient cloud that releases musical raindrops. The Soup Dragon and the Iron Chicken both also have their own infant offspring, whose juvenile eccentricity can sometimes prove puzzling and frustrating even to Tiny Clanger.

While they all chatter away in an assortment of whistles, ribbits, metallic clucks and what can only be described as reverberating burbles, apparently unaware that they are being observed, Oliver Postgate narrates in the manner of a celestial observer way beyond the reach of a telescope, like a cosmic deity permitted to watch but forbidden by an ancient vow from interfering. His warm delight in their joys and detached alarm at their mishaps make the Clangers and company feel less like funny little characters and more like an intelligent parallel species with their own outlook, culture and conventions, although it was Oliver's introductory monologues that particularly resonated with viewers.

Over a slow camera pan to the Clangers' planet from ours, lasting barely forty seconds but feeling both longer and more profound than that might suggest, viewers are reminded — in a different manner in each episode — of the noise, clamour and pressure of life on Earth and how despite the dense population and warmth it is also a cold and lonely place; they are urged to look to the stars and the tranquil emptiness, stillness and silence of space, and imagine what better ways of living there may be out there somewhere. Smallfilms' productions were of course well known and widely celebrated for Oliver's opening narrations, but whereas the others tended to invite the audience to look ever more inwards and focus on what they could have found around the corner, or at least a historical longboat ride away, this was a step outside of the usual and the ordinary, inviting young minds and old alike to consider their place in the universe and what nonsense they took for granted or just plain put up with in their day-to-day existence.

Not that the Clangers themselves were immune to this, and they often found themselves initially seduced by an aspect of life on Earth before realising that it possibly wasn't quite their mug of soup after all. In their first set of adventures, Tiny finds a stash of glistening gold coins that are jealously hoarded until they turn out to be foil-wrapped chocolate; an attempted firework display brings the Iron Chicken down to the ground with a bump; horseplay with a balloon necessitates an inventive cave roof rescue; a Lunar Rover causes disruption to a peaceful family day; and a machine churning out useful household items proves incapable of being switched off. And then there was the incident with a television: after catching an orbiting portable set in a net, the Clangers are initially entranced by the strange sounds and lights when they tune in to a signal from Earth, but are taken aback by a ranting, self-aggrandising politician and deafened by a bunch of headbanded hippies blasting out heavy rock, so they elect to catapult it back into space where it belongs. 'It's nice to have visitors,' notes Oliver, 'but sometimes it's even nicer to see them go.' Everything invariably works out fine by the end of the episode, however, and there are plenty of healthier and more wholesome pursuits to enjoy around their rocky home terrain, including 'fishing' for metal with a magnet, Tiny's discovery that the notes from the Music Trees can be arranged into a tune, and lots of time for soup and blue-string pudding.

Just as the Nogs had helped the Moon Mouse travel back to the stars using the limited resources that they had to hand, Smallfilms' cheerful lack of flashy top-of-the-range resources – the Clangers themselves were knitted by Peter's wife, Joan, and the shimmering letters hanging in space that made up the show's title were cut out from discarded wrapping paper – actually made *Clangers* feel more 'alien', with a curious mix of the familiar and an unfamiliar setting, although the production setup was not without its headaches. Notably, the stories called for a good deal more flashes, bangs and rocket launches than Tog and Pippin ever had to contend with, and on one occasion the set briefly caught fire; eagle-eyed viewers can actually spot a single frame with a flame flickering into shot.

Meanwhile, the 'dialogue' – performed on a series of differently sized slide whistles by Oliver and Stephen Sylvester, an occasional Smallfilms contributor who had previously provided Tog's voice in *Pogles' Wood* – was actually written out in full in the scripts, using language that felt appropriate to each Clanger's character and disposition, complete with relevant stresses and emphases. It took some persuasion on Oliver's part to convince the BBC that Major Clanger's exasperated 'Sod it – the bloody thing has stuck again', on finding a door not opening on demand, would not actually be detectable to the viewing audience.

Certainly, sufficiently few of them noticed to prevent a series of *Clangers* storybooks and annuals from turning up in pillowcases over the next couple of Christmases, not to mention a *Clangers* knitting pattern available to anyone who wrote in asking for one, or indeed to stop them from returning for a second run from 18 April 1971. This time around they scored a natty new tablecloth when an astronaut planted a flag on their planet; dissuaded another space pioneer from collecting rocks by accidentally startling him into falling into some soup; learned how vanity can cause you to miss supper if you won't stop looking at yourself in a mirror; encountered a gramophone that recorded your voice as sound bubbles; took a tour of the Glow Buzzers' caves; and accidentally mistook a Gladstone bag for an alien life form. They also turned out to have acquired an unexpected celebrity fan; in the 1972 *Doctor Who* story 'The Sea Devils', the Doctor's arch adversary the Master was seen in his sea fort cell watching *Clangers* and trying to whistle along with their language. He did not seem especially pleased to learn that they were just puppets.

Perhaps getting a nod of recognition from the BBC's biggest sci-fi show shouldn't have been too much of a surprise. Intelligent, cerebral, esoteric and with a convincing feel that you actually were eavesdropping on events on another planet, few other shows ever captured the absence of sights and sounds of space that viewers could only visit in their imaginations as strongly as *Clangers*, and it had an appeal that went way beyond its intended audience. A large part of the reason for this was Vernon Elliott's music, which twinkled like stars and whizzed like comets using nothing more futuristic than his usual brass, woodwind and percussion, and which won rave reviews when it was released as an album many years later. Nowhere did all of these elements combine more effectively than in what was originally supposed to be the final episode of *Clangers*, 'The Music of the Spheres', first broadcast by BBC1 on 10 November 1972. To thank Tiny Clanger for helping them to construct a new pipe organ, the Hoots take Tiny Clanger to their planet, where she gets to conduct an orchestra of living instruments and spinning cluster formations in a grand cosmic ballet based on a two-and-a-half-minute symphonic arrangement of the tune she has been toying with since first discovering the Music Trees. Then it's time to go home, and home they go – away through the silent emptiness of space to their home planet, and green soup for supper.

Except, bizarrely, that wasn't actually the last episode of *Clangers*. The general election of February 1974, in which Labour found themselves seventeen seats short of an overall majority but unable to agree on a coalition with the Liberals, resulted in a minority government that led to a second general election being called for October. With children's programmes being shunted all over the place to allow for hasty electioneering and unexpected news updates, the BBC accepted Oliver's offer to make a short film that both explained to younger viewers why there were boring men going on and on about boring things in place of *Scooby-Doo, Where Are You!*, and more subtly to voice his own personal frustrations about petty interparty arguments that he felt were putting the politicians first and the voters pretty much nowhere in particular at all.

Broadcast while the polls were still open on 10 October 1974, 'Vote for Froglet' unusually features the Clangers being able to hear and interact with Oliver as he guides them through a mock election in which the prospect of free soup unexpectedly becomes a policy flashpoint. Eventually they get bored of politics, which they denounce as not 'nice', and head off back into the planet, with Major Clanger responding to Oliver's exasperated query over whether they are listening to him with a prolonged 'No' and an indignant slam of a dustbin lid. Presumably the BBC was too preoccupied with discussing the suitability of the blunt satire for its audience to notice Mother Clanger's weary, 'Sod off! This whole thing is a waste of time.'

'Vote for Froglet' was only shown once, and for many years was not regarded by Smallfilms as part of the series proper, but *Clangers* itself was far from a waste of time. The show made its last appearance in the pre-news slot just before Christmas 1978, but it remained a firm favourite with viewers, and perhaps more so than anyone involved with it had quite realised. It formed a huge part of the promotion for the BBC's 'Sixty Years of Children's Programmes' celebrations in 1983, and when an accompanying exhibition was held at the Liverpool International Garden Festival the following year, a visitors' book inviting attendees to suggest favourites from the archives saw page after page filled with one word again and again – Clangers.

In response to popular demand, it was given a couple of outings in an early-morning weekend slot, and in the early nineties, along with several other Smallfilms productions, it was purchased by

Channel 4, where it achieved the possibly unique feat of simultaneously appearing both as part of their children's programming and in the small hours chill-out slot aimed at winding-down clubbers. It just kept on reappearing too, firstly on Channel 5 and then across numerous newly launched digital channels, before finally alighting on CBeebies in a brand-new series of adventures. Written by Oliver's son, Daniel Postgate, who presumably favoured *Clangers* over *Pogles' Wood* on account of not having to deal with the witch, and narrated by Michael Palin, the new episodes used modern visual techniques and gentler music but – crucially – not only still used stop-motion animation in preference to CGI but also retained the flavour and setting of the original series, only introducing a handful of new characters while expanding the roles of the existing ones and revisiting old storylines, scenarios and encounters with unwelcome extra-terrestrial objects in a new context.

Eventually, long after everyone had given up on hoping to hear from aliens, whether through regional news broadcasts or otherwise, the fad for all matters cosmological dimmed like a distant pulsar. David Bowie charted Major Tom's downfall in his 1980's 'Ashes to Ashes', and most fans of *2001: A Space Odyssey* would probably prefer it if you didn't mention *2010: The Year We Make Contact*. The Clangers, however, kept on transmitting their signals back to Earth – and that's because they were so much more than just science fiction. They took small-screen animation at its lowest tech and highest quality far beyond the reaches both of our galaxy and our imagination, and they forced us to take a step outside our own orbit and take a look at our world and where we might be getting everything a little wrong and indeed a little right. More importantly, however, they were funny pink moon mice who ran around comically misunderstanding everyday objects and whistling.

Bringing matters full circle, Oliver's autobiography, *Seeing Things*, included a drawing by Peter depicting Tiny Clanger reading about her ancestor's encounter with Noggin the Nog in a history book. It's difficult to think of a more perfect illustration – literally – of what can happen when old and new ways of storytelling collide. Especially if they collide in a horse trough.

Interlude 1

Watch It!

It might well be any self-respecting broadcaster's primary consideration now, but for a long time, children's television didn't have any 'branding', and it was almost as though you'd just stumbled across it in the middle of regular programmes.

On the BBC, children's shows were introduced as usual by an announcer over the BBC globe. There were continuity slides cut into the shape of jigsaw pieces or surrounded by balloons to afford a sense of levity – which didn't exactly sit easily with *Spine Chillers* – and the occasional schedule rundown decorated with either rainbow-hued montages of Captain Pugwash, Paddington and company, or artwork of old-fashioned youngsters toting polite smiles and massive wooden toy trains, but that was pretty much the extent of it. In the school holidays, you didn't even get cursory jigsaw effect, with regular continuity slides to the fore. If you got up before television 'started', you'd just get the same again, usually with a poorly cropped extreme close-up of MacWomble or Roobarb in a pirate's hat and either 'Baby Elephant Walk' or a record with 'singing' dogs playing over it, which at least allowed the announcer to make a gag about hoping Bagpuss wasn't scared away.

Over on ITV, you got the continuity announcer, usually mispronouncing the name of the show in a maddeningly disinterested and patronising manner, and that was your lot. Even schools television – with the counting-down stiffly formal pie chart; the hypnotically pulsating prog jazz-backed diamond; the dots with their accompanying freewheeling AOR instrumental on the BBC; and the more formal clock and time-filling, light orchestral-soundtracked picture rolls of splurgey paintings of the Muppets by infant school children on ITV – had more effort put into creating an identity.

Once ITV was ordered by the IBA to buck its ideas up, that all changed, and 1980 saw the launch of 'Watch It!', a full strand-branding exercise involving dancing kids in natty T-shirts, synthpop 'stings' and a logo that looked like it would be more at home introducing a new crisp flavour. In 1983 this shifted to in-vision continuity, with Children's ITV favourites like Matthew Kelly, Marmalade Atkins, Super Gran, David Rappaport, Rod Hull and Emu, The Krankies, Bill Oddie and Roland Rat – who memorably responded to a schedule change to make way for the Budget by asking why the Chancellor can't just keep it in a cage like everyone else – at the controls of a programme-cueing spaceship.

The BBC's initial response was to reach straight for the BBC Micro to create a series of MODE 2 graphical representations of minimally animated witches and robots to introduce shows via a slight change of text; an approach that was as technically underwhelming for anyone with their own home computer as it was unpredictable, with the opening fireworks 'sting' once accidentally cued over the top of an episode of *Grange Hill*. In 1985, they finally gave in and installed human presenters doing live links in the Broom Cupboard, almost unbelievably giving the likes of Andy Crane and Debbie Flint freedom to fill in during the handover to *Neighbours* with whatever prop-based silliness they cared to indulge in. ITV followed suit with Gary Terzza and Debbie Shore in 1987, and nothing was ever quite as off-kilter again.

5

Lunchtime Shows

'As if by magic – the shopkeeper appeared'

So, you've had a busy morning. You've got up, got everyone else up, and you've repeatedly refused then furiously demanded to eat your breakfast and put your clothes on sensibly in no particular or logical order. You've been to playgroup and questioned the absence of a single letter from the alphabetical frieze of animals running around the walls until the teacher very pointedly gives you a Fisher-Price toy telephone to play with. You've got back home and fulfilled your daily quota of slapping the windowsills and laughing, continually opening and closing every single cupboard door you can find and poking a mug until it falls off the table and smashes. Now it's lunchtime, and you need a rest. Not like your mother, who has all those exciting things like the kettle and the blender and that booklet from *Living* magazine with a list of calorie counts in it and is not at all wishing that she could replace that instant coffee in her second favourite mug with something stronger.

The relentless stresses of everyday life for mothers of very young children were not really taken seriously by the rest of the world for a very long time – and some particularly harassed mothers reading this would no doubt contend that they still aren't – but at least the BBC had been trying to give them a moment of respite since as far back as January 1950. The BBC Light Programme was very much the product of its age, with imaginative show titles like *Housewives' Choice* and *Sports Report*, but *Listen with Mother* (BBC, 1950–82) was in every other respect a forward-thinking effort designed to engage children and, more importantly, give their parents an opportunity for a sorely needed fifteen-minute feet-up.

After asking their rapt audience, 'Are you sitting comfortably? Then I'll begin...', presenters such as Daphne Oxenford, Julia Lang – who invented the introductory phrase as a panicked ad-lib – and Eileen Browne formally but jauntily made their way through a collection of stories, songs, poems and counting games in a tiny radio studio where, legend has it, they often had to dash across from the storytelling microphone to a piano to play the closing theme – an arrangement of Fauré's 'Berceuse' – if there wasn't a musician present. Featuring stories from published authors and eager audience members alike, and introducing young listeners to such one-time favourites as 'Mitten the Kitten', 'The Little Blue Engine' and Dorothy Edwards' 'My Naughty Little Sister', who went on to inspire a series of best-selling books, *Listen with Mother* might have been widely mocked for its genteel tones, tinkly piano accompaniment and endless repetitions of 'The Grand Old Duke Of York' even at the time, but it certainly kept the comfortably seated listeners in rapt attention and gave the mothers doing the listening a glimmer of hope that they might get a bit of peace and quiet for the duration of *Woman's Hour* too. Even by that time, though, there was already competition in another corner of the living room.

Introduced by *Radio Times* as a 'baby clown', the first occupant of what would soon come to be known as the 'Watch with Mother' slot – *Andy Pandy* (BBC, 1950–52) – made his conspicuously stringed debut on 11 July 1950. Wandering around his playroom and adjoining garden inviting viewers to join in with games and songs, Andy initially appeared on his own but was eventually joined by two friends — the endearingly over-enthusiastic, polka dot bow tie-sporting Teddy, who threw himself with limb-flailing abandon into games with toy boats and jack-in-the-boxes, and Looby Loo, a rag doll who only came to life whenever Andy and Teddy were out of the room. Andy himself, meanwhile, was hastily remodelled from the original slightly terrifying puppet to a more recognisably humanlike look, reputedly based on puppeteer Audrey Atterbury's young son and future *Antiques Roadshow* presenter Paul Atterbury. Their exploits may not look like much now, but between the sprightly opening song promising 'Andy Pandy's coming to play' and the closing refrain of 'time to go home', those simple stories kept younger viewers diverted and entertained for more than twenty-five years; in 1970, some of the episodes were remade in colour — and with a new Teddy to replace the slightly motheaten original, who was still noticeably 'different' even on a black-and-white set — to prolong the show's shelf life and Andy's enduring appeal.

Andy Pandy was created by the BBC's Director of Children's Programming — and co-creator of *Listen with Mother* — Freda Lingstrom, with her co-writer and the show's narrator Maria Bird, through their independent production company Westerham Arts. Impressed with the cost-effective popularity of *Andy Pandy*, the BBC was only too keen to ask them to develop more shows, with the aim of establishing a full weekly schedule.

Flower Pot Men (BBC, 1952–53) Bill and Ben were the first to join the roster, taking up the Wednesday slot with their clanky backyard antics, while the unseen man who worked in the garden was otherwise engaged, in cahoots with upbeat monosyllabic untended flower Little Weed and very gradually visiting tortoise Slowcoach, with their celebrated babbling nonsense language – which still had its own lexicographical structure – created by voice artist Peter Hawkins. Making Slowcoach look like a Formula 1 champion, hand-puppet hedgehog, mouse and rabbit *Rag, Tag and Bobtail* (BBC, 1953–54), whose exploits never seemed to involve very much more than transporting an object from one side of a strip of artificial grass to the other, very slowly took their time in making their way into the Thursday slot.

Flick-haired Patricia Driscoll – the only actual human seen in any of the original five shows, and better known to older siblings as Maid Marian in early ITV hit *The Adventures of Robin Hood* (ITV, 1955–59) – flicked through the pages of *Picture Book* (BBC, 1955–57) every Monday for a look at an assortment of photographs, drawings, simple makes, visiting in-studio animals and short films, some of which occasionally featured cameo appearances from her more hand-operated 'Watch with Mother' co-stars. Finally, farm-dwelling clothes peg-like family *The Woodentops* (BBC, 1955–56) – Daddy, Mummy, Willy, Jenny and Baby – joined on Fridays for light comic vignettes with their yowling ear-flapping scene-stealing upstager, 'the very biggest Spotty Dog you ever did see'. With Andy, Teddy and Looby Loo clambering in and out of the wicker basket, where they bizarrely appeared to reside in between shows every Tuesday, and with a large number of episodes of each programme in the bank, the classic 'Watch with Mother' line-up was in place and continued to delight viewers for over a decade.

Well, some did. Even by the early sixties, some of the original 'Watch with Mother' line-up were starting to look more than a little creaky; they had all been filmed more or less as live and in one take, and while that may have worked fine for Bill and Ben's gibberish, Teddy's excitable leaping and Spotty Dog's attempts at crooning lullabies, the others really were starting to show their age in an

LUNCHTIME SHOWS

exciting new world of Capri pants and The Tornados. A new set of episodes of *Picture Book* presented by Vera McKechnie and lolloping puppet dachshund Sossidge were made in 1963, and the following year a new show – which the BBC had been trying in a couple of different slots since 1960 without it really catching on – was introduced to rotate with the existing shows and, hopefully, liven matters up a bit.

Starring carefully photographed genuine animals as Hammy Hamster, Roderick Rat and the rest of their band of waterside mischief-makers, *Tales of the Riverbank* (BBC, 1960) was actually made in Canada in 1959, but for the BBC showings, their excursions on sailing rafts and setting up woodland newspapers were redubbed by celebrated storyteller and giver of voices to animals Johnny Morris. This immediately lent *Tales of the Riverbank* more of a sense of dry humour and narrative structure than the existing 'Watch with Mother' shows, and there were some that just couldn't be livened up in a rapidly changing world. *Rag, Tag and Bobtail* were given their marching orders late in 1965 – they elected to trudge – and *Picture Book* closed its covers for the last time over Christmas that same year. In their place, on 3 January 1966, came the first entirely new 'Watch with Mother' show in over a decade.

Although Bill, Ben, Andy, Teddy, Looby Loo and the Woodentops would stay part of 'Watch with Mother' well into the early seventies, *Camberwick Green* (BBC, 1966) was very quickly joined by a number of similarly up-to-date shows – many of which were forward-thinkingly made in colour – including their county neighbours in *Trumpton* (BBC, 1967), *Pogles' Wood* (BBC, 1966–67) and *Bizzy Lizzy* (BBC, 1967).

Previously regularly seen as a more two-dimensional, animated insert in *Picture Book*, Lizzy was a young puppet girl with a stylish bob and a magic wishing flower on her dress which could make even the wildest imaginations come true for her and ever-present doll Little Mo. However, she invariably fell foul of both a strict four-wish-a-day limit and the perpetual adage that you should be careful what you wish for, with a visit to the Moon and a desire for longer hair amongst the imaginative schemes that didn't quite work out how she had hoped. The final series made by Westerham Arts, *Bizzy Lizzy* was still evidently the work of Freda Lingstrom and Maria Bird, but the difference between it and the other shows that were now pushing fifteen years old could not have been more marked. Certain other shows, however, were just that bit *too* modern for 'Watch with Mother'.

Writer Alison Prince and artist Joan Hickson were walking their young children in the park when a chance discussion about how out of touch they felt some of the older 'Watch with Mother' shows were led to an agreement that they could do better. The result of their shared disdain was *Joe* (BBC, 1966), a show about a boy whose parents ran a transport café and whose day-to-day adventures arose from curiosity about jukeboxes, street-sweeping lorries and the local market; he was also, in a notable sign of changing times, regularly joined by his Black friend Abel. Narrated by Lee Montague, with a with-it modern jazz score from Laurie Steele, *Joe* boasted exceptional artwork and clever and relatable stories but was not entirely universally popular, albeit apparently with parents rather than the children it was intended for. Conspicuously repeated less often than the other shows, *Joe* was eventually shelved in favour of a somewhat less radical and urban new set of colour episodes narrated by Colin Jeavons in 1971, with the family now relocated to a seaside guest house and seemingly forever waiting for 'a man' to come round and fix something. Even the music had been toned down.

LUNCHTIME SHOWS

Although *Mary, Mungo and Midge* (BBC, 1969) and its similarly jazzy soundtrack still raised similar levels of wariness amongst the sort of parents who didn't want their children to catch 'common', it seemed to provoke less outright hostility, possibly on account of the fact that it was rendered in the distinctive animation style of *Captain Pugwash* creator John Ryan and narrated in the reassuring tones of BBC newsreader Richard Baker. Introduced by a celebratedly lengthy monologue about the workings of a city centre that concluded by asking the viewer, 'Do you live in a town?', quasi-latchkey kid Mary and her talking pet dog Mungo and mouse Midge lived at the top of a very modern block of flats with an adjoining perfunctory 'garden', travelling up and down in the lift on their quests to answer such burning questions as how post reached its destination and how much a crane could lift. Unlike *Joe*, their adventures were repeated regularly into the late seventies, by which time a certain prominently displayed toy in Mary's bedroom was starting to look a little uncomfortable. The residents of Trumptonshire similarly wrestled with the march of modernity in the factory-strewn district of *Chigley* (BBC, 1969), and it was left to *The Herbs* (BBC, 1968) to cultivate the psychotropic possibilities of children's television, albeit to significantly less consternation than poor old *Joe* had provoked.

In fact, as the seventies and the exciting new world of colour broadcasting rolled around, there was a sense that 'Watch with Mother' wanted to remain very much down to earth – literally so in the case of a series of new documentary-styled shows, including the Keith Barron-narrated *On the Farm* (BBC, 1970), Gordon Rollings' look at goings-on *In the Town* (BBC, 1973) and a triumvirate of more pastoral efforts with Rick Jones' travels *Along the Seashore* (BBC, 1970), *Along the River* (BBC, 1970) and *Along the Trail* (BBC, 1972), all of which essentially took the form of glorified *Play School* window films. What was more, they were joined in 1970 by the new set of colour *Andy Pandy* episodes, shot on surprisingly battered film stock but otherwise more or less exactly the same show that was now a whopping twenty years old; by the time that these colour prints were retired in 1976, Andy had been waving goodbye for over a quarter of a century. Everything might have felt as tranquil as Rick Jones making a wry comment about finding a starfish amongst some seaweed, but the BBC suddenly found themselves having to move with the times – and quickly.

Prior to October 1972, ITV hadn't really bothered with daytime broadcasting at all, as the limited hours they were afforded in the afternoons would not really have proved cost-effective for their advertising-driven model. Their equivalent to 'Watch with Mother' was in fact a late-afternoon slot hovering around 4 p.m., most famously home to the storytelling miscellany slot 'Small Time' (ITV, 1955–66) – which at one point included Westerham Arts' lone ITV excursion *The Magic Doll's House* (ITV, 1959–60) – and 'Auntie' Jean Morton reading out letters from viewers between cheeky exchanges with the titular varispeed-voiced koala bears and a gallery of marsupial associates in *The Tingha and Tucker Club* (ITV, 1972–80). But it was also home to such long-forgotten puppet-led delights as *Fergus Fish* (ITV, 1967); Bella Donna the witch and Sebastian Cat toiling and troubling up stories in *Hubble Bubble* (ITV, 1969–71); sub-Supermarionation travels through history with a disconcertingly *Joe 90*-like lead in *Jimmy Green and his Time Machine* (ITV, 1968); and, notoriously, *Sugarball the Little Jungle Boy* (ITV, 1968–69), the saga of the resourceful junior tribesman and his wacky attempts to meet the unlikely demands of Big Chief Bilbo, both of whom were unfortunately rendered in a manner that could perhaps be most generously described as 'caricatured'. Sometimes, long-forgotten shows are really best left that way.

Newly relaxed rules had allowed ITV to launch a full daytime service, and in amongst such out-of-office delights as *Emmerdale Farm* and *First Report*, younger viewers were treated to not one but two shows at midday – one educational effort like *Rainbow* or *Pipkins*, and another that was – even if not all of them were quite as entertaining as others – out and out entertainment. To hit the ground running, however, they needed to bring in some content already seen elsewhere in the Children's ITV schedules – and in the process discovered the production teams that gave ITV some of their biggest lunchtime smashes.

Left at a loose end when production had shifted to live action, Gerry and Sylvia Anderson's former puppeteers Mary Turner and John Read had scored something of a post-Supermarionation coup when Lew Grade secured the rights to the enduring *Daily Express* strip 'Rupert Bear'. Opening with a live-action mother and child reading a *Rupert* book and a storming theme song sung by Jackie Lee – which quickly made the top twenty, allaying *Daily Express* concerns over it hinging around the non-canonical refrain 'Rupert The Bear' – *The Adventures of Rupert Bear* (ITV, 1970–77) was a lively adaptation of the exploits of the chirpy check-trousered ursine and his chums, including Badger Bill, Edward Trunk and, notoriously, Raggety – a minor figure from the strips who was essentially a man made of sticks who constantly screeched at Rupert to go away. Viewers were either terrified of him or felt compelled to concede that he had a point.

Mary and John went on to score similar successes with similarly catchy theme songs with *Here Comes Mumfie* (ITV, 1975), based on Katherine Tozer's novels about a well-mannered young Nellifant and his struggles to outwit aspirant manner-purloiner Witch-Up-In-The-Sky with the aid of fellow pachyderm Uncle Samuel, stockbroker turned vagabond Nattysocks and imaginatively named crow-scarer Scarecrow. There was also quasi-medieval timely satire *Cloppa Castle* (ITV, 1978–79), which saw pointedly named 'friendly enemies' the Bygones and the Hasbeenes at comically inept war over a territory-straddling oil slick, with neither Queen Ethelbruda, King Woebegone and court inventor Cue-E-Dee on the one side, or Beosweyne and his lunk-headed hordes on the other, prepared to enter into meaningful negotiation when backfiring catapults would do just fine. And there was the society-building saga of Corny-On-The-Cob, Lizzie Leek and their fellow grocery store escapees in a series based on the popular children's storybooks, *The Munch Bunch* (ITV, 1980–82).

Slightly further up north, Brian Cosgrove and Mark Hall had met at Manchester College of Art and were both working as artists at Granada when they decided to form their own animation house. Setting out their stall from the outset, *The Magic Ball* (ITV, 1971), made for Granada and written and narrated by Eric Thompson very much in the style of *The Magic Roundabout*, revolved around a young boy called Sam who found a crystalline musical ball in his Aunt Mil's antiques shop that took him off on surreal and faintly psychedelic adventures. It was their work with Thames on *Rainbow*, however, that led to a partnership with the company and a string of fondly remembered shows.

Named after the Manchester district their studio was based in, *Chorlton and the Wheelies* (ITV, 1976–78) concerned a relentlessly upbeat Northern 'Happiness Dragon' and his efforts to protect a town-council-like assortment of Wheelies from the machinations of Fenella, a drawling head-spinning Welsh witch who shared her scorched kettle residence Spout Hall with Teutonic spellbook Claptrap Von Schbilderbeanz and genial telescope O'Reilly, neither of whom were ever especially on board with her schemes, and the suitably named snickering miniature minions the Spikers and luridly coloured evil-eyed mushrooms the Toadies. *Chorlton and the Wheelies* was so popular, in fact, that it was granted an almost unheard-of honour for a lunchtime ITV show – the feature-length Boxing Day special *Chorlton in the Ice World* in 1977.

As the opening miniature rock opera related in riff-rocking detail, *Jamie and the Magic Torch* (ITV, 1977–79) saw a young boy in natty orange and red pyjamas wait until his parents thought he was asleep before activating a flashlight that sent him and loyal if reticent Old English Sheepdog Wordsworth hurtling down a strobing helter-skelter before bouncing out of a tree and off a trampoline into the aptly named Cuckoo Land, where they invariably had to help Mr Boo and all the others to resolve some minor conundrum before whizzing back up home backwards, without his parents ever suspecting a thing.

Based on Enid Blyton's original stories featuring the bell-hatted Toytown denizen, rumours abound that the jauntily themed Richard Briers-narrated *Noddy* (ITV, 1975) also retained some of the more dubious culturally insensitive aspects of the original books, but in fact they were very carefully omitted and, in this instance at least, Big Ears has been very unfairly accused. Their familiar visual style did, however, mean that Cosgrove Hall's decidedly non-lunchtime-friendly Captain Kremmen inserts for *The Kenny Everett Video Show* (ITV, 1978–81) led to a fair few arguments about what it was acceptable to be allowed to 'stay up' for.

Elsewhere, S.G. Hulme Beaman's original BBC radio scripts were reworked for the unwieldly titled *Stories from Toytown featuring*

Larry the Lamb (ITV, 1972), with a blockbusting big band theme tune raising the curtain for Larry and Dennis the Dachshund's chaotic attempts to do unsolicited favours for the mayor, invariably attracting the ire of Toytown's oldest and most respected resident Mr Growser, who would summarily adjudge their actions 'a disgrace' that 'ought not to be allowed'. Meanwhile, *The Enchanted House* (ITV, 1970) played surely extremely cramped host to Mini Moke-loving Tiny the Giraffe and his friends to the relentless backdrop of an over-elaborate toe-tapping Johnny Dankworth soundtrack.

By this time, however, 'Watch with Mother' was also moving with the times and alongside *Bagpuss* and his friends, a new set of shows made by equally make-do-and-mending animators introduced a new set of similarly unlikely characters having similarly odd adventures.

David McKee's *Mr Benn* (BBC, 1971) took a daily stroll to the accompaniment of some of the UK's top jazz musicians from his home at 52 Festive Road to a local costume shop, where – after the suspiciously exotically attired shopkeeper had appeared 'as if by magic' – he would try on a costume that had caught his imagination and sidle out through the changing room's alternate door 'that could lead to adventure', enjoying an ensemble-appropriate adventure before returning home and invariably finding a souvenir in his pocket which he kept 'to help me remember'. Memorable door-led escapades included assisting with a game of hide-and-seek between cowboys and Native Americans; helping a dragon win the King's favour back from a Machiavellian matchmaker; embarking on a balloon race against notorious cheat Baron Bartram; and accompanying an astronaut to a planet where an abundance of precious stones became non-precious if they left the atmosphere. The BBC, however, stopped short of agreeing to an episode based on convict-costumed storybook *123456789Benn*.

Celebrated French literary bear Colargol became *Barnaby* (BBC, 1973), courtesy of a quick spot of redubbing from character actor Colin Jeavons and a song demanding that you should 'never call me Jack or James'. Barnaby ran away from home – exiting via the window – to join the circus, sparking off a chain of events that took in everything from a ride on a whale to donning a cardboard beak to become King of the Birds, with more than a few disturbing interludes involving sobbing behind bars and other such cheerful scenarios. It was difficult to avoid the suspicion that something had got lost in translation.

Medallion-sporting *Teddy Edward* (BBC, 1973), on the other hand, was very much a UK-specific literary sensation, based on the best-selling photo books about Patrick and Mollie Matthews' globe-trotting medallion-sporting bear and brought to the small screen with a Richard Baker voiceover and a deep funk theme tune ending on a wild shrill flute excursion which possibly put off a few potential viewers. Formerly a cobbler until he was exiled to the woods for insulting the mayor's feet, Czech outlaw Jak Rumcajs became *Boris the Bold* (BBC, 1973) for English-speaking audiences, and slightly more well-behaved Swedish toddler Totte and his oddly depressing theme music made new friends as *Thomas* (BBC, 1975).

By far the most prolific and creative contributors to 'Watch with Mother' during the seventies, however, were husband-and-wife team and former *Play School* producers Michael and Joanne Cole. Inspired by Michael finding himself gesturing for inspiration while trying to come up with a programme idea, *Fingerbobs* (BBC, 1972) saw Rick Jones adopt the guise of paper-rolling hippy artist 'Yoffy' with suitably acid folk-tinged musical accompaniment as he sent his elemental-representing finger puppet assistants Flash the tortoise, Gulliver the gull, Scampi the scampi and Fingermouse – who could of course 'get past cats so easily with my famous body swerve' – out on surreal and cerebral quests to collect the scraps and bits and pieces he needed to tell a Taoist-inspired tale involving basic animation and a simple and positive message, most famously one concerning a hand-puppet crow who very slowly deposited pebbles in a jar to raise the water inside it to a drink-facilitating level.

Wearing his Zen-dispensing influences even more prominently on his yellow kasaya sleeve, *Bod* (BBC, 1975) – who had originally appeared in a series of stories in *Play School* – and his friends Frank the Postman, Farmer Barleymow, PC Copper and Aunt Flo embarked on urban odysseys narrated by John Le Mesurier that invariably taught them that whatever they had been looking for had been right under their noses all along, while Derek Griffiths yodelled over the top of an assortment of free-jazz solos. The shows also featured stories of Alberto Frog and his Amazing Animal Band, who performed civic good deeds in exchange for a milkshake – viewers were invited to guess which flavour, allowing elder siblings with longer memories to impress their younger counterparts with their powers of prediction – and a Maggie Henderson-dealt game of snap.

Over on ITV, matters were just as offbeat but not necessarily always as upbeat. The distinctly melancholy *Simon in the Land of Chalk Drawings* (ITV, 1974–76) came with a plaintive theme song that masked a bleak tale of a boy who found that whatever he drew 'came true' in another world over a nearby wall, exposing him to such distressing scenarios as a hospital full of incomplete stick men and a city centre he had inadvertently caused to become choked with traffic. Retooled for an English-speaking audience with a cast of Tim Brooke-Taylor voices and downtempo synth noodlings from Alan Hawkshaw, *Gideon* (ITV, 1979–81) – *Gédéon* in its native France – concerned an ungainly long-necked duck who, as the lengthy opening titles chronicled, was shunned by society and in particular some tone lowering-fearing hens before proving his worth by, primarily, using his neck as a bridge for some mice to cross a river. Often alarmingly brutal for its timeslot – one episode infamously depicted animals being maimed by an unwitting fisherman's equipment until Gideon finally upended him into some fast-flowing water to unspecified consequences – it never quite succeeded in fully obscuring its more moody and philosophical origins.

Already marked out by being a schoolboy elephant moving freely amongst human society, *Little Blue* (ITV, 1977) was literally tarnished when, while playing in the bath one day as some of us do, he took his mummy's fountain pen and broke it in two, causing a fusion of ink, water and bodily hue that the more they tried to scrub it out the more it scrubbed in, leaving him defeatedly signing off his theme song with a resigned acceptance that 'I'll have to stay a little blue'. Textbook puppet on a black background *Oscar the Rabbit in Rubbidge* (ITV, 1978) took a Lance Percival-narrated tumble into a dustbin and ended up in the garbage-hewn home of Gnashers the Pterodactyl and the Great Wooferoo.

Most startlingly of all, *The Magic Fountain* (ITV, 1973) was a serial combining heavily stylised prog rock-friendly animation, eye-hurting psychedelic film effects designed by *2001: A Space Odyssey*'s Zoran Perisic – who also wrote and directed the show – and ominously burbling atonal Moog synthesiser outbursts again from Alan Hawkshaw. It concerned a boy called Timothy who, while on holiday in a seaside town, becomes involved in a centuries-old time-travel murder mystery revolving around a bid to wrest ownership of some hidden treasure. Terrifying enough as all that might sound, it also featured some jaw-droppingly graphic violent and horrific details that would have raised eyebrows in pretty much any timeslot.

If that felt a little too full-on, you could always have your mind blown by a bunch of shows that were gaudy, glamtastic and just plain weird even by the spangliest standards of the seventies. Arriving on Earth from 'Popland' by flying saucer, *Animal Kwackers* (ITV, 1975–78) – Rory the lion on rhythm guitar, Boot the tiger on lead guitar, Twang the monkey on bass, and Bongo the dog on drums – were a pop group made up of actors in huge cartoony animal costumes that, it has to be said, bore more than a passing conceptual resemblance to the Banana Splits. Possibly the ultimate inevitable stylistic mutation of glam rock, the band would perform a couple of fifties and sixties oldies that could be vaguely reinterpreted as having some sort of literacy- or numeracy-related meaning, and relate one of their thankfully un-Led Zeppelin-like tales of life on the road in response to the stomping riff-driven request, 'Rory! Rory! Tell us a story!'; completing the illusion of Womble-level rock stardom, they also did actual records and concert tours.

Inspired by Palmer Cox's nineteenth-century humorous strips about the impish Brownies, the silent movie piano-heralded *Topper's Tales* (ITV, 1977) presented the whimsical doings of rakish elfin toff Topper and his decidedly un-modest tendency to lead his 'Little Friends' into a spot of bother, requiring reluctantly tolerated bailing out from their more cautious associate 'The Old One' ('bo-ring!'), coming across as something roughly akin to a Jeeves and Wooster story rewritten by a Dutch progressive rock band.

Anita in Jumbleland (ITV, 1970–71) saw sixties popster Anita Harris and her multi-coloured beach buggy pull up in a scrapyard full of abandoned steampunk fairground gadgets, antique flying carpets and gaudily dyed puppets for fantastical stories and groovy songs. And sewing box offcut safari gang *Jungle Ted and the Laceybuttonpoppers* (ITV, 1974) went about their sub-*Goon Show* business to the sound of a classy cabaret-styled theme from Peter Doyle of The New Seekers.

Keith Chatfield's stories of walking and talking hats with vocation-related personalities, *Hatty Town*, had originally appeared as part of 'Small Time' in 1966, narrated by Peter Hawkins over a series of still images, but later in the decade FilmFair turned his tales of Posty the Postman, Mr Wimple the Mayor, Sancho and Carrots the donkey and assorted other millinery-sourced occupation-appropriate walking and talking headgear into *Hattytown Tales* (ITV, 1969–73). His later *Issi Noho* (ITV, 1974–78) told the occasionally cliffhanging serial of a supernaturally mathematically adept panda, who had taken his name from the shrub-obscured crate labelled THIS SIDE UP USE NO HOOKS that he had been hiding out in, and the efforts of plucky youngsters Andrew, Sally and Neil to conceal his whereabouts from the authorities – efforts that ultimately proved to be in vain when he made his way into the wider world and nobody seemed to be very much bothered.

If all of that was still a little too mind-blowing for you, there were always a handful of human presenters on hand to offer you, well, *A Handful of Songs* (ITV, 1973–80), in which acoustic guitar-toting duo Maria Morgan and Keith Field strummed their way through the titular Tommy Steele number to introduce witty inter-song exchanges about the scrawly letters and drawings that viewers had sent in requesting them to play 'Yellow Submarine', 'A Windmill in Old Amsterdam', 'Sippin' Cider Through a Straw' and other easily singalong-able child-friendly favourites. Susan Stranks demonstrated simple card and string makes with the aid of high-pitched panicked-sounding puppet spiders Itsy and Bitsy in *Paperplay* (ITV, 1974–81); PC 254 Deryck Guyler doled out a couple of tips for good citizenship between 'listening' to some collapsing puppets miming to pop records on a wind-up gramophone that was handily sitting around in the street in *The Laughing Policeman* (ITV, 1974–76); Ulf Goran cheerfully trilled about how he came from down your way before rattling through a few basic guitar chords in *Music Man* (ITV, 1976); and *The Learning Tree* (ITV, 1977–80) was essentially just a tree in a watercolour woodland clearing with the superimposed face of radio presenter Tony Brandon singing songs about how to tell the seasons apart.

Over at the BBC, a brace of new shows with human presenters – the first since *Picture Book* was put back on the shelf – strove to combine education and gleeful to-camera silliness. Derek Griffiths improvised around stories with accompanying songs like 'Ricky's Aeroplane' and 'The Paper Family' in the jubilantly no-budget *Ring-a-Ding* (BBC, 1973). And Michael and Joanne Cole got to indulge their shared love of The Goons and Monty Python in *Ragtime* (BBC, 1973–74), in which Fred Harris and Maggie Henderson traded puns, riddles and wordplay with Cole family homemade toys, including Humbug the tiger hand-puppet, philosophical cushion man Fred Bubble, Dax the plush dachshund and a band of musicians who looked like they'd been fired from Frank Zappa's The Mothers of Invention for looking too much like 'freaks', while some of the UK's top session musicians cranked up some serious funky grooves in the background.

Ian Allen's Playboard Puppets were the stars of the obviously named *Playboard* (BBC, 1976), with narrator Christopher Lillicrap observing as inquisitive rodents Hedge and Mo made their way through acres of fake foliage to watch Max the Magician, Shahid the Snake Charmer, Jo the Clown and other employees of the Bright Family's Circus putting on Big Top interpretations of the likes of 'The Gingerbread Man' and 'The Great Big Enormous Turnip'.

LUNCHTIME SHOWS

How Do You Do! (BBC, 1977) focused on interactive musical and counting games with Carmen Munroe and classical percussionist Greg Knowles along with Joan Hickson's stories of Miss King and her impressively diverse nursery school class. *Over the Moon* (BBC, 1978), with Sam Dale, boldly sought to explain basic scientific concepts with the aid of animated songs, including Kim Goody's cautionary tale of time-travelling Rat Van Winkle; Carole Leader's projectile's eye-view voyage of the hapless Archer's Arrow; Jasper Carrott's wry reportage on the antics of wildlife photographer Angus McBluff; and most memory-searingly of all, Derek Griffiths' life and times of Obadiah Blank, an inventor — mostly of pointless or destructive innovations — who proved so prolific that he eventually had to invent a machine to invent for him, just to keep up with himself. Derek Griffiths also energetically presented *Heads and Tails* (BBC, 1977–79), linking an assortment of wildlife footage with a mixture of animal kingdom facts and figures and tongue-in-cheek in-character songs about zoological lifestyles, ending each episode with a grandparent-alarmingly out-of-control scat-yodel version of the theme song.

New animated shows included Gordon Murray's 'Historical Trumptonshire' comedy *Rubovia* (BBC, 1976) and quaintly themed animated retellings of Roger Hargreaves' *Mr Men* (BBC, 1974–78) by Arthur Lowe, featuring two stories bridged by the 'what a lot of Mr Men there are . . . I wonder which one we shall be meeting next . . . can you guess?' guessing game. There was also Julie Holden and Gay Soper's slices of life with furry Northern family *The Flumps* (BBC, 1978), with juveniles Posey, Perkin and Pootle trying their hardest not to disturb Grandpa Flump's 'Flumpet' practice while querying what a carrot is and trying to shake off a raincloud that had decided to hover permanently above Perkin's head.

There was one aspect of the timeslot, however, that had failed to move with the times – the name. In an age of wider pre-school education and where the idea of working mothers was no longer frowned on in the same way, the basic notion of watching with mother itself felt increasingly outdated and, tellingly, it had scarcely been used on air or in print for several years. On 12 October 1980, using a name that they had already tried to introduce via a spin-off comic in the mid-seventies and an icon in the *Radio Times* listings in 1977, a repeat of *The Flumps* became the first programme to be officially billed as 'a See-Saw programme'. This basically involved nothing more than a rebranding using a continuity slide with images of two characters awkwardly pasted onto opposing sides of a heavily stylised see-saw – or, if it was difficult to represent, left completely empty – but it was a significant and effective break with the past and a step into the present. It is a moment probably seen by many as the end of an era, but many of the new programmes ushered in to accompany the old favourites – most of which would be retired within a couple of years – managed to combine the appeal of 'Watch with Mother' with a refreshingly new approach.

In *Chock-A-Block* (BBC, 1981), Chock-A-Bloke Fred Harris and Chock-A-Girl Carol Leader 'clocked on' at a factory of indeterminate purpose which housed the titular supercomputer, capable of generating stories about a grandfather clock that had mislaid its tock and a pig who refused to dance without hearing six pairs of rhyming words. *Stop-Go* (BBC, 1981) welded the tried and tested 'round window' documentary film approach to very modern and urban machinery and a raucous reverb-drenched sax-wailing soft-rock theme song.

Play School alumni Chloe Ashcroft, Don Spencer and Carol Chell energetically served up a hotchpotch of fun and facts with the aid of two dishmop-resembling clown puppets in *Hokey Cokey* (BBC, 1983–85), while their fellow Humpty propper-upper Iain Lauchlan teamed up with a newly repurposed *Fingermouse* (BBC, 1985), now redeployed as a Scampi-less treble clef-fixated 'musical paper mouse'. Brian Cant rifled through a junkyard conveniently full of items beginning with that week's featured letter in *Bric-A-Brac* (BBC, 1980–82), and David McKee contributed the Ray Brooks-narrated childlike court and cat-exasperating antics of *King Rollo* (BBC, 1980). *Little Misses and the Mr Men* (BBC, 1983) simply bolted new adaptations of Roger Hargreaves' later equality-conscious books onto the existing Mr Men films.

The show that gave the greatest reflection of changing times, however, was the work of old hands at the newly relaunched slot. Alan Rogers and Peter Lang of the Cut-Out Animation Co. had been working on a number of children's shows – including *Over the Moon* – when they came up with the concept of *Pigeon Street* (BBC, 1981), set amongst the high-rises and terraced rows of a modern inner city, with residents of all ages, races and vocations, and an inordinate amount of local pigeons pursued with negligible success by Tom the cat. Backed by authentic South London Dub from agit-prop outfit Soulyard, lorry driver 'Long Distance' Clara Newman, warring houseproud pensioner neighbours locked in an ongoing 'pigeon feud' Rose Fogg and Daisy Waldron, manual workers with a secret passion for ballroom dancing Reg and Doreen Pottage, and all of the other locals, converged where pigeons meet and their wings-wings beat for light storylines based around lunchbreaks and planning permission documents. *Pigeon Street* was well loved and widely praised for its closeness to the everyday experience of a large share of the audience, and Alan and Peter continued their collaboration with Soulyard's Benni Lees for ITV's collection of anthropomorphic animal-overstaffed nursery rhyme retellings *Rub-A-Dub-Dub* (ITV, 1984).

ITV, conversely, struggled to come up with anything that was to any degree as iconic and memorable as *Jamie and the Magic Torch* or *Rainbow* in the eighties – although, to be fair, *Rainbow* was still running throughout the eighties anyway – but they did at least start the decade in style. Originally conceived as a stage play, *Button Moon* (ITV, 1980–88) was another vehicle for Ian Allen and the Playboard Puppets which had been initially intended as a serial within *Rainbow* before Thames decided it had sufficient potential to be a series in its own right. Initially charting utensil-formed Mr Spoon's quest to visit the large yellow button shining in Blanket Sky in his tin-can-and-funnel rocket ship, the show soon settled into a format when he realised that he could observe the odd goings-on of other planets through a moon-mounted telescope. As well as being visually arresting and driven by droll knockabout humour, *Button Moon* also benefited from a suitably cosmic theme song performed by Peter Davison and his then-wife Sandra Dickinson. In fact, perhaps in recognition of the fact that the age of the digital watch and VHS video recorder was upon us, outer space featured unusually heavily during the decade.

Operated by Roland Rat creator David Claridge, green lunar feline Mooncat had come to learn about life on Earth – not the last animated alien who would find themselves in this educative predicament – in the company of Beryl Reid, Stephen Boxer and a sprightly reggae-inflected instrumental theme in *Get Up and Go!* (ITV, 1981–85). As related at great length by the whistling children of Trinity Comprehensive School, Nottingham, and a wonky synthesiser on a generic 'brass' setting, the Jon Pertwee-voiced *The Little Green Man* (ITV, 1985) and his pulsating light-based sidekick

Zoom-Zoom took a look at life on Earth with the guidance of surprisingly underwhelmed schoolboy Sydney 'Skeets' Keats. And Flying Pencil-propelled alien Giddy – who sounded suspiciously like Yorkshire Television announcer Redvers Kyle – Professor Gus and hard-of-thinking lab technician Gorilla set the animated puzzles in *The Giddy Game Show* (ITV, 1985–87).

Back down on earth, FilmFair contributed the coastal capers of a bunch of nautical navigators named after 'Shipping Forecast' regions in *The Adventures of Portland Bill* (ITV, 1983) and the prehistoric exploration of an evolving Earth by *Moschops* (ITV, 1983) and his dinosaur brethren. Nondescript, cordially aligned dog and cat *Teetime and Claudia* (ITV, 1983) mused on how 'we're like each other in our ways' in a theme song that sounded like it belonged to a programme from a decade earlier, while John Ryan made a rare on-camera appearance in a procession of natty cravats to draw and tell the biblical problem-solving antics of Noah's young shipmates Jannet and Jaffet in *Ark Stories* (ITV, 1981).

Collectively known as the Black Theatre Group of Prague, whose distinctive 'puppets on a black background' style was well known from dozens of light entertainment shows around the time – not to mention *Daisy, Daisy* and *Once Upon a Time* – Rosta Cerny and Susan Kodicek created *Pullover* (ITV, 1982), featuring a scrawny toy made from a discarded sweater who enjoyed surreal under-bed adventures when his young owner had turned in for the night. They also made Grandpa Fox's unashamedly expressionist and literally dark retellings of European folk tales 'in the wood where stories grow', *Fox Tales* (ITV, 1985), narrated by Peter Davison to a creepy 'knock knock' percussive backing and more than once requiring a post-transmission announcement warning not to copy the mushroom-picking exploits of Bear and company.

Sometime pop star and co-lead in BBC1's hugely successful sitcom *Just Good Friends* Paul Nicholas related the sundial-dwelling daily routine of Cosgrove Hall's alarmingly realistic collection of arthropods and gastropods that made up the *Creepy Crawlies* (ITV, 1987–89), and George Cole took time out from starring in ITV's hit comedy crime drama *Minder* to brave the spooky theme music and roll his eyes at the hapless *Heggerty Haggerty* (ITV, 1982–84), a well-meaning witch struggling to cast spells with the assistance of a slightly less well-meaning broomstick. Folk singer and 'Streets of London' hitmaker Ralph McTell and actress Nerys Hughes pooled their talents for *Alphabet Zoo* (ITV, 1983–84), an Alligator to Zebra of animal facts relayed in stories, sketches and songs, and went on to do much the same from the general store of Tickle Village near the River Tum in punningly named *Tickle on the Tum* (ITV, 1984–88). Chat show host Michael Parkinson wrote and narrated *The Woofits* (ITV, 1981–82), a family of anthropomorphic bluff Northern dogs not entirely unlike their creator who lived in a terraced house in non-existent Grimsworth, including brass band enthusiast John Willie Woofit, aspirant rock star Elton Woofit, Uncle Gaylord who had got 'ideas' following a win on the football Pools and, confusingly, their pet actual dog, Gershwin.

Formerly of the Bonzo Dog Doo-Dah Band and Beatles parody outfit The Rutles, Neil Innes wrote, narrated and sang the naggingly catchy theme song for Sad Sack, Dotty, Hi-Fi, Lucy, Back-To-Front, Claude and Princess, the Reject Bin-residing 'dolls like you and me' collectively known as *The Raggy Dolls* (ITV, 1986–94). He also played the resident conjurer in the large house at the end of *Puddle Lane* (ITV, 1985–89), telling stories about Tim Catchamouse the kitten and confusingly named mythical creatures the Gruffle and the Griffle to Tony Robinson-voiced puppet dragon Toby with the aid of a magic cauldron and a handful of musical motifs that might well have been familiar to followers of his musical career. Tony Robinson also wrote and presented *Tales from Fat Tulip's Garden* (ITV, 1985–87), a wild and freewheeling narrative about such unlikely named garden-dwelling characters as Lewis Collins the Tortoise, Gilbert Harding the Sheep and Jim Morrison the Cockle, delivered directly to camera at large in the grounds of Little Monkhams in Woodford Green.

Richard Briers-voiced puppet friends Orm the worm and Cheep the bird lamented the latter's inability to fly – pointing out that if he could 'then I a proper bird would be' – in the melancholy theme from *Orm and Cheep* (ITV, 1984–87), which by then slightly older viewers couldn't avoid noticing bore a distinct resemblance to The La's 1990 hit 'There She Goes'. Pat Coombs' sentient scrap-hewn accidental train journey-prone associate *Ragdolly Anna* (ITV, 1982–87), who according to her formal forties-style theme song was fine and fat, with a bunch of paper roses in her big straw hat, enjoyed prim and proper excursions around the streets of Leeds. And the same production team's *Wil Cwac Cwac* (ITV, 1982), originally produced for S4C, was an extremely Welsh tale of a young duck in a sailor suit – presumably with no awareness of the more celebrated Donald – who was forever being sent to bed early on account of scarcely qualifying misdemeanours in cahoots with his farmyard chums, invariably concluding with a plaintive and self-pitying cry of 'cwaaaaaaac'. In fairness, you couldn't really blame his perpetually put-upon mother. If only she'd had something on television at lunchtime to distract him with.

'Never too quickly, never too slowly'

One day early in January 1967, guitarist Jimi Hendrix – newly arrived in the UK from America – had a row with his girlfriend, journalist

Kathy Etchingham, who promptly stormed out. When she returned, she found that he had written a new song as an apologetic gesture, using her middle name Mary as inspiration – and that wasn't all that inspired 'The Wind Cries Mary'. According to Kathy, the line 'after all the jacks are in their boxes, and the clowns have all gone to bed' was inspired by BBC Test Card F, but that didn't make its debut on screen until 2 July 1967, whereas 'The Wind Cries Mary' had been recorded on 11 January and released as a single in May. Instead, it's entirely likely that Hendrix had actually been watching an altogether different clown, and one that was often seen in close proximity to a certain box.

Camberwick Green (BBC, 1966), *Trumpton* (BBC, 1967) and *Chigley* (BBC, 1969) were all set within the fictional county of Trumptonshire, populated by an assortment of stop-motion puppets with very clearly defined vocations – usually spelled out in no uncertain terms in their accompanying song – and equally clearly defined characters, dealing with minor mishaps, unfulfilled errands and pretty much anything that required the use of a fire engine elevator box in their own public-spirited way. Set in a timeless fusion of the 'old ways' and modernity, they rotated in the 'Watch with Mother' schedule for decades, and between them would clock up nigh on a hundred showings.

An amateur puppeteer since childhood, Gordon Murray turned his hobby into a profession in the late forties with the launch of his theatrical company Murray's Marionettes; after one of their shows he was introduced to Freda Lingstrom, who was sufficiently impressed by his skill and knowledge to invite him to operate Spotty Dog in *The Woodentops*. Such was that skill and knowledge, in fact, that within months he had been appointed as a producer within the Children's department, where one of his earliest projects was helping to bring John Ryan's *Captain Pugwash* (BBC, 1957–66) to the screen; Gordon's most important contribution was arguably plucking accordionist Tom Edmonson's 1954 recording of the traditional sea shanty 'The Hornblower' from the BBC's own archives to act as the theme music.

Gordon also acted as head of the BBC Puppet Theatre, which may appear archaic as a concept now but in the simpler days of live television was responsible for a series of lavish and critically acclaimed productions, initially in the same tin shed at the BBC's Lime Grove studios where Westerham Arts had staged the early 'Watch with Mother' shows. He oversaw more than fifty original productions for the BBC Puppet Theatre, and a measure of their prestige can be seen both in the fact that production was quickly transferred to a purpose-built facility in BBC Television Centre, and that a 1957 production of *The Emperor's Nightingale* was selected as one of a handful of programmes to be experimentally filmed in colour.

The Puppet Theatre was also responsible for a lengthy series of restagings of S.G. Hulme Beaman's BBC Radio plays featuring Larry the Lamb and company in Toytown between 1956 and 1958, and thirty-three instalments of Murray's own comic tales of life in a magical medieval Middle-European kingdom, *A Rubovian Legend* (BBC, 1955–64).

Alongside the young husband-and-wife design team Andrew and Margaret Brownfoot, puppeteers John Hardwick, previously a member of the Murray's Marionettes company, and Bob Bura were also regular contributors to the Puppet Theatre's productions. With a keen shared interest in the innovative process of stop-motion animation, Bura and Hardwick quickly formed Stop Frame Productions as a sideline, and their work was soon being featured everywhere on the BBC, from *Blue Peter* to Schools television and wildlife documentaries.

Although Gordon's background was very much with string-and-rod puppets, he found himself excited by the possibilities suggested by Bura and Hardwick's work, and in 1964 he presented the BBC with a detailed proposal and some test footage for 'The Minute Men', a show about diminutive characters at large in a full-scale human world. When this was turned down, already unhappy at the direction he felt that the Children's department was taking – it had been subsumed into the broader Families department earlier that year, and the Puppet Theatre would be closed down shortly afterwards – Gordon took the risky decision to leave the BBC and strike out as an independent animated filmmaker.

He had in fact discussed the idea of making a new 'Watch with Mother' show with Bura and Hardwick and the Brownfoots as far back as 1961, but at that point nobody saw any need for a new show when they already had a large number of episodes of five shows available. By the time he left the BBC, however, not everyone was necessarily so happy with *Rag, Tag and Bobtail* in particular, and his proposal for a new stop-motion series set in a rural village full of realistic characters could not have arrived at a more opportune moment. Early in 1965, the BBC expressed interest in seeing a pilot film, and thanks to a fortuitous typing error, 'Candlewick Green' became *Camberwick Green*.

Even just making one fifteen-minute pilot film without the full resources and backing of the BBC, however, was a huge technical undertaking and financial risk. Working from scripts by Murray, Andrew and Margaret Brownfoot designed the settings and buildings – often based on real-life architecture that had caught their attention – and Murray created the puppet characters using ping-pong balls and a poseable metal framework. Working with their studio assistants George Debouch, Pasqaule Ferrari, Colin Large and Len Palace, Bura and Hardwick set to work animating the stories, supervising the lighting and camera positioning as well as manipulating the puppets, although they found a clockwork camera timing device that Gordon had created to save time on set too restrictive to work with, and the system was unsurprisingly very quickly dropped. They also devised a method of pinning the puppets in place on a soft base rather than the more time-consuming traditional process of securely fastening them, while the Brownfoots insisted that a traditional wooden post mill mentioned in the scripts should be replaced by a taller stone tower mill for practical reasons; this decision would take an unexpected turn when Bura and Hardwick accidentally assembled the prop the wrong way round and affixed the sails to the front of the tower. If this all suggests that everyone involved was learning as they went, then that was very much the case.

Although the scripts had been very carefully tailored to avoid anything that could not easily be realised in stop-motion, some details still proved beyond their resources; notably, in the finished series, there is a shot of a beehive being sprayed that clearly had to be filmed in real time. Another unforeseen complication, however, did not come to light until the completed pilot film was played back – nobody had considered that the prop trees might very slowly and imperceptibly wilt under the heat of the studio lamps, with the unfortunate consequence that in the finished film, they appeared to loom menacingly towards the puppets. Otherwise, Bura and Hardwick's attention to detail was impeccable, and they were able to produce two and a half minutes of footage each week that never required any further editing.

With each character intended to have their own introductory song, classical guitarist Freddie Phillips was engaged to set Gordon Murray's lyrics to music. An acclaimed musician who had played with the Royal Ballet and the BBC Symphony Orchestra, he also had a sideline in soundtrack music that had taken in accompaniment for Lotte Reiniger's pioneering silhouette puppet film shorts, a series of 'Network Openings' that played at the played at the start of the BBC's daily television schedules throughout the sixties, hundreds of performances on BBC Radio music and variety shows and – although he reputedly did not like to be reminded of this – the controversial Michael Powell horror film *Peeping Tom* (1960).

Despite his classical background, Freddie also had a keen interest in the possibilities of new recording techniques; using a self-devised multi-track tape system, he created the music for *Camberwick Green* making extensive use of reverberation effects and altered tape speed to create different moods and textures, not entirely unlike the processes that pop producers like George Martin and Joe Meek were experimenting with on top ten hits at the time. He also provided the actual sound effects, many of which were recorded 'live' while out walking with a tape recorder, although the sound of the windmill mechanism was created from an assortment of manipulated percussion instruments; he later also made the cost-conscious discovery that a slowed-down alarm clock sounded sufficiently similar to a fire station bell to convince viewers.

What this pilot film still needed, though, was a narrator. Brian Cant had originally intended to be a commercial artist, but soon developed a taste for amateur theatre and very quickly found his way into professional work. By the early sixties he was regularly securing small roles in shows like *Dixon of Dock Green* and *Doctor Who*, but it was an otherwise unremarkable turn as a figure on a

LUNCHTIME SHOWS

Roman urn for a schools' television show that had the most significant effect on his career. Producer Cynthia Felgate felt he would be a good fit as a *Play School* presenter; he made his debut in *Play School*'s third week in May 1964 and was still there in 1985, even continuing to make regular guest appearances after he had nominally left the show. While Murray was casting around for suggestions for a potential narrator, *Play School* producer Joy Whitby drew his attention to Brian, who he adjudged to have a similar tone to a storytelling young father and as such considered him an ideal fit for *Camberwick Green*. Brian – who had not seen any of the puppets at this point – worked closely with Gordon to sketch out each character's tone and 'voice' and recorded the narration in a soundproofed cupboard, insisting on removing his shoes before each session to avoid creating any extraneous noise, although he had significantly less control over the fact that the makeshift studio was beneath a busy flight path, occasionally necessitating a pause while a plane passed overhead.

All of the innovation, improvisation and indeed interrupting aircraft proved to be well worth it when the BBC immediately commissioned a series of thirteen shows to be broadcast from January 1966, but there was one further spot of minor turbulence to navigate first. By 1965, it was obvious that a full-colour television service would be rolled out in the near future, and Bura and Hardwick both expressed concerns that if this expensive and ambitious series was made in black and white, it could prove to have a very limited shelf life indeed. Murray was initially wary due to the exorbitant cost of colour film stock, but after prolonged persuasion from his animators, the rest of *Camberwick Green* was filmed using a system whereby cameras loaded with colour and black-and-white film were set up in line with each other. This did also mean that the first episode then had to be remade in colour, and while this time the nightmarish descending trees were kept under control, a number of small changes were made to the script, notably with local confectioner Bertie Baker becoming the somewhat less nominatively determined Mickey Murphy. It did, however, retain one detail that rarely ever featured anywhere else in any of the Trumptonshire series – the puppets are depicted as having mouths. By the time that the rest of *Camberwick Green* made it to television screens, they were gone, and the distinctive mouthless puppets proved to be the final key detail of Gordon Murray's charming animation style.

Each episode of *Camberwick Green* – a small village centred around a huge tree and surrounded by old-fashioned shops plying old-fashioned trades and staffed by puppets in varying forms of traditional dress – essentially followed one of the local residents through their daily routine, beginning with Peter Hazel the postman on his frequently interrupted round, during which he not only raised the alarm over a fire at the bakery that wasn't, but also somehow managed to get his postbag caught on the local windmill's sails.

Other local business figures included Mr Carraway the fishmonger, Mrs Dingle the postmistress, oddly Victorian Dr Mopp – who even drove a car with 1901 licence plates – and Mickey Murphy the capaciously hatted baker, whose children Paddy and Mary often helped in the bakery in between bouts of conspicuously polite and responsible mischief. Many of their trades relied heavily upon supplies from nearby Colley's Mill, whose rustically smocked proprietor Windy Miller enjoyed a just about friendly rival with 'modern mechanical' farmer Jonathan Bell, while on the village outskirts – and not especially fussy about who they got their breakfast from – the soldier boys at Pippin Fort were being drilled into soldier men by Captain Flack and Sergeant Major Grout. If anyone's vintage car, baker's van or army truck broke down during their working day, as they did surprisingly often, Mr Crockett's garage was on hand to help with their cheery slogan 'Gets you up the 'ill'. Also frequently often to be found somewhere in the vicinity of the post office were gossiping housewife Mrs Honeyman and her much fussed-over baby, milkman Thomas Tripp and his cat Tabatha, PC McGarry (Number 452), Roger Varley the chimney sweep and Mr Dagenham, a trendily attired sports car-driving salesman who was forever attempting to persuade all of the above to invest in the latest mod cons.

At the opening of each episode, over footage of a desk covered in academic books and reading lamps, Brian asked, 'Here is a box – a musical box, wound up and ready to play, and this box can hide a secret inside. Can you guess what is in it today?' upon which an antique wooden box on the desk began to rotate with a hefty clunk and a loud whirr until one of the above characters emerged from it. Following a story which usually began with a delivery being made or a surprise gift being arranged but could end up anywhere from Farmer Bell and Windy Miller staging a tractor versus tricycle road race to determine the relative superiority of modernity and the 'old ways', a major incident when a swarm of bees is discovered outside the bakery, and a multi-handed plot to prevent an electricity substation from being built on the green – which turned out to be a misunderstanding on the part of an eavesdropping Mrs Honeyman, who suddenly felt the need to make herself very scarce indeed – they would return back into the music box at its conclusion.

It took the best part of a year to complete work on *Camberwick Green*, with Gordon Murray delivering the thirteenth and final episode to the BBC days – or, by some accounts, hours – before the first one was scheduled to be broadcast. Introduced by a half-page feature in *Radio Times* explaining how stop-motion animation worked for the benefit of question-plagued parents, *Camberwick*

Green made the first of its dozens of appearances as part of 'Watch with Mother' on 3 January 1966 and was an instant success. The charmingly stylised puppets and settings, Brian Cant's upbeat narration, Freddie Phillips' quaintly rolling folky music and the accompanying songs – especially those introducing 'big friendly policeman' PC McGarry, 'sharper than a thorn' Windy Miller and the soldier boys 'riding along in an army truck', although few could quite match the boast that Mr Dagenham could sell 'a bathtub or a button, a bugle or a bike' for lyrical dexterity – all played their part; although what became the highlight of the show for many came about almost entirely by accident. Owing to the mistake in assembling the windmill, Windy Miller was obliged to dash in and out through momentary gaps while the sails were in motion, somehow managing to avoid them every time – and what's more, he did this during filming too, without a single retake required.

Despite some initial discontent in the press about the likelihood of it replacing longstanding favourites, *Camberwick Green* was such a success that it was immediately followed by a repeat run, and within months shops were full of everything from tie-in toothpaste to an intricately recreated village playset.

Not everyone was quite so taken with *Camberwick Green*, though. Each episode opened and closed with a clown operating a roller blackboard bearing the credits, who occasionally abruptly turned his head to inspect them but mostly just stared forwards, seemingly both directly at and right through the viewer and into the void beyond. To make matters worse, thanks to Freddie Phillips' music having to be curtly edited to fit the credits, it ended on a sudden jangling unresolved chord as the image faded away, not generally helped by the fact that BBC Test Card F and another unsettling-looking clown was liable to appear on either side of the show as well. Some may have been too amused to by the typographical contrivance required to fit Andrew Brownfoot's name onto the just slightly too small credit scroller to ever be properly unsettled by it, but many more would trepidatiously wait outside the door until parental assurance had been received that 'the clown' had gone.

Even so, the BBC was sufficiently pleased with *Camberwick Green*, and sufficiently prepared to stand up to the clown, to commission Gordon Murray and what he touchingly referred to as his team of 'cottage industries' to produce a new follow-on series. In contrast to the tranquil surroundings of Thomas Tripp and Son Dairies, *Trumpton* was set in a bustling neighbouring town centre dominated by the imposing town hall and its huge clock tower — famed for 'telling the time, steadily, sensibly, never too quickly, never too slowly' — that acted as the commercial focal point for local residents, tradesmen and dignitaries.

There was the mayor, town clerk Mr Troop, chauffeur Philby, carpenter Chippy Minton and his apprentice son Nibs, Mrs Cobbitt the flower seller, Miss Lovelace the milliner — and her three pampered and yappy dogs Mitzi, Daphne and Lulu — Mr Munnings the printer, Mr Platt the clockmaker, Mr Clamp the greengrocer and Mr Craddock the park keeper. From hats blown into trees to abandoned paint pots preventing the clock from chiming, their minor emergencies and comic mishaps were all attended to in record time by Captain Flack and his intrepid troop of firefighters Pugh, Pugh, Barney McGrew, Cuthbert, Dibble and Grubb, who also entertained the locals with a daily brass band concert in Trumpton Park. Their alarm bell-heralded line-up and race through the streets of Trumpton was the centrepiece of every episode and edge-of-the-seat excitement for young viewers — and it also has something of a mystery attached.

Conscious of the production schedule and the need to tailor the storylines to a busier setting, not to mention to a fire brigade who were prevented by the limitations of animation technology from encountering any actual smoke, fire or water, Gordon Murray had engaged Alison Prince to write the scripts for *Trumpton*. Fresh from working on *Joe*, and having been a member of the BBC's review panel for proposed new children's series, Alison was shown some test footage of the fire brigade roll call and, at least as she recalled it, thought up the names of the firemen based on their appearance. Gordon Murray, however, more than once asserted that he had come up with the 'rhythm' for the roll call inspired by a suggestion from his wife, ballerina Enid Martin, and as was usual practice had chanced upon the character names while flicking through the telephone directory. Meanwhile, Freddie Phillips recalled that the earliest scripts he received only listed five firemen, and he had suggested adding a second 'Pugh' to allow for a more coherent musical structure. Whatever the reality of their origin was, as with all inspired moves of genius, the explanation was no doubt somewhere between all three.

With a more confident production schedule – although once again work on the series was only finished shortly before the first episode went out – Bura and Hardwick were able to pull off more ambitious effects, including in one episode the demolition of a chimney. The Brownfoots drew design inspiration from the industrial-era architecture around Harrow – although the inclusion of a map of Florence in the fire brigade's control room served to confuse eagle-eyed viewers. Freddie Phillips adopted a brisker and more strident musical approach to reflect the more modern surroundings, from Mr Munnings' mechanically driven explanation of how his printing press worked to Mr Platt's chiming rumination on how 'clocks are like people', and a gentle ballad about the joys of feeding the ducks in the park; the latter accompanied by some actual ducks recorded in Ewell and an almighty splash as Cuthbert teeters – inevitably offscreen – into the pond, resulting in the flooding of the Phillips family bathroom.

The *Trumpton* credits appeared on simple white text on splodgy black shapes on a blue background, and were accompanied by two memorable sequences. Each episode opened with the clock ticking down the seconds to striking 9 a.m., with gilt figures of town founders Sir Basil and Lady De Trompe emerging to chime the hour while the businesses below rolled up shutters, put out awnings and parked up vans and the mayor surveyed the activity from the Town Hall balcony. Each episode closed with the fire brigade merrily tootling away on the bandstand as a sizeable crowd rolled up to watch them, which included numerous otherwise rarely sighted residents of Camberwick Green.

Rather than concentrating on individual characters, Alison's script tended to focus on specific local events and incidents and how they would all play their part in resolving it. For example, the Trumpton residents found themselves having to contend with crossed telephone lines caused by Miss Lovelace's uncontrollable dogs, a race to stop Chippy Minton's rocking horse-stored life savings from being incinerated on a park bonfire, a window cleaner stranded on the roof of the hat shop, and a road blocked by a fallen tree, necessitating the emergency deployment of one of Mr Platt's previously disregarded homing pigeons. The fire brigade proved adept at reattaching dislodged crowns to statues, removing old water tanks from high lofts and locating wandering artists from a distance – although Nick Fisher was comically unimpressed at their attempts at sticking up bill posters – but they never had to deal with anything even halfway approaching an actual blaze ('A fire? A real fire? Oh, a bonfire . . .').

Possibly even more successful than its predecessor – as the fleets of talking toy fire engines will attest – *Trumpton* made its debut exactly one year after *Camberwick Green* on 3 January 1967. Viewers clearly wanted to see more of Trumptonshire, but it would be almost three years before they got a glimpse of *Chigley* (BBC, 1969). Identified in the opening titles as 'Near Camberwick Green, Trumptonshire' – Gordon Murray intended the three locations to be in an equidistant triangular formation – Chigley was dominated by light industry, cottage industries and the opulent Winkstead Hall, ancestral home of local philanthropist Lord Belborough.

The employees of the Creswell family's celebrated high-tech biscuit factory held daily dances after the six o'clock whistle, accompanied by Lord Belborough and his butler Brackett on his Dutch organ; potter Harry Farthing and his daughter Winnie catered for everyone's ceramic needs; and bargee Mr Rumpling and crane operator Mr Swallow at Treddle's Wharf were on hand to ensure the smooth delivery of supplies and materials. If anything defeated even them – not to mention builder Mr Clutterbuck, dustmen Mr Gubbins and Mr Sneed, Winkstead Hall gardener Mr Bilton and other local workers – then a call would be put through to Winkstead Hall, necessitating Brackett to take a famously lengthy stroll along the corridors to find his Lordship so that they could rush to assist via his own private steam railway. Depicted almost as a sentient entity in its own right, 'Bessie' the vintage steam engine is possibly the most well remembered detail of *Chigley*, not least on account of Lord Belborough's chuggingly memorable song about how 'time flies by when I'm the driver of a train'.

In fact, *Chigley* is generally not nearly as well remembered as *Camberwick Green* and *Trumpton*, and there are a couple of possible reasons for this. Each episode opens with a well-known character from one of the other shows being asked by Brian Cant if they are on their way to Chigley ('May we come with you?'), and the repeated motifs of the six o'clock dance and Bessie on the rails mostly only appear towards the conclusion of each episode. The storylines were more gentle vignettes with a comic twist than character studies or big event setpieces, ranging from the accidental partial demolition of a wall by a runaway lawnmower to arranging a charity balloon ride with the mayor of Trumpton, a crate of books tumbling into the canal – eventually retrieved by one of the Pippin Fort soldier boys in frogman gear – and an abundance of apples in the Winkstead Hall orchard, literally pressed into cider-making service by Windy Miller.

Chigley also had something of a troubled genesis, which not only saw a neighbouring doughnut factory, a local candlemaker, a modern housing estate, a private zoo and even a Lady Belborough disappear from the original format proposal but also led to it temporarily disappearing for a couple of years in the late seventies while some contractual issues were ironed out. Despite this low profile, *Chigley* was every inch the equal of its two more famous counterparts, and the creative team had reached new heights: Bura and Hardwick pulled off some difficult effects including steam issuing from Bessie's funnel; Andrew and Margaret Brownfoot turned in a convincingly modernist factory and based the huge Winkstead Hall set on the real-life Kedlestone Hall near Derby; and Freddie Phillips furnished the onomatopoeic lyrics about 'wheezing pistons, smoking funnels, turning wheels go clickety-clack' with a shunting guitar rhythm and authentic sound effects recorded from the platform at Sheffield Park station – but by the time it arrived on 6 October 1969, it really did feel like the end of an era. All three shows continued to be repeated into the mid-eighties, but although Gordon Murray did briefly toy with the idea of a further series set in a coastal town, that was the last that viewers saw from Trumptonshire. At least in the present day.

In 1976, Gordon Murray remade six of his original *Rubovian Legend* plays as *Rubovia* (BBC, 1976), revisiting the magical kingdom ruled by King Rufus and Queen Caroline with their son Prince Rupert and pet dragon Pongo, and various associates including court magician Mr Wetherspoon, Rubina the cat, Farmer Bottle, the Lord Chamberlain, King Boris of Borsovia and MacGregor, a visiting Native American with a Chinese accent who dispensed wisdom over the garden wall, with music from Freddie Phillips and narration by Gordon himself and voices from Roy Skelton. Originally intended for a later timeslot aimed at a slightly older audience, the high-spirited pantomime sitcom antics of *Rubovia* ended up as an odd fit for 'Watch with Mother' and was only shown a handful of times, destined to forever be a frustrating memory of erstwhile Pongo-loving viewers who were roundly accused of just having made up a 'fourth' Trumptonshire show. It is also fair to say that the entirely coincidental similarity to ITV's contemporaneous *Cloppa Castle* did not exactly help. After making the similarly inclined *Skip and Fuffy* (BBC, 1977) and *The Gublins* (BBC, 1978) as inserts for a more appropriate audience in *Multi-Coloured Swap Shop*, Gordon Murray quietly retired from television to concentrate on his miniature collectable 'Silver Thimble' storybooks.

For the residents of Trumptonshire, though, the six o'clock dance, the fire brigade band concert and indeed disappearing back into the music box were only really the prelude to another working day, and while we might have stopped getting to see them at work, they never quite stopped themselves. Recently, after years of resurfacing as battered and unsteady old prints, the original episodes were restored in high definition with as much care and attention as is afforded to any archival Jimi Hendrix recording, allowing viewers to guess who was in the music box, recite along with the fire brigade roll call and indeed hide behind the door from the clown all over again. Whoever *Chigley*'s resident film restoration engineer was, they definitely deserve their own song.

6

Comedy

'Give me a P! Give me an L! Give me an A! Give me a Y!'

Let's be honest – everyone tried it, and hardly anyone got away with it. You'd very politely, casually and vaguely ask your parents if you could stay up to watch 'the funny programme' on the black-and-white portable. With official parental assent, you'd watch a couple of tamer ITV sitcoms to throw them off the scent, until the moment came. Then, eleven seconds into the opening titles of *The Young Ones*, you'd be rumbled and sternly sent off to bed, then have to keep your head down as best you could on the playground the next morning. Nobody's quite sure why, but the comedy you weren't allowed to watch always seemed so much funnier than the comedy that you *were* allowed to.

It wasn't always this way. The Goons may have responded to their wartime experiences by babbling nonsense into the faces of authority figures, and Tony Hancock may have cast a weary eye over the latest fads and crazes of the modern world, but nothing you'd find on the television or radio, even the gay slang bandied about – 'Ooooh, innee bold!' – by Kenneth Williams and Hugh Paddick as 'Julian and Sandy', was anything that you couldn't watch or listen to with the whole family in tow. Hardly surprisingly, what few children's comedy shows there were – such as the comic mishaps of hard-of-thinking Mr Small of the petty criminal world in *Bonehead* (BBC, 1960–62), Jimmy Edwards' un-headmasterly pocket-lining schemes in *Whack-O!* (BBC, 1956–72) and the comic strip-derived antics of scoffing schoolboy *Billy Bunter of Greyfriars School* (BBC, 1952–61) – were really just junior versions of what you could watch later on that evening. Tony Hancock's notorious dismissal of the idea of being asked to write for 'flippin' kids' eventually spurred his gagman Terry Nation into creating the Daleks, but The Goons even found their way into children's television courtesy of *The Telegoons* (BBC, 1963–64), a set of radio scripts remade with puppets that, frankly, looked as though they had been dredged from a canal.

Then on 22 August 1960, Peter Cook, Dudley Moore, Alan Bennett and Jonathan Miller took to the stage at the Royal Lyceum Theatre, London, for the first performance of their satirical revue *Beyond the Fringe*, and everything changed. Although not everyone was especially happy about it, everything from politics and religion to tradition and equality was suddenly fair game and a valid target for barbed lampoonery and comment, and a lot of it had to be put safely out of the way where children couldn't see it. The chances of being allowed to stay up to watch *That Was The Week That Was* (BBC, 1962–63) or *The Frost Report* (BBC, 1966–67) were slight, to say the least. The 'radio custard pie thrown by' the cast of *I'm Sorry, I'll Read That Again* (BBC, 1964–73) might suddenly be snapped off by parents who understood the jokes that you didn't, and although Peter Cook and Dudley Moore might have been as big as the pop stars of the day, their chartbound singles might have been the closest that younger fans came to actually seeing any of *Not Only . . . But Also* (BBC, 1964–70). Ironically, though, those younger fans got their own show that had adults racing home from work determined not to miss out on the fun.

COMEDY

Michael Palin, Terry Jones and Eric Idle had all been working as writers and occasionally performers on many of the late-night satire shows when they were approached by producer Humphrey Barclay, who was putting together a team for a Children's ITV sketch show and felt it needed to be a little different and more 'now'. Along with comic actors Denise Coffey and David Jason, the trio were joined for the aptly named *Do Not Adjust Your Set* (ITV, 1967–69) by animator Terry Gilliam, who added a dash of psychedelic surrealism, and the Bonzo Dog Doo-Dah Band, the absurdist parody pop troupe led by Vivian Stanshall and Neil Innes. Ostensibly engaged to perform an appropriate song for each show, the Bonzos were soon adding their own brand of mayhem into the sketches and generally causing polite havoc for their own amusement, notoriously once asking the props department for an oil tanker out of sheer mischief and left feeling sheepish when they found out efforts had actually been made to acquire one. This may all sound like an odd fit for a children's show, but the limitations placed on them by their audience was what made *Do Not Adjust Your Set* work. Subversions of traditional knock-knock and shopkeeper jokes sat seamlessly alongside gags about Harold Wilson and John Lennon and Yoko Ono, and the three lead writers in particular found that the budgetary and suitability restrictions taught them a valuable lesson about what you could achieve through thinking sideways, as well as fostering a keen taste for poking fun at the boundaries – sometimes literally – of television itself.

Jason and Coffey's cliffhanging serialised adventures of Captain Fantastic and his battles to foil the fiendish plots of Mr Black and her cardboard box-headed henchmen the Blip Men inspired countless playground recreations, and the studio audience rowdily sang along with the Bonzos, clearly having 'got' all of their arcane gags and absurdist prop comedy. It was a show that credited its viewers with intelligence, and it's hardly surprising that, after years of trying to make a breakthrough with more sophisticated audiences, the Bonzos immediately scored a top ten hit with 'I'm the Urban Spaceman'.

Palin and Jones went on to make *The Complete and Utter History of Britain* (ITV, 1969), a sketch show imagining great historical events as if they had occurred in the age of investigative journalists and football commentary, which was possibly a little too ambitious for its resources but led to John Cleese – who had been exploring similar comic ground in the adult comedy show *At Last the 1948 Show* (ITV, 1967) with Graham Chapman, Marty Feldman and Tim Brooke-Taylor – phoning Palin to suggest that he, Jones, Gilliam and Idle might want to join forces with himself and Chapman for a new sketch show. David and Denise's only consolation for not being invited to join the Monty Python team was the odd job-toting canine team-up sitcom *Two D's and a Dog* (ITV, 1970).

Elsewhere in the ITV children's schedules, another familiar face from late-night shows – wry and lugubrious singer-songwriter Jake Thackray – joined Bernard Bresslaw and Janet Henfrey for *Tickertape* (ITV, 1968), which saw them perform silly material in a minimalist setting informed by silent cinema and expressionist theatre at the behest of a clown-shaped news ticker. By the early seventies, the satire boom was all over bar the shouting – usually at Edward Heath – but children's television had gained a little sophistication from its dalliance with the more daring end of comedy, and everyone was that bit happier to try something new.

An unlikely combination of a chance sighting of a gatepost sign while lost in the country and a bedraggled old man in Hieronymus Bosch's painting 'The Crowning with Thorns' led writer Richard Carpenter to come up with *Catweazle* (ITV, 1970–71), an eleventh-century magician flung forward in time while casting a spell to escape Norman soldiers. Played to perfection by Geoffrey Bayldon, the stranded superstitious time-traveller and his toad familiar Touchwood sought refuge in a water tower he renamed Castle Saburac, hidden and aided by local farmer's son Edward 'Carrot' Bennett, whom he erroneously believed to be a master magician privy to the secrets of 'electrickery'. Despite his struggles to comprehend the mysteries of 'the sun in a bottle' and the vexatious 'telling bone', Catweazle did eventually find his way home, only to find himself imprisoned by a crooked lord determined to discover the secret of alchemy. Escaping by 'flying' into the future once more, Catweazle this time arrives at abandoned railway station Duck Halt, where local aristocrat's son Cedic 'Owl Face' Collingford helps him to recover the thirteen – yes, thirteen – signs of the zodiac he will need to right the wrongs of his own time.

In between a vast number of adventure series, Richard Carpenter followed *Catweazle* with *The Ghosts of Motley Hall* (ITV, 1976–78), in which a suitably motley assortment of phantoms – Arthur English as wily medieval jester Bodkin, Freddie Jones as retired Victorian military man turned boozing bore Sir George Uproar, Nicholas Le Provost as failed Georgian man-about-town Francis 'Fanny' Uproar, Sean Flanagan as Regency stable boy Matt and Sheila Steafel as the White Lady, whose identity was lost to the ages – conspired to help their crumbling ancestral home's custodian Mr Gudgin, as played by Peter Sallis, to prevent it from falling into the hands of redevelopers. Technically ambitious – two separate identical sets had to be built to facilitate the multiple materialisation effects – and with a heavyweight cast better known for their stage work, it's little wonder that *The Ghosts of Motley Hall* was furnished with scripts that were as affecting as they were ingeniously funny, with the mismatched allies much given to contrasting their lamented lot in life to the comradeship they had found in spectral form. Sadly, they were spirited away before viewers got any long-term assurance that Motley Hall's future was secure.

Although elements of the supernatural were oddly predominant in children's entertainment in the seventies, everywhere from *The Usborne Book of Ghosts* to Trebor Mummies and Crosse & Blackwell's Haunted House game, there is no rational or sceptical explanation for the fact that two other uncannily similar sitcoms made their debuts almost in the same week as *The Ghosts of Motley Hall*. *Nobody's House* (ITV, 1976), starring Kevin Moreton as a nameless Victorian sweep ectoplasmically holed up in a modern family home and much given to addressing the camera directly, would as good as pass straight through a wall into obscurity, but the spooks-for-hire at *Rentaghost* (BBC, 1976–84) made a more tangible intangible impression.

Rentaghost wasn't writer Bob Block's first fantasy slapstick sitcom for children. Over at ITV he'd already created *Pardon My Genie* (ITV, 1972–73) with Hugh Paddick as a lantern-bound misunderstanding-prone sorcerer accidentally summoned by exasperated stores apprentice Hal Adden, and the malfunctioning microchip palaver that followed inventor Robert Sommerby and *Robert's Robots* (ITV, 1973–74) – but it was the self-employed hired hands at *Rentaghost* who really caught on; and to begin with, it was something of a different series to the one most viewers might recognise.

Determined to be more of a success as a spectre than he had been in life, and keen to avoid his parents finding out that he'd been even more of a failure than they realised, Fred Mumford (Anthony Jackson) formed Rentaghost with two more experienced spirit-world associates – ageing Victorian dandy continually fussed over by his much younger mother Hubert Davenport (Michael Darbyshire) and mischief-prone court jester to Queen Matilda Timothy Claypole

(Michael Staniforth), with occasional assistance from sharp-shootin' Wild West gal Catastrophe Kate (Jana Shelden) – to take on any job any time, with the covert aid of their teleportation and telekinetic abilities, which unfortunately none of them were especially adept at. Not particularly business-savvy couple Harold and Ethel Meaker (Edward Brayshaw and Ann Emery) looked after their bookings – usually by department store manager Adam Painting (Christopher Biggins) – despite the chaos they invariably wrought; with their uptight houseproud neighbours the Perkins forever trying to catch them out and expose whatever it was that was going on next door. Called on to act as everything from classical musicians to bus conductors, the unlikely trio also found themselves confronted with such topical concerns as trade-union conflict, tenancy agreements and massive delays at airports in between all of the mishearing-fuelled mishaps.

The three leads formed a deep personal bond; although for the children watching at home the undisputed star was the resolutely zany Staniforth, a veteran of musical theatre who also furnished the show with its memorable theme song, extolling the virtues of employing them 'if your mansion house needs haunting', and closing with 'an apparition quipped from deep inside a crypt, "Ring Rentaghost!"' followed by echoing mocking laughter that possibly did not sit well with some viewers.

Rentaghost was even afforded a feature-length Christmas special in 1979. First made in 1978, the special was not shown until 1979 due to BBC industrial action; it introduced Dobbin, a pantomime horse brought to life by Mr Claypole, which insisted on becoming a devoted yet destructive pet to the Meakers. And their closeness meant that when Michael Darbyshire became unavailable for the most ironic reason in 1979 (his death at the age of 62), Anthony

Jackson refused to continue without him. Instead, Mr Claypole and Dobbin were joined by a succession of even more eccentric apparitions, including Hazel the McWitch (Molly Weir), Tamara Novek (Lynda Marchal) and her cousin Nadia Popov (Sue Nicholls) who were both afflicted by uncontrollable sneeze-activated teleportation, clueless Whatisname Smith (Kenneth Connor), variety glamour girl Susie Starlight (Aimi MacDonald) and temperamental dragon Bernie St John ('DON'T GO INTO THE CELLAR!'), and the storylines became more driven by slapstick and pantomime, but *Rentaghost* still worked just as well for younger viewers eager for a high-speed barrage of comic chaos.

As the success of *Rentaghost* showed, nothing succeeded with children more than slapstick with wild escalating plots about next to nothing descending into mayhem while the boring 'normal' world looked on baffled, and happily – and more than likely not a coincidence considering the popularity of *The Monkees* – there was plenty of it around and in ready supply. Spun off from a series of cinema shorts featuring *The Magnificent Six and ½* (1968–72), *Here Come the Double Deckers!* (BBC, 1971) was even wilder than its title warned, with a gang of over-energetic kids – Scooper, Spring, Sticks, Doughnut, Brains, Billie and Tiger, the latter invariably accompanied by her stuffed toy also named 'Tiger' – launching a reality-challenging procession of plots and plans from their mechanically modified Routemaster clubhouse, finding themselves prevailed upon to do everything from stopping a runaway go-kart to repelling what they believed to be an alien invasion. Equipped with a suitably brash cast-performed pop song theme, they had the sort of adventures that you always hoped might somehow happen on a long hot summer day but never actually did because, well, even reality isn't THAT weird.

With one foot in the Merseybeat boom and the other in the satire boom, and doubtless they would have claimed a third in a bucket of custard, The Scaffold — poet Roger McGough, comic John Gorman and musician Mike McGear, who just happened to be the brother of a certain Paul McCartney — hit the big time with an unlikely fusion of blunt social satire, collaborations with top rock stars and family-friendly nonsense songs, including 1968 chart-topper 'Lily the Pink'. Although they had first come to prominence through late-night topical shows, they proved to be an ideal fit for Children's BBC, and while *Score with the Scaffold* (BBC, 1970–71) was ostensibly a quiz show aimed directly at the 'contestants' watching at home, it was really little more than an excuse for them to run riot around the supposed 'rounds'.

Cousins from a veteran variety family, Mike Hope and Albie Keen were regular faces on light entertainment shows but never really caught a break until they moved into *Hope and Keen's Crazy House* (BBC, 1970–71), a sitcom set in a suitably wacky mansion with that week's pop star guests 'staying' in the guest bedroom. *Hope and Keen's Crazy Bus* (BBC, 1972) saw them commandeer a double-decker with an unshiftable resident ticket inspector and head off in search of Uncle Ebenezer's lost fortune, while *The Hope and Keen Scene* (BBC, 1974) reverted to a more traditional sketch show format, albeit with a weekly theme.

Michael Bentine, who had previously explored his post-Goons mastery of radio-controlled puppetry in visiting alien sitcom *The Bumblies* (BBC, 1954) and variety show *Michael Bentine Time* (BBC, 1972), perfected his art in *Potty Time* (ITV, 1973–80), a current affairs reportage-style show in which he interrogated his jabbering creations as they re-enacted major historical occurrences, more than once veering a little too close to comment on real-world current events for the IBA's comfort.

Norman Rossington's inept P.C. Fogg found himself at the bidding of canine partner Parry in *Follow That Dog* (ITV, 1974); Jack Woolgar wrestled with Norman Hunter's unlikely literary contraptions in *The Incredible Adventures of Professor Branestawm* (ITV, 1968); *Bright's Boffins* (ITV, 1970–72) came up with gadgets that would hardly have impressed 007 in their forgotten-about Whitehall laboratory; comic Freddie 'Parrot Face' Davies wrangled the zoologically bizarre inmates of Chumpton Green Pet Shop in *The Small World of Samuel Tweet* (BBC, 1974–75); and mime artist Ben Benison got up to all manner of street-based Jacques Tati-like antics in *The Up and Down In and Out Round About Man* (ITV, 1973).

Pauline Quirke, Linda Robson and assorted pupils of the Anna Scher Theatre School teamed up with similarly youthful pop group Flintlock for frequently taste- and decency-challenging larks with the studio audience in *You Must Be Joking!* (ITV, 1975–76) and *Pauline's Quirkes* (ITV, 1976), before Pauline was joined by a new younger troupe for *You Can't Be Serious!* (ITV, 1978).

Clive Dunn reprised the persona from his 1970 chart-topping sentimental novelty song of the same name for the Bob Block-penned *Grandad* (BBC, 1979–84), in which spectacularly unhandy handyman Charlie Quick – who as the cockney pub singalong theme song had it, 'played the pianner in the strangest manner' – and his pet parrot the Captain unravelled local authority red tape usually more by accident than by design. Possibly having exhausted all of the unlikely comic scenarios on this planet, Bob Block blasted off into space for *Galloping Galaxies!* (BBC, 1985–86), an intergalactic farce with the just about competent crew of the *Starship Voyager* and their RAM-deficient contingent of androids unwittingly joined by inadvertently teleported housewife Mabel Appelby and a glorious turn from Kenneth Williams as the voice of the pompous and impatient on-board Space Investigation Detector – or S.I.D., for short. If there wasn't enough comic mayhem in the actual episodes, the sci-fi disco pastiche *Galloping Galaxies!* theme song actually impatiently referenced the fact that it *was* the theme song. Shrieklingly enlivened by Bonnie Langford's unforgettable turn as Violet Elizabeth Bott, *Just William* (ITV, 1977–78) brought Richmal Crompton's tales of the chaotic cap-askew schoolboy – who crashed through the LWT logo in the opening titles – to the screen with suitable piano-demolishing abandon.

If you wanted witty, fast-moving and fast-talking comedy with more than its fair share of gleefully awful puns, though, there was really only one place to look – BBC2 on Saturday afternoons. Funded by revenue generated from overseas sales of *Play School* and inspired by the presenters' joke-telling habit between takes, *Play Away* (BBC, 1971–84) gave them the opportunity to run riot with part-improvised gags, sketches, puzzles, riddles, quizzes, tongue-twisters, party games, songs and slapstick, with Brian Cant and *Play School*'s resident pianist Jonathan Cohen emerging as the stars of the show. At various points they were joined by Toni Arthur, Derek Griffiths, Chloe Ashcroft, Carol Chell, Johnny Ball, Lionel Morton – who also provided the rambunctious theme song urging all and sundry that 'it really doesn't matter if it's raining or it's fine, just as long as you've got time to p-l-a-y' – and many others, including up-and-coming acting talent like Jeremy Irons, Anita Dobson and Tony Robinson, apparently running on more energy and indeed noise than an actual children's birthday party.

There were numerous attempts to replicate *Play Away*'s unique brand of mayhem, including interruption-fuelled witticism contest *Excuse Me!* (BBC, 1980) and musical mischief with Chris Wear and Justin Case in *Chopsticks* (BBC, 1980), but nothing really ever came close to matching its unashamed brand of deliberate silliness. Floella Benjamin, who had proven an especially popular part of the *Play Away* cast, was chosen to lead its eventual successor, and was joined by Anna Monro, Nick Wilton and Andrew Secombe for *Fast Forward* (BBC, 1985–87), an up-to-date sketch show with a computer-voiced theme song riffing on the fact that you could record it on video and watch your favourite moments again. Although the cast did well with sketches poking fun at McDonald's adverts and Indiana (Rubber) Jones, and running gags about their unseen gigantic pet 'Tiny' and visiting aliens from the planet Zymaron, ultimately it just wasn't different enough – unlike *Play Away*, which had seemed to exist in its own universe entirely – and the BBC pressed Stop soon enough.

The greatest outbreaks of anarchy, though, could always be found at the hands – or indeed on the hands – of exasperated puppeteers with a less than obedient furry sidekick. Harry Corbett's magic wand-wielding show-off orange bear Sooty had been a favourite from as far back as the mid-fifties, with *The Sooty Show* (BBC, 1955–67) featuring the duo and their close associates, goody two-shoes panda Soo and permanently bemused squeaking sausage-fixated dog Sweep, joining the hysterical studio audience for a parade of sketches and songs, most of which resulted in Harry being squirted with a water pistol. A move to ITV in 1968 for a new iteration of *The Sooty Show* (ITV, 1968–92) moved in a different direction, particularly once Harry's son Matthew took over in 1975, with a more sitcom- and running serial-based approach, including an epic playground-exciting race to unmask their untidying nemesis, the Black Hand.

Well-spoken laugher at his own jokes Basil Brush emerged from supporting roles in children's television and a spell as stooge to magician David Nixon for *The Basil Brush Show* (BBC, 1968–80), a variety show where some of the biggest names in light entertainment were prevailed upon not to wince at his terrible puns and attendant jubilant cry of 'BOOM! BOOM!' as assorted hapless 'Mister's – Rodney Bewes, Derek Fowlds, Roy North, Howard Williams and Billy Boyle – tried not to roll their eyes at his tall tales about Blast-Off Basil and Basil d'Farma, the Knight in Shining Armour. Jim Henson's tales of the song- and dance-prone fuzzy subterranean dwellers at *Fraggle Rock* (ITV, 1983–87) were made as inserts for international broadcasters to add their own linking material around; British audiences got to see Fulton Mackay, John Gordon Sinclair and Simon O'Brien as a succession of lighthouse keepers remaining blithely oblivious to Sprocket the dog's attempts to alert them to Goober and company making off with needles and paintbrushes for their latest harebrained scheme.

Most unpredictable of all – by pretty much anyone's standards – Rod Hull and his tetchy glittery blue bird Emu even threatened the integrity of your television itself in *Emu's Broadcasting Company* (BBC, 1975–80), in which the pair poked fun at schedules and continuity announcements as they operated their own BBC station EBC1 complete with no-budget programming – most infamously the not at all pointed 'Doctor Emu Meets the Deadly Dustbins' – and Hull's incredible gift for physical comedy, which once saw Emu hurl the pair of them convincingly into a supermarket freezer. A change in broadcasting company for *Emu's World* (ITV, 1981–84) relocated them to the Pink Windmill, where a literal song and dance was made every time there was somebody at the door, and introduced the similarly singing and dancing Pink Windmill Kids alongside Carole Lee Scott as scheming witch Grotbags and her inept sidekicks Robot Redford and Croc. Capitalising on the show's enormous popularity, it evolved into *Emu's All-Live Pink Windmill Show* (ITV, 1984–88), adding an element of Pink Windmill Kid-helmed live interactivity and the lengthy non-Emu saga of 'Tudor Rod in Boggle's Kingdom', but nothing ever went quite off the rails as much as it had over at EBC1. That said, when your puppet has attacked Michael Parkinson, Snoop Dogg and the Queen Mother's bouquet on live television and lived to tell the tale, that's a bar set pretty high.

There was always room for a gentler form of comedy that your parents wouldn't be left too exhausted and disorientated by, however, and this was very much the case for one of the biggest unexpected hits in television history. *Worzel Gummidge* (ITV, 1979–81) wasn't the first adaptation of Barbara Euphan Todd's novels about a talking scarecrow with a heart of gold and an interchangeable head of straw, but writers Keith Waterhouse and Willis Hall had seen a potential for heartwarming family comedy that had never really been explored before. Jon Pertwee agreed with them, attaching himself to the role before the series had even been commissioned and staying with the project through many rejections before Southern finally picked it up.

Filmed entirely on location in Hampshire, in and around Stockbridge, King's Somborne and Brashfield, the cheerful rustic adventures of Ten Acre Field's cheeky resident bird-scarer, his friends John and Sue (Jeremy Austin and Charlotte Coleman) from Scatterbrook Farm, his highly strung would-be paramour fairground attraction Aunt Sally (Una Stubbs) and a host of semi-regular moving mannequins, including Dolly Clothes-Peg (Lorraine Chase), Saucy Nancy (Barbara Windsor) and Jolly Jack (Bernard Cribbins), were warm and uplifting slices of rural farce that captivated the audience. From the opening chirping birdsong and rambunctious theme tune to Worzel toppling backwards on his stave at the end of the closing credits, it was quintessential Sunday afternoon viewing, although it wasn't afraid to go dark either, with constant threats of characters being unwittingly burned on bonfires, stern rebukes and disciplinary action meted out by the sinister Crowman (Geoffrey Bayldon), and Worzel's nightmarish self-created scarecrow with malign intent Dafthead (Frank Marlborough). Only ever cancelled due to Southern losing their ITV franchise – it returned on Channel 4 as the New Zealand-made *Worzel Gummidge Down Under* (Channel 4, 1987–89) – it was such a hit that Jon Pertwee even made a bid for chart stardom with a vocal version of the theme song explaining how to speak the confusing tie-in language 'Worzelese'. Children routinely putting a 'wor' after 'w' and a 'wor' after 'o' and a 'wor' after 'r' were, sadly, decidedly thin on the ground.

If you were of a more traditional persuasion, an industrial-strength procession of gags were printed out by *The Joke Machine* (ITV, 1985–89) with the varying assistance of Andrew O'Connor, The Krankies, Jimmy Cricket and Basil Brush, while *The End of the End of the Pier Show* (ITV, 1981) recreated the glory days of music hall in the fictional town of Smallhaven, safe in the knowledge that the audience couldn't ask the performers to kindly leave the stage. Richard Beckinsale led a troupe of theatrical players through in-character readings of Hilaire Belloc and Spike Milligan poems in *Elephant's Eggs in a Rhubarb Tree* (ITV, 1971), and Edward Lear's celebrated absurdist verse formed the Halas and Batchelor-animated basis for *Tomfoolery* (ITV, 1970), in which the exploits of the likes of the Umbrageous Umbrella Maker and the Yongy-Bonghy-Bo rubbed shoulders with a very modern form of silliness taking in ridiculous recipes and songs celebrating 'good old nonsense', in which, crucially, 'pennies are pence to me'.

The unlikely combination of Denise Coffey, Roy Hudd and sixties hitmaker Gerry Marsden made up the thought bubble-assisted editorial staff of *The Weekly Bizarre* as they sought to expose a local rug scandal in *Hold the Front Page* (ITV, 1974), while Thames' comedy anthology *Funny Ha-Ha* (ITV, 1974) tried to give a leg-up to the dismal fortunes of Wormwood Rovers in 'Football Crazy', saw Eric Idle's gang of inept crooks planning to return an overdue library book in 'Commander Badman', and included improv sketch show 'Don't Blame Us', family prank comic playlet 'Who's Afraid of the Big Bad Bear?' and visiting alien mayhem 'Me 'n' Meep', but only the adventures of a juvenile gang named after a reputed local spook *The Molly Wopsies* (ITV, 1976) graduated to a full series.

Loosely based on Peter Eldin's series of tongue-in-cheek classroom self-help guides, *The Whizzkid's Guide* (ITV, 1981) cast Arthur Mullard, Rita Webb, Patrick Newell, Kenneth Williams and Sheila White as a gaggle of overgrown schoolchildren in outdated uniforms offering twisted tips on such topics as how to get ahead on sports day without even trying, with regular appearances by copyright-busting comic and cinema character-costumed acrobatic troupe The Dingbats. Meanwhile, Derek Griffiths linked classic Warner Bros. cartoons in the GET ON WITH IT!-shouting guise of Reg the projectionist, Doreen the usherette and the entire staff of the Roxy Cinema in *Film Fun* (ITV, 1982). On a more abstract tangent, *A Bundle of Bungles* (BBC, 1979) followed silent comedy character Mr Ree through a series of odd and downbeat mime vignettes; it went largely unnoticed at the time, but Rowan Atkinson later put this experience to particularly effective comic use.

There was little getting away, however, from the fact that the late seventies in particular were a time of huge unrest, tension and associated irreverence. This provided powerful fuel for a string of critically lauded movies and television series that, while not without their lighter moments, were understandably grim and pessimistic — but one of the earliest examples of a response to this was an out and out children's sitcom with a far more hopeful tone. Starring Phil Daniels and Ray Burdis — who went on to star in many of those movies and series themselves — *4 Idle Hands* (ITV, 1976) followed the mixed fortunes of school leavers Mike Dudds and Pete Sutton as they navigated the workplace with a teacher's parting shot that they will amount to nothing ringing in their ears and a determination to avoid a life on the dole. Neither qualified nor adept, nor indeed especially well-suited to workplace politics, Mike and Pete stumble through a procession of jobs, trying their hand at pretty much anything until a social worker eventually finds some purpose and potential in their can-do and want-to-do attitude. In a very different sign of the times, *The Square Leopard* (ITV, 1980) starred sixties heartthrob John Leyton as a solicitor who suddenly finds himself without a roof over his head and has to reluctantly move in as a lodger with a large single-parent family, none of whom especially take to him but both parties frequently find themselves in mutual need of assistance to pull off the schemes and shortcuts they need to keep their heads above water. *Graham's Gang* (BBC, 1977–79) even struck an unlikely blow for equality with the permanently bickering teenage rabble-rousers invariably finding that their attempts to exclude female associate Mildred, for being a 'girl', end up being to their detriment.

End of Part One (ITV, 1979–80) was the work of writers Andrew Marshall and David Renwick, then well known to a huge cult following for their wildly deconstructionist radio sketch show *The Burkiss Way* — which famously saw one edition 'dropped' on the floor and smashed, and then glued back together in the wrong order — who were asked to turn their astute parodic attention to television. Neither prepared to rein themselves in for, or talk down to, their intended audience, they came up with a series of savage sendups — as observed by viewing couple Mr and Mrs Straightman — not just of such obvious and deserving targets as the lazy stereotypes bandied about by sitcoms like *Are You Being Served?*, the contempt for the audience shown by game shows like *The Generation Game* and the obvious faked illustrative footage in current affairs shows like *World in Action* and *Panorama*, but even the station logos, the schedule rundowns and the patronising warnings not to 'copy' the elaborate underwater setpieces in ITV's big action import of the day *The Man from Atlantis*. Other times however, like when they replaced the cat on the roof in the *Coronation Street* opening titles with a lobster, they were just being silly for the sake of it, and the audience loved it. *End of Part One* was, without a shadow of a doubt, far funnier than most comedy shows aimed at adults at the time.

Two of the 'kind' featured in BBC's early eighties late-evening irreverent sketch show *Three of a Kind* (BBC, 1981–83), Tracey Ullman and Lenny Henry, went on to even greater national and international fame; third team member David Copperfield is often considered to have missed the boat, but in fact he enjoyed – and very much personally enjoyed – a couple of years as Children's BBC's biggest comedy star in shows like elevator-linked sketch show *Lift Off! With Coppers and Co!* (BBC, 1987) and its sitcom spin-off *Coppers and Co!* (BBC, 1988), with his 'Wally' character sparking more than a few playground impressions.

Based on an idea by cartoonist Gray Jolliffe of 'Wicked Willie' infamy, *Stainless Steel and the Star Spies* (ITV, 1981) followed a crack team of puppet 'Metalians' – not remotely influenced by the robots from the Cadbury's Smash adverts – as they sought to retrieve the vital Kleptonite Ball from under the noses of unwitting humans after the original assigned agent failed in his mission by falling in love with a hoover, and was every bit as bizarre as it sounds. Overseen by original *Doctor Who* producer Verity Lambert and with a high-profile cast including Ed Bishop, Deryck Guyler and Bob Hoskins, huge things were clearly expected of this eccentric one-off, but thanks to ATV losing its ITV licence, it didn't go much further.

Over at LWT, former Monkee Micky Dolenz had been hired as a producer by the comedy department, where he was responsible for a series of sitcom hits that were nearly as wild and indeed nearly as popular as his own small-screen escapades. Over-affectionate Atomic Thunderbuster-gobbling android *Metal Mickey* (ITV, 1980–83) – who as the theme song reminded everyone was a lot of fun, weighed half a ton and wanted to be your number one – graduated from *The Saturday Banana* to living with a family whose genius inventor son Ken (Ashley Knight) had ostensibly constructed him, getting up to all manner of shenanigans in cahoots with punk brother Steve (Gary Shail) and impishly young-at-heart Gran (Irene Handl).

Delivered in futuristic sub-Nadsat neospeak 'blurb', *Luna* (ITV, 1983–84) starred Patsy Kensit – and latterly, in her second generation, Joanna Wyatt – as the artificially created batch diminibeing – or in less futuristic terms 'adolescent' – diligently processing data pertaining to life in the far-flung futuristic year or of 2040, in the company of her fellow havibiron residents, ageing punk Gramps (Frank Duncan), appropriately named youngster Brat (Aaron Brown) and well-meaning domestic android Andy (Colin Bennett, who also co-wrote the series). *Luna* could get a good deal darker than its twinkly neon stylings might suggest, echoing works of genuine dystopian fiction with the assembled company dreading the officious visitations from the 'Bureaubeing', and on one occasion Luna was threatened with deactivation for the crime having mislaid her ID card. On a lighter and more contemporary note, if not necessarily a more realistic one, *From the Top* (ITV, 1985–86) was written by and starred Bill Oddie, relating the very Goodies-like fortunes of William Worthington, a middle-aged bank manager who suddenly quits to enrol in stage school alongside some ferociously ambitious teenagers.

Metal Mickey and *Luna*'s popularity seemed to inspire a wave of similarly quirky children's sitcoms that were very much on the side of the kids without upsetting the adults *too* much. Already well known from Forrest Wilson's top-selling series of novels, accidentally sensory and strength-enhanced by Inventor Black's experimental ray, Granny Smith jumped to even greater heights when Gudrun Ure walloped her way onto television as *Super Gran* (ITV, 1985–87). She was assisted in her ongoing battle against the devious Scunner Campbell by her grandson Willard, askew baseball-capped aspirant girl tech whiz Edison and a rambunctious Billy Connolly theme song challenging Al Pacino, Robert De Niro and Sylvester Stallone to come and have a go if they thought they were hard enough.

Introduced by a suitably scarpering brass band, Joan Edington's literary mishap-prone Northern juvenile hero *Jonny Briggs* (BBC, 1985–87) and his unpredictable pet dog 'Our Razzle' continually found his attempts to pursue normal healthy stamp collecting-adjacent activities overridden by the conflicting machinations of his elder siblings, academically ambitious 'Our Humph', stroppy and argumentative 'Our Rita' and the spectacularly feckless and indolent 'Our Albert', whose collective antics meant that he was never far away from having to help cover for the fact that they'd already eaten an elaborate anniversary cake. Helen Cresswell's series of novels similarly formed the basis for *The Bagthorpe Saga* (BBC, 1981), in which young Jack Bagthorpe affects to have developed psychic abilities to compensate for being the 'normal' one trying to navigate a family of unhinged eccentrics headed by arsonist cousin Daisy, a psychotically devoted Scrabble-cheating grandmother and their suitably named spectacularly useless dog Zero.

Then, of course, there were the expulsion-baiting exploits of spectacularly ill-behaved schoolgirl Marmalade Atkins, but some of the best and most popular children's comedy of the eighties was hidden away in Cosgrove Hall-forged animated form.

Danger Mouse (ITV, 1981–92) wasn't any old cliffhanging James Bond send-up – its dashing David Jason-voiced hero was a large white mouse with an eyepatch who, with the assistance of his loyal sidekick Penfold and the impressively moustached Colonel 'K', jetted out by flying car from his headquarters beneath a pillar box on Baker Street to take on the fiendish plots of Baron Greenback and his snickering underlings Stiletto the crow and Nero, regularly taking time to comment on the outlandish plots to the audience and the exasperated narrator, with plenty of punning cultural allusions that presumably went way above the heads of the target audience.

'Wanted' on account of the awfulness of his aspirant variety act being considered tantamount to a terrorist weapon, vegetarian vampire *Count Duckula* (ITV, 1988–93) spun off into his own similarly horror-lampooning series which turned the use of punningly highbrow-referencing episode titles into an art-form, notably with the gloriously contrived Bob Dylan nod, 'I Don't Wanna Work on Maggot's Farm No More'. *Count Duckula*, in turn, led to a further spin-off for inept employees of Naughtiness International, *Victor and Hugo: Bunglers in Crime* (ITV, 1991–92); although the unrelated adventures of Middle Ages-stranded time traveller bold Alias, whose ship got stuck by pure bad luck in the Earth's magnetic hold, *Alias the Jester* (ITV, 1985) created less of a legacy despite its audaciously plot-overexplaining theme song. Cosgrove Hall also enjoyed slightly more sedate success with their award-winning stop-motion adaptation of *The Wind in the Willows* (ITV, 1983–90), with P.G.

Wodehouse-style whimsy noticeably higher on the agenda than it had been in the original novel.

There were still plenty of more traditional offerings around – usually with conspicuously weedy theme tunes – including the Elizabeth Spriggs-led gentle classroom high jinks of *Simon and the Witch* (BBC, 1987–88), Stanley Baxter's turn as bumbling Earth-exiled wizard *Mr Majeika* (ITV, 1988–90), and the very first ball-retrieving scramble of long-running boy–dog bodyswap *Woof!* (ITV, 1989–97). But the example set by Marmalade and company could not be kept at bay for long, and the next generation found their somewhat more subversive comic thrills in the likes of *Uncle Jack* (BBC, 1990–93), *The Queen's Nose* (BBC, 1995–2003) and *The Demon Headmaster* (BBC, 1996–98), and perhaps most memorably of all, Tony Robinson's riotous gender-swapped retold legend *Maid Marian and her Merry Men* (1989–94). After all, when you'd had your mind irretrievably frazzled by *Wizbit* (BBC, 1986–88) – Paul Daniels' tales of the titular trebly voiced conical yellow conjurer and a vast collection of actor-in-costume stage illusionist implements in the eye-hurting Puzzleopolis, with a theme tune featuring a rapping Paul over Mungo Jerry's reworking of a children's song by Depression-era bluesman Lead Belly – maybe it was time for a change.

'Mischief is her stock in trade'

School drama lessons. They should have been the most fun and free-spirited part of the timetable, but so often they weren't. If it didn't involve following flutey music-backed instructions issuing from the radio to contort yourself into an approximation of a cement mixer, then you'd be feeling self-conscious reading out earthy dialogue from a kitchen sink drama – complete with a mild profanity that the teacher panic-strickenly asked you all to 'just skip over' to a backdrop of sniggers. Meanwhile, woe betide anyone who saw fit to give one of Shakespeare's 'comedy' characters a 'comedy' accent.

In 1981, with comprehensive schools on the rise and the rigours of the eleven-plus examination rapidly becoming a distant memory, Thames Television did their best to shake up drama lessons for an exciting new world of social studies and lab equipment that was actually younger than the pupils using it – but even they can't have realised what a monster they were about to unleash. *Theatre Box* (ITV, 1981) was a series of thoroughly modern playlets for young aspirant thespians with accompanying script books, designed to be used in class in conjunction with off-air recordings. Whether Indian folk tale-inspired 'The Prince and the Demons', the Dibble family's camping trip at the behest of patriarch Brian Murphy in 'Reasons to Be Cheerful', Charles Dickens-focused comedy drama 'You Must Believe All This' or Ken Campbell's translation of F.K. Waechter's 'School for Clowns' – in which he played Professor Molereasons alongside Jonathan Pyrce as Drippens – enlivened any dull lessons is something you would have to ask anyone who was actually in them. Meanwhile former professional wrestler Brian Glover's horror-tinted tale of a ringside robbery gone wrong, 'Death Angel', seems to have proved to be memorable for entirely the wrong reasons. It was the first play in the run, however, that gave any children doing their vocal warm-ups what they really wanted – and more than likely had teachers running for cover.

'The Worst Girl in the World', Marmalade Atkins, had first appeared in Andrew Davies' 1979 novel *Marmalade and Rufus* – later reprinted as *Marmalade Atkins' Dreadful Deeds* – in which she introduced her own brand of disobedient havoc to an unsuspecting world, in cahoots with a like-minded donkey with a penchant for stepping on people. Cleverer — or at least less prepared to accept nonsense for the sake of a quiet life — than the adults around her, and able to see through the empty hot air of the establishment and formal tradition, Marmalade is capable of creating mayhem on a scale that would even have had Minnie the Minx and the pupils of St Trinian's suggesting she might want to dial it back a bit. She nihilistically rejected how a child, and a girl in particular, might be expected to behave. A riotously funny creation from her name alone, but still with a serious and relatable 'message' underpinning her demolishing rampages, it's hardly surprising that Marmalade was picked up for a project aimed at getting children to engage more with language and performance. Few involved can really have been prepared, however, for the whole new level of outrage and adulation she would provoke in television form.

Marmalade Atkins in Space (ITV, 1981) posited a solution to Marmalade's disruptive influence both inside and outside the classroom that dozens of parents and teachers doubtless wish that they had thought of first. At the instigation of her ruthless social worker Mrs Allgood, and to the relief of head girl Cherith Ponsonby and the previously unassailable and suspiciously masculine Sister Purification and Sister Conception at Convent of the Blessed Limit — the tenth school she has been expelled from — Marmalade is blasted off into space on a spurious mission that nobody seems to be sure about the purpose of other than that it gets her as far away from them as is physically possible. Her mother and father, who are too houseproud and secretly proud of Marmalade to acknowledge the extent of her behaviour, and only tolerate each other because 'he's practically a millionaire', have no major objections to this course of action. Sent on an exploratory trip with a crew who pride themselves on being the most boring astronauts in the entire solar system, Marmalade – with supporting wisdom from a suspiciously Obi-Wan Kenobi-like dashboard-mounted nodding dog – arrives at the conclusion that her naughtiness is needed to maintain the balance of cosmic order, and that 'If I'm not bad, I'm not me, and if I'm not me, they can't be them'. Arriving back on Earth, she catches Mrs Allgood on television discussing how the brainwashing treatment has been a success, which prompts a quick spray-painting of the screen. It is safe to say that universal balance had been restored.

Crammed with digs both at *Star Wars*-mania and – via Mrs Allgood's suggestion of implementing 'Very Extreme Treatment', sending up Home Secretary Willie Whitelaw's recently implemented and much questioned 'Short Sharp Shock' young offender punishment regime – the sort of people and policies that were creating the real-life Marmalades, the play set out its subversive and anarchic stall from the outset in no uncertain terms. Few sights on television have ever felt as genuinely subversive and anarchic as Charlotte Coleman's wild portrayal of the dishevelled gum-fiddling Marmalade, with her school uniform invariably yanked in multiple directions and her tie permanently knotted around her forehead, hair that was more disobedient than plain boring old 'messy', and a habit of addressing everyone – the great, the good and the otherwise – as 'cock'. A masterclass in slovenly rejection of meaningless rules and conventions, and about as far from the traditional image of the 'naughty' pupil playing tame pranks on a mortar-boarded teacher as it was possible to get, Marmalade Atkins was a heroine – if that's the right word – in waiting, and few can have been surprised when she came back for a full series. Although a lot of parents were very, very surprised indeed.

With outer space no longer on the curriculum, *Educating Marmalade* (ITV, 1982) followed the inevitably doomed attempts to find an educational establishment that could comfortably accommodate, or at the very least contain, Britain's Naughtiest Schoolgirl. Opening with a blaring klaxon-accompanied flashing 'Bad Girl Warning', an undaunted Marmalade effortlessly weathered the best efforts of her father's alma mater Eton, an Italian finishing school, Dartmoor Prison and the inane stage school-dropped aitch conversations of the pupils of 'Cringe Hill', and a rematch showdown with the Convent of the Blessed Limit ended up as two–nil to Marmalade as she locked her nun nemeses in the heavily secured 'Bad Girl Cupboard'. Unbelievably – or perhaps not so much given the dwindling alternative options – she gets sent there a third time after absconding from prison, where hopes that her role as the innkeeper in the school nativity might have helped her turn a corner are immediately dashed when she informs Mary and Joseph that there's 'Plenty of room in the inn, bring the donkey and all – the drinks are on me!' Even dog behavioural expert Clara Coalhouse – no relation to the famously no-nonsense real-life celebrity animal trainer du jour Barbara Woodhouse – was incapable of bringing her to heel. With an increasingly exasperated Mrs Allgood on the verge of jumping from her office window, and her parents still not that bothered really, it was only too obvious – as the theme song put it – that *Educating Marmalade* really was 'the worst mistake they ever made'.

That suitably rowdy theme song, which continually sounded like it was going to spiral out of control live on air, was performed by Bad Manners, a reliably boisterous ska band fronted by the hulking and over-energetic Buster Bloodvessel, who enjoyed a string of hits in the late seventies and early eighties including 'Special Brew', 'Lip Up Fatty' and their idiosyncratic take on 'The Can Can', and who could frequently be found adding to the mayhem and even adding some extra craziness of their own everywhere from *Tiswas* to *Cheggers Plays Pop*. Their assertion that Marmalade 'tops the bad girl hit parade' wasn't just a convenient rhyme – like Bad Manners, a whole raft of bands had emerged that combined punk's spiky-haired multi-coloured outrageousness and exuberance with a less offence-provoking comic strip-attitude, embodying all of the politics and attitude with none of the swearing at local news anchors. These bands found and enjoyed a following with a generation of schoolchildren who identified with their unidentifiable sense of irreverence and inclusivity, and Marmalade Atkins looked and acted the way that they all sounded.

Although *Marmalade* was scarcely as taboo breaking as *The Comic Strip Presents* or *The Young Ones*, it was the closest that children's television got to its own alternative comedy show, and perhaps tellingly, director John Stroud went on to create *Hardwicke House* (ITV, 1987), a sitcom about a failing and feral school that most specifically was not aimed at children, but ITV took a gamble and put it in a timeslot where they could see it anyway. It lasted two episodes before it was yanked from the schedules and never mentioned again.

Marmalade wasn't as popular with everyone as she was with would-be dinner queue disruptors, though. A barrage of uproar from politicians, taste and decency campaigners – some of them drawing unfavourable comparisons to reliable fresh-faced old *Grange Hill*, which was as laughable for the fact that Gripper Stebson and Imelda Davies would have hightailed it in fear if they'd seen Marmalade coming up the corridor, as it was for the inevitability that they would be back blaming *Grange Hill* for anything and everything a fortnight later – and it wasn't unusual for parents to bar their own potential Bad Girls and Boys from watching. All of whom seemed to have gleefully missed the fundamental point that Marmalade never actually did anything quantifiably 'wrong' – she just didn't do what she was expected to, and that's a lesson that none of those doing the mouth-frothing about the series and anything else like it ever seem to have learned in real life.

Even the naughtiest schoolgirl can only be the secondary educational system's responsibility for so long, however, and *Danger: Marmalade at Work* (ITV, 1984) followed the not especially missed school leaver as she sought to channel her undeniable if undesirable talents in a suitable direction. With a theme song decrying the fact that 'Jobs – I've had a few, and most of them, were pretty grotty' in the manner of Sex Pistol Sid Vicious' rendition of 'My Way', Marmalade tries her hand at a procession of eminently unsuitable vocational callings with the assistance of vocational guidance counsellor Wendy Woolley. These include becoming a butler and an air hostess, enlisting in the army, helping out in the kitchen at a five-star restaurant and following in Mrs Allgood's footsteps – even though she probably still had nightmares about Marmalade following in her footsteps – as a social worker.

The BBC's celebrated procedural police drama about the sexism-challenging struggles of Inspector Kate Longton in *Juliet Bravo* was sent up by 'Marmalade Bravo', and the glossy star-reaching singing and dancing imported teen drama sensation du jour became the vacuous, vain and arrogant pupils of the New York School for Bigheads and Show-Offs – or 'The Kids from Shame!' for short.

Marmalade Atkins never did find consistent gainful employment, but she did later end up at the controls of a spaceship herself – hosting Children's ITV's Watch It! strand in April 1983 and not allowing the likes of Gammon and Spinach to get off lightly. By this time, however, Charlotte Coleman was keen to move on to other challenges, and although Andrew Davies had novelised both series and went on to write *Marmalade Hits the Big Time* in 1984, he was soon at work on the acclaimed BBC2 campus comedy drama *A Very Peculiar Practice* (BBC, 1986–92), set in a university staffed and attended by such a parade of eccentrics and lowlifes that even Marmalade would have thrown up her hands in horror and considered her second-choice offer.

Marmalade wasn't the only one in detention around that time, though, and a series of similarly irreverent sitcoms and sketch shows with a pronounced disdain for school – and for spelling 'skool' correctly – handed in their extremely untidy homework, many of them featuring more than one dig at *Grange Hill*; it's odd to think that even then, there were some for whom it was just that little bit too 'square'. Comedy punk band Alberto y Lost Trios Paranoias offered alphabetically themed tips on how to *Teach Yourself Gibberish* (ITV, 1982); Michael Fenton Stevens and Jo Unwin were amongst the adults on the side of chore-averting kids in *Stop That Laughing at the Back* (ITV, 1987); and the appositely named *Your Mother Wouldn't Like It* (ITV, 1985–88) drew on the up-and-coming talent of the Central Junior Television Workshop – who included such names of the future as Simon Schatzberger, Alison Hammond, Pui Fan Lee and Gail Kemp – for a series of sketches poking fun at the ups and downs of adolescent life, including a pointedly named school-set running serial which proved so popular that it became a series in its own right; *Palace Hill* (ITV, 1988–91).

Headmistress Megan Bigge – or 'Megapig' – ruled over the unruly pupils of Fulley Comprehensive in musical comedy *Behind the Bike Sheds* (ITV, 1983–85), which boasted a regular cross-airwaves dig at 'John Raving's Newsround', a *Phantom of the Opera*-style puppet pupil who had been left disfigured in the Great School Canteen Disaster, and an early writing and acting engagement for Tony Slattery.

Who, Sir? Me, Sir? (BBC, 1985) saw a bunch of pupils at unruly Hawkswood Comprehensive entered – much to their surprise – into a triathlon against neighbouring private school Greycoats, with comic mishaps underscoring their flawed but flattered bids to succeed. And twelve-year-old Kevin Doyle obsessively turned the comings and goings at 13 Tindale Close, Biddlecombe, into stories in his disconcerting fantasy of being a newsreader in *News at Twelve* (ITV, 1988). Most outrageously of all, Brian Arthur Derek Boyes – or *BAD Boyes* (BBC, 1987–88), for short – operated his money-making self-advancing schemes with the efficiency of a master conman, continually outwitting school bully the Slug and managing to fool just about everyone bar his mother, whose furious shout of 'BRI-AN!' would usually herald some form of comic comeuppance. She wasn't the only one who wasn't impressed by his innocent demeanour – despite massive popularity, the series was allegedly cancelled on the instructions of BBC Director General Michael Checkland, who had received disconcerting letters from do-gooders expressing alarm at the dubious behaviour and apparent lack of consequence on display. Quite how Brian exacted his revenge for that slight is perhaps best not speculated on, though we can be quite sure Marmalade Atkins would have approved.

7

Factual Shows

'We cannot return your paintings'

No matter how boring school got, and no matter how simultaneously daunting and unfair the prospect of homework may have been, you could always count on one thing to break up the stultifying and unending cycle of education. When you staggered in from the sweltering condensation-riven school bus, complete with the additional existential angst occasioned by the unpredictably loud-mouthed semi-feral kids from the 'other school' in the seat in front, there was a couple of hours of television just for you. In that all too fleeting gap between the bell that signified freedom and having to wrestle with homework, you could count on children's television to entertain you. Except that sometimes, it also tried to teach you.

Children's television attempting to educate and inform as well as entertain – and sometimes even not that – was nothing new, and early favourites included Desmond Morris' light-hearted set of chimp-hindered anthropological profiles *Zoo Time* (ITV, 1956–58) and Huw Wheldon's weekly roundup of fresh-faced healthy hobbies and interests, *All Your Own* (BBC, 1952–61), which once saw him interview a polite young aspirant guitarist named James Page, but their sole concession to making learning fun was to adopt a still rather formal variant of informality. That was pretty much considered the acceptable approach until BBC Bristol's newly established Natural History Unit had the bright idea of combining their acclaimed wildlife programming style with Johnny Morris' gift for creating 'characters' out of animals.

Filmed in and around Bristol Zoo, *Animal Magic* (BBC, 1962–83) saw 'Keeper Morris' add appropriate character voices to the animals he encountered, dispensing facts about the natural world in amongst the skidding polar bears exclaiming, 'Look out below, fellars!' Already well known to younger viewers for spinning semi-improvised comic yarns while standing next to a brazier as *The Hot Chestnut Man* (BBC, 1953–1961), Johnny Morris had a gift for finding characters and stories where others would just see animals minding their own business, and was only too happy to make himself the frequently soaked hapless victim of the splashing penguins and squirting elephants. The format worked a literal charm for decades, with viewers little suspecting they were increasing their knowledge at the same time as laughing at the funny animal antics, though as the eighties loomed this approach was beginning to fall from favour.

Various attempts at bringing the show up to date included refitting the original showbizzy theme music with an ill-advised light funk wah-wah arrangement, bringing in long-haired youthful co-presenter Terry Nutkin and the occasional mention of Space Invaders or a special effects-assisted sub-sci-fi incursion into the undergrowth, not to mention Tom Baker showing up in-character and mid-adventure as Doctor Who to recount some of his weirder alien foes.

Meanwhile, close associate *Wildtrack* (BBC, 1978–85) saw Tony Soper and Su Ingle hitting the trail with a more energetic to-camera style and a bizarre theme choice of John Barry's 'Florida Fantasy' from *Midnight Cowboy*, but it was all to little avail. In 1986, after over four hundred editions, *Animal Magic* gave way to *The Really Wild Show* (BBC, 1986–2006), presented by Terry Nutkin with the even younger and even more relatable Nicola Davies and punky-haired Chris Packham and a sub-hip hop theme tune, which defied the usual youth-courting trajectory by becoming a massive favourite, inspiring a postbag-challenging barrage of regular viewer correspondence. Last seen leading a choir through an interminable song about how to pronounce Gemini the Sea Lion's name, poor old Keeper Morris never quite found his niche again.

His contemporary Tony Hart, in contrast, seemed to have no such difficulty in adapting to changing times, usually by completely refusing to change his own idiosyncratic cravat-favouring demeanour and delighted reactions to the deployment of 'our old friend pastel'. Already a familiar face from contributing to a variety of children's shows both as a presenter and an artist – including designing the *Blue Peter* ship – Tony was a natural choice when the BBC was putting together a replacement for the well-meaning but possibly not quite well-meaning enough *For Deaf Children* (BBC, 1952–64).

Inspired by research indicating that hearing-impaired viewers were actually drawn to *Top of the Pops*, ever-inventive producer Patrick Dowling set about creating a show that adopted its fast-moving format and use of up-to-the-minute video trickery for a non-dialogue dependent parade of art, animation and sign-language comedy. *Vision On* (BBC, 1964–76) cast Tony and fellow presenters Pat Keysall, Ben Benison, Sylvester McCoy and Wilf Lunn into suitably abstract and absurdist – and largely wordless – studio-based situations punctuated by similarly abstract and absurdist animated inserts, notably the philosophical musings of Humphrey the Tortoise and squabbling grandfather clock-dwelling speech bubbles the Burbles, and David Cleveland's silent scientific slapstick antics as 'The Prof'. Activity was frequently interrupted by vain attempts to capture Sylvester's high-speed art-destroying fuzzy feather boa pet the Woofumpuss, Wilf's inventions seldom helped to facilitate calm and order, and the only real respite from the glorious mayhem came in the Gallery, a parade of paintings sent in by viewers while jazzy library music played in the background and the audience at home scoffed in the belief that they 'could do' that. In the middle of all the madness, Tony – who also designed *Vision On*'s logo, a mirror-image of the title in the form of a creature nicknamed 'Grog' – gave simple yet ambitious demonstrations of fun art you could create yourself with the aid of just a few everyday objects, gradually revealing what he was painting or making in a relaxed but wry style with an uncanny ability to shorten or extend the process to fit the available screen time.

In fact, there was a sense of relaxed wryness and jazzy library music all over *Vision On*, and combined with high-concept comedy silliness and the unusual techniques favoured by the animators – many of whom had fled from the Eastern Bloc – it was about as cinematic as children's television got. By the mid-seventies, however, that dash of style was starting to show its age a little, although the presenter who remained resolutely unfashionable throughout wasn't. *Take Hart* (BBC, 1977–83) relocated Tony and the Gallery – now disconcertingly accompanied by John Williams' 'Cavatina', also more famously used as the theme from *The Deer Hunter* – to a somewhat more conventional art studio, where he attempted to explain technique and form around continual interruptions from well-meaning accident-prone caretaker Colin Bennett and paintbrush box-dwelling plasticine man Morph.

Created by animators Peter Lord and David Sproxton, the chirpy but quick-tempered nonsense-babbling shape-changing Morph appeared in short, filmed inserts, generally wreaking havoc with items on the art desk while attempting to 'help' Tony, but quickly became a star in his own right, especially once he was joined by his reflection-turned-rival Chas, and eventually graduated to his own series. Originally introduced by a catchy theme song from British jazz legend Georgie Fame – replaced for repeats by a raspy synth instrumental due to rights complications – *The Amazing Adventures of Morph* (BBC, 1980–81) saw the duo and Tony joined by a host of other art material friends, including Grandmorph, Delilah, Gillespie, Folly, Gobbledygook, the Very Small Creatures and Morph's eccentric 'dog' Nailbrush, for a series of suitably art critic-testing off-the-wall adventures in the pre-news slot.

Then in 1984, with *Take Hart* itself starting to look a little dated in the face of an imminent Children's BBC relaunch, Tony, Morph and Mr Bennett were simply moved over to *Hartbeat* (BBC, 1984–93), a more updated version of the existing format with electronic music, early computer animation effects, and the addition of a team of young co-artists with experience of the fashion and textile industries, including Margot Wilson, Joanna Kirk, Gabrielle Bradshaw, Alison Millar and Liza Brown. All of which might well sound like a desperate attempt to appear trendy and stay relevant, but it was a revamp that really did work; *Hartbeat* was the most popular of Tony Hart's shows by far and he remained a much-loved cornerstone of children's television right through to his retirement.

Play School polymath Johnny Ball was given the opportunity to explain scientific and mathematical concepts to an audience of overexcited children in *Think of a Number* (BBC, 1977–84), using nothing more logarithmic than enthusiastic patter, over-the-top oversized experiments, corny comedy sketches and camera trickery-effected double-bluffs enabling him to affect to carry a bar of gold on his back. So popular was his refreshingly energetic approach that *Think of a Number* evolved into an entire franchise in its own right.

Think Again (BBC, 1981–85) invited viewers to apply rational questioning to aspects of their everyday lives; *Think! Backwards* (BBC, 1981) presented a week of themed number-based facts counting down from ten to one; *Think! This Way* (BBC, 1983) considered the societal and geographical implications of directions; *Think It . . . Do It* (BBC, 1986–87) looked ahead to how scientific advances were informing the boom industries of the future; and *Knowhow* (BBC, 1988–90) sought to address the answer to questions about why water is wet, with the assistance of residents at the near-futuristic Hyperspace Hotel. Such was his enthusiasm and expertise that when the BBC began to lose their enthusiasm for the long-running strand of shows, he was able to successfully transfer it to ITV with *Johnny Ball Reveals All* (ITV, 1989–94). Less successful, however, was an attempt to make learning fun with *Johnny Ball Games* (BBC, 1980–81), in which teams of over-earnest families attempted to outdo each other's logic puzzle-solving skills on a dining room set jarringly surrounded by a go-getting 'light entertainment meets keep fit' atmosphere, with a song and dance introduction that seemed to last for almost the entire programme.

If straightforward facts and figures that didn't require any further work on your part were more your thing, Roy Castle presented a comprehensive guide to the fastest, the slowest, the fattest, the thinnest, the newest, the fewest and the largest tattoo in the *Guinness Book of World Records*-scouring *Record Breakers* (BBC, 1972–2001). Ideally suited to Roy's otherwise less exploited light-entertainment talents in a rapidly changing world – he wrote and performed the jazz-funk opening theme, with its list of potential achievements and promise that if you could lift twenty tonnes or score 99,000 runs, 'the whole sporting world would applaud it, the McWhirters, they would record it', and the closing theme's assertion that if you want to be the best and you want to beat the rest, dedication's what you need, complete with a breathless summary of that week's facts and feats crowbarred into the closing line, *and* successfully broke a huge number of tap-dancing and trumpet-playing records himself – *Record Breakers* existed to celebrate achievements in any and every way they saw fit, not least an extended song and dance number celebrating the life and times of the world's tallest man Robert Pershing Wadlow. While elsewhere, The 'Norris on the Spot' slot saw the not entirely genial *Guinness Book of Records* compiler Norris McWhirter being grilled by the studio audience about, say, the identity and dimensions of the world's biggest leaf.

An earlier spin-off, *Roy Castle Beats Time* (BBC, 1974–75) concentrated on meeting musicians who could play 'anything from the bagpipes to the kitchen sink'. But *All-Star Record Breakers* (BBC, 1974–82) was essentially just an excuse to stage an unofficial Children's BBC panto featuring presenters and stars from all of the other current shows in the timeslot, and it became a much-loved mainstay of the Christmas schedules.

If for some reason you wanted to watch the 5.45 p.m. News but were a little put off by the bombastic theme music and alarming headlines, you weren't exactly out of luck. Created in response to audience research suggesting that only seven per cent of children watched the news, John Craven's *Newsround* (BBC, 1972–) presented a palatable and carefully considered five-minute round-up of the day's main headlines. Contrary to popular belief, it was never sanitised or patronising, perfectly prepared to explain events in Northern Ireland or Afghanistan and even on occasion, thanks to its then-unique position in the schedules, left to break some heavyweight stories including the Challenger Space Shuttle disaster and the Windsor Castle fire.

Sporting an impressive selection of gaudily coloured jumpers, former BBC Bristol reporter and a familiar face from Children's BBC's hard-hitting documentary strand *Search* (BBC, 1971–75) and historical reportage *The Story Behind the Story* (BBC, 1972), John Craven was the main *Newsround* anchor right through to 1989, with assistance and occasional deputising from Lucy Mathen – the first female British Asian news presenter on any UK programme – Paul McDowell, Howard Stableford, Roger Finn, Helen Rollason and Terry Baddoo, with weekly in-depth twenty-five-minute reports under the banner *Newsround Extra* (BBC, 1975–2006).

Helped in no small part by the stylised 'daily' studio backdrops and the catchy theme music – a whistly Golden Age of Hollywood stop the presses-style alert derived from bandleader Ted Heath's arrangement of jazz standard 'Johnny One-Note' – and a closing electronic 'sting' snipped from the end of the BBC Radiophonic Workshop's theme for Radio 4 documentary strand, *New Worlds*, *Newsround* benefited from a more informal approach that allowed it to both engage and reassure easily alarmed viewers at the same time. The programme also staged regular campaigns and competitions to get youngsters interested in collating and reporting the news. One notable recipient of a *Newsround* Newshound badge, thanks to a justifiably angry written report about playground racism which was commended on air by John and Lucy, was writer and broadcaster Samira Ahmed.

Just in case you'd somehow missed the two years out of date 'Ever Thought of Sport?' awareness posters on the school walls, Peter Purves, Susan King – who in a great outdoors double-whammy also presented rural affairs update *Country Search* (BBC, 1975–78) – and

FACTUAL SHOWS

Rugby Union legend Nigel Starmer-Smith were on hand to answer your questions about why sport was the tops in *Stopwatch* (BBC, 1978–81). Heralded by bombastic brass fanfares and animated knights and bishops looming towards the camera, *Play Chess!* (BBC, 1980–87) elbowed its way onto school holiday mornings with hints and tips from international champion Bill Hartston, a running puzzle-solving Wild West-themed serial about 'The One They Called the Bishop', and voice-activated matches 'played' by self-levitating chess pieces. You could only very, very occasionally make out the hapless 'backroom boy' wearing black against a black background who was moving them.

We Are the Champions (BBC, 1973–95) was technically a game show, but considering that it consisted of sports commentator Ron Pickering presiding over teams from rival schools taking part in rounds of typically school sports-styled activities, with proper sporting stars on hand to explain why taking part in sports was good sportsmanship, there was no getting away from the brutal and bullying truth of the matter. It was, to all intents and purposes, the double PE lesson on a cold and wet afternoon being sold back to you as entertainment. Fortunately, they threw in a weekly conclusion where Pickering shouted, 'AWAY YOU GO!' and all of the participants jumped into a swimming pool for show-closing larks in noted contravention of those 'No Diving No Bombing No Petting' notices that always used to be up in the local swimming baths, to the accompaniment of a terrace chant-styled theme song played out in that sort of water and tile ambience where complete silence was every bit as cacophonous as a riot.

Meanwhile, those who concerned themselves more with local legends of a bike so light you could lift it with your little finger were more than adequately catered for by *BMX Beat* (ITV, 1984–87), anchored by world champion stunt-cyclist Andy Ruffell live from Carlisle's finest car parks with a theme song that promised 'BMX boys have a lot of fun, riding a bike out in the sun' in a less than BMX-friendly arrangement, and Channel 4's *Trak Trix* (Channel 4, 1984), which widened the scope to include go-karts and roller-skating but only ever achieved notoriety over an occasion when they dared a young researcher named Jonathan Ross to have a bash himself.

If you were looking for a less strenuous new pursuit, veteran topical songsmith Richard Stilgoe wandered around a mocked-up house demonstrating easily cobbled-together hobbies and interests and offering tips for how to amuse yourself when you're 'imprisoned indoors, feeling pale and wan' for a disproportionately rowdy studio audience in *Stilgoe's On* (BBC, 1986); while Shelagh Gilbey presided over the offices of aspirant visual lifestyle supplement *Do It!* (ITV, 1984–88) and David Bellamy 'logged on' to an early primitive manifestation of what we might now recognise as 'the web' to keep an eye on international developments in conservation in *Bellamy's Bugle* (ITV, 1986–88).

Nanette Newman and a bunch of cuisine-crazy inmates of the Anna Scher Theatre School, including a young Jesse Birdsall, donned the dinner lady hats for *The Fun Food Factory* (ITV, 1976–77), striving to promote healthy eating as creative fun, although a massive warning siren and flashing light still went off whenever they had to use a sharp implement. Flautist Atarah Ben-Tovim and her band of rock-crazy escapees from the Royal Liverpool Philharmonic Orchestra – whose live kids' show was a sell-out sensation at the time – showed you how the harp could groove just as hard as the Yamaha DX7 in *Atarah's Music* (ITV, 1982–84), and Michael Bentine and Matthew Kelly cast an enthusiastic eye over everything from trains to 'chucking out planes' in *Madabout* (ITV, 1981–84).

Slightly less successfully, the essentially improvised *Ad Lib* (ITV, 1981) attempted to spread a happy-clappy do-gooding message courtesy of a large ensemble cast including – bizarrely – celebrity swimmer Duncan Goodhew and the minimally animated adventures of Swiss storybook favourite *Yok-Yok*. Having met with mixed success at best, it returned the following year as almost exactly the same programme under the suitably slapped-on grin title *Sunny Side Up* (ITV, 1982), but nobody was really fooled.

For those who would have rather had their nose in a good novel, *The Book Tower* (ITV, 1979–89) was possibly initially more of a hindrance than a help, with a combination of a dark crumbling manor house setting, an ominous *Exorcist*-evoking theme from Julian and Andrew Lloyd-Webber, and Tom Baker at his most stark-voicedly mysterious ostensibly pulling out a couple of recommended reads from the grand house's spiral staircase-festooned library, and thereby ensuring that most viewers ended up hiding behind books rather than watching. Subsequent hosts, including Alun Armstrong, Neil Innes, Roger McGough and Victoria Wood, did their best to lighten the mood slightly.

Mel Smith and Bob Goody, and their elongated theme song bickering about the joys of reading wisely, went straight for the laughs in *Smith and Goody* (ITV, 1980), interspersing raves about their latest literary favourites with tips on 'How Not to Read in the Shower' and, with brilliant pointlessness, attempting to present their Christmas Special 'on ice'. Meanwhile, Chris Kelly went behind the scenes of the movie industry in *Clapperboard* (ITV, 1972–82), and took a look at television production in the company of Gareth 'Gaz Top' Jones in *Kellyvision* (ITV, 1988).

If after all that you really just wanted straight-up learning, you might have been better off pretending to be ill so you could stay off and watch schools' television, but there were still a handful of notable exceptions. Isla St Clair might well have been better known to television audiences as Larry Grayson's seemingly indefatigable co-host on *The Generation Game*, but she had started her career as a hardcore traditional folk musician, and – doubtless to the surprise of many viewers – that's the role she returned to for *The Song and the Story* (BBC, 1981–83). Relating the history of everything from seventies prog-folkie favourite ballad of female highwayman 'Sovay' to wailing laments for when King Harold was away-kayed, and chirpy utensil-clattering loom-scrubbing rounds, Isla gleefully dressed up in as many traditional costumes as whatever was left over of the budget after all the location filming would allow, and declined to gloss over harsh and macabre historical detail in an approach that might now be termed 'folk horror'.

Mark Curry didn't get to go to quite such elaborate extremes in *Treasure Houses* (BBC, 1982–87), limited instead to roaming around museums and historical residences of note and outlining biographies and tales of invention and adventure with whatever exhibits were to hand. He did, however, never fail to deliver a wry look to camera at an unintentionally amusing name or description, in a manner that suggested a National Trust employee determined to take down the 'system' from within.

Tom Tom (BBC, 1965–70) was essentially a junior counterpart to the BBC's flagship science show *Tomorrow's World*, with the nattily attired likes of Jan Leeming and Janet Kelly heading off to find out how those big computers with spools of tape on them worked. *Erasmus Microman* (ITV, 1988–89), on the other hand, was typical fare for avant-garde deconstructionist theatrical one-off Ken Campbell – even down to the fact it was pronounced 'Meecro-man' – and by everyone else's standard just plain weird.

FACTUAL SHOWS

Dragging a group of bored children, including a very young Naomie Harris, into a grey neo-techno microverse through their televisions, Erasmus took them off on a whistle-stop time travel tour of history's greatest scientific innovations with his history-changing arch-nemesis Dr Dark hot on their heels.

Meanwhile, if you fancied yourself as something of an amateur armchair critic, there were plenty of ways of entitling yourself to your opinion in those pre-social media days. Granada continuity announcer Sue Robbie chirpily tolerated endless complaints about how it wasn't fair for *Blockbusters* to have one individual contestant against a team of two in *First Post* (ITV, 1983–85), chiefly remembered for closing with a heavily accented child urging viewers to write in to the show at 'Manchester M60 9EA'. Over on the BBC, disgruntled viewers could write in to argue over whether or not the comedy bits in *So You Want to Be Top?* were funny on *Take Two* (BBC, 1982–96), variously presented by Phillip Schofield, Lucie Skeaping, Josephine Buchan, Sarah Greene and Juliet Morris, conspicuously introduced by a slinky robot-voiced theme tune from chart-bothering jazz-funk collective Shakatak, and accompanying the read-out correspondence with a very un-Children's BBC illustration of some youngsters throwing vegetables at their television.

Consumer rights-conscious youngsters complained to *The Pocket Money Programme* (Channel 4, 1986) about not hearing back from the Boy George Fan Club while the guest host likes of Kim Wilde and Paul Hardcastle issued sage advice on how to navigate the barrage of teen-aimed advertising. Keith Chegwin went in for a spot of more risky foot-in-door business investigation, looking at where the money you spent on pop singles went and how much a burger should really cost you, in *Chegwin Checks It Out* (BBC, 1987–88). For viewer interaction at its most basic, *Hey, It's My Birthday Too!*

(ITV, 1981) involved nothing more than a continuity announcer sending greetings to year-older youngsters, introduced by remarkably elaborate eight-second opening titles depicting a cartoon boy announcing to a saluting crowd with the traditional knees-bending policeman that it was indeed his birthday too. A less palatable variety of public access came in the form of *Who's Next?* (ITV, 1987), in which aspirant 'provocative' columnists were ushered into a 'Video Box' in a shopping centre to play devil's advocate over subjects that they really would have been better advised leaving well alone.

Then again, if you just didn't fancy any of the above full stop, you could always stop watching altogether. *Why Don't You Just Switch Off Your Television Set and Go Out and Do Something Less Boring Instead?* (BBC, 1973–96) filled up the school summer holiday mornings with demonstrations of potential homespun hobbies and games, taking a trip around the British Isles at the same time as you probably weren't courtesy of a series of regional 'gangs' of varying ages – and varying ability to make it from one end of a sentence to the other – careering around a warehouse/scrapyard-styled den making ham sandwich towers and 'Squashy Grannies' while trying to avert the attentions of their map-straddling unseen stripy sock-heralded nemesis 'The Dorris'. Originally introduced by George Martin's undisciplined kazoo-led 'King's Road Raspberry Parade' before opting for a Janis Joplin soundalike roaring 'sittin' at home, watchin' TV, turn it off, it's no good to me' over animation of a goggle-eyed viewer kicking his screen in, it was intended as the ideal complement to a miserable wet British summer. And felt like it, too.

By the eighties, however, they had got a little better at this making-learning-fun lark, so much so that you often didn't realise you were learning anything at all. Clive Doig's puzzle-solving jamboree, with more than its fair share of absurdity, *Jigsaw* (BBC, 1979–84), followed

FACTUAL SHOWS

Janet Ellis, top-hatted mime artist Adrian Hedley and floating orange know-all jigsaw piece Jig as they rifled through clues to identify a six-letter word. All with the aid of pedantic puppet pterodactyl Pterry, private eye Cid Sleuth, foot-represented Biggum the Giant, the nominal 'Pig of the Week', vowel-fixated David Rappaport and Sylvester McCoy-portrayed less than super superheroes the 'O' Men, who were summoned by six words with a double 'o' in a row and – infamously – Mr Noseybonk, a mime character acted out by Hedley in an enormously nasally advantaged white mask, who presented cryptic clues and sent a generation scurrying for out-of-vision safety. In another Clive Doig-devised venture, *Eureka!* (BBC, 1982–86) featured hosts Jeremy Beadle, Sarah Greene, Paul McDowell and Wilf Lunn revisiting great moments of historical innovation courtesy of recreations from a rep company who weren't prepared to take any of it too seriously, including Sylvester McCoy, Simon Gipps-Kent and – with delightful incongruity – former Hammer scream queen and Bond girl Madeline Smith.

Following Channel 4's early brief as good as to the letter, *Everybody Here!* (Channel 4, 1982–83) featured Michael Rosen and a diverse assortment of urban youngsters presenting entertainingly rendered mini-documentaries on their culturally disparate yet unifyingly playground-centric day to day lives; at least if there was any room for them left after the famously lengthy opening titles, which against a sitar and steel drum-clashing backdrop included both Rosen's far from easily imitable 'everybody-verybody-erybody-rybody-ybody-body-ody-dy-y' tongue-twister and a seemingly infinite procession of children holding up signs saying 'YES!' in as many languages as was geographically possible.

Evidently named by someone who knew next to nothing about computers other than that children were 'into' them, *Video and*

Chips (ITV, 1985–88) took a more irreverent and game-fixated feet-up-in-trainers look at the latest news from the home computer boom, with Capital Radio DJ Mick Brown on hand to lend an all-important veneer of pop credibility. Meanwhile, Craig Charles exhorted pop stars, classical musicians and thrash metal outfits to jam together under a belief that all music was equal in *What's That Noise?* (BBC, 1988–95), in strict adherence to the imperative that 'It's GOT to be funky!' *Corners* (BBC, 1987–91) took matters to a much younger audience, with Sophie Aldred, Simon Davies, Diane-Louise Jordan and roundly viewer-mocked green puppet Jo Korna deploying a combination of comic exchanges, and a computer running a distant relative of Windows 1.0, to answer audience-sourced queries about how things worked. The unending rigmarole of homework that still needed to be done while everyone else was watching *Full House* and *Roll Over Beethoven* was still ahead, of course – but they got better at fooling you about that too . . .

'Here's one I made earlier'

Quite how you felt about children's television trying to educate you after you'd just spent an entire day in school might well have depended on how you'd approached that day yourself. If you were the sort of pupil who couldn't wait to stick their hand up to let everyone know that they knew what a cosine was, then you were probably more than happy to have a handful of further facts and sums to wrestle with in your own time. If, on the other hand, you were a creatively minded junior philosopher with a hankering for art and English, you probably wanted to be left well alone, only with more *Battle of the Planets*.

FACTUAL SHOWS

There was, of course – and still is – one show that harnessed the achievement-hungry eagerness of the former group in a genuinely positive manner, with presenters who were more like elder siblings, albeit slightly leaning too far on the polite and clever-clogs side for some tastes. This programme encouraged a sense that civic-minded generosity and helping out with charitable endeavours could be rewarding in and of itself, in amongst fun features sharing the thrills of learning about nature and history and sporting achievements and 'makes' you could try at home with minimal expenditure and supervision. The latter group probably hoped against hope for a technical breakdown and the sudden deployment of an emergency episode of *Help! It's The Hair Bear Bunch!*, although they secretly liked it when they went behind the scenes of *The Tripods*.

Borrowing its name from the flag flown to indicate a ship is about to set sail, producer John Hunter Blair launched *Blue Peter* (BBC, 1958–) on 16 October 1958. Billed by *Radio Times* as 'a weekly programme for younger viewers' featuring 'toys, model railways, games, stories and cartoons', the show was initially presented by actor Christopher Trace and 1957's Miss Great Britain Leila Williams, initially doing little more than demonstrating what were very much presented as separate hobbies for boys and girls. As the weeks went by, however, the likeable pair, and their enthusiastic if only just slightly less than formal presentational style, caught on with viewers, and the show – broadcast weekly on Thursdays – expanded its remit to take advantage of this, bringing in competitions, short documentaries and the very first if not exactly particularly distinguished stirrings of what would become a much-loved institution; the *Blue Peter* 'make'.

By 1960, *Blue Peter* was so popular that it was moved to a longer slot on Mondays, but behind the scenes all was not well. A succession of unsuitable replacement producers saw Leila leave early in

1962 after creative clashes, and her replacement Anita West only lasted eight weeks before she opted to leave, in light of an impending divorce. By the end of 1962, however, arguably the two most significant figures in *Blue Peter*'s history were on board; the formidable no-nonsense Biddy Baxter, who fought tirelessly to get the show as much recognition and resources as any adult programme and invariably won, took over as producer, and Valerie Singleton – of whom, Biddy observed, if the studio had collapsed in the middle of a broadcast, she would have stepped out from under the rubble and continued word perfect with the scheduled item – joined as co-presenter. One of Biddy's first innovations was to replace the previously standard *Blue Peter* presentation area with a huge open set and a few items of furniture in front of a white backdrop, with guests and featured items simply ushered on and off as required. It made absolutely no attempt to disguise the fact that it was a live broadcast from a television studio, and *Blue Peter* as it is still known and loved today was born.

Biddy was never one to stand still, however, and kept on introducing new innovations that just seemed to make *Blue Peter* more vibrant and more popular. The first *Blue Peter* Appeal, famously raising funds for charity by asking viewers to send in easily collectable recyclable items like silver paper, used stamps and broken watch straps rather than money, took place in December 1962, followed in the new year by the introduction of the much-coveted *Blue Peter* Badge, awarded to competition winners and other exceptional achievers, and which granted them free entry to museums and National Trust properties. Never simply distributed freely and idly, the *Blue Peter* Badge itself is difficult enough to get hold of; the corresponding Gold *Blue Peter* Badge is only ever awarded to those who have shown exceptional acts of bravery, participated in a prominent activity in the face of considerable odds or are, quite simply, as remarkable as Paul McCartney.

The 'makes' became ever more ingenious yet straightforward to achieve, as the presenters showed viewers how to make everything from budget-conscious improvised pet beds and Christmas decorations to a tobogganing outfit for a teddy bear, famously using everyday unwanted implements like used washing-up-liquid bottles and what BBC rules on advertising obliged them to refer to as 'sticky-backed plastic', with the time-saving conveyor belt of examples of 'here's one I made earlier' quickly becoming national shorthand.

Having twice received a disinterested pro-forma response from Enid Blyton as a youngster herself, Biddy insisted that every child who wrote in got a personalised reply. The first ever *Blue Peter* Expedition, where the presenters spent the summer exploring a foreign location and presented filmed reports of their exploits in the autumn, saw them head off for Norway in 1965, and artist William Timym's stories of Bengo the boxer dog puppy, and intrepid futuristic boy and alien from Planet Miron duo 'Bleep and Booster' were introduced as running serials. The *Blue Peter* Book, a fixture of Christmas Day pillowcases for decades to come, made its debut in 1964, and Biddy also instituted a close association with a certain other newly launched BBC show that went on to benefit both at different difficult times and continues to this day; when Russell T. Davies brought back *Doctor Who* in 2005, his first official act as showrunner was to contact the *Blue Peter* production office.

Mindful that a large percentage of the viewing audience might live in circumstances where they were unable to have a pet of their own, Biddy also introduced the idea of the show having resident animals, and the tradition of their names being chosen from viewers' suggestions. Mongrel Petra – a secret last-minute replacement for another puppy who had been introduced on screen but died of distemper shortly before the following edition – joined in December 1962 as *Blue Peter*'s very first pet. Irritable and prone to on-set stroppiness, Petra nonetheless became beloved of the viewers and presenters alike, to the extent that when she died in 1977 Timym created a bronze statue of her, which was erected in her honour in the *Blue Peter* Garden. Petra was joined by Fred the tortoise – who later revealed himself to be a Freda – in 1963, Jason the cat in 1964 and her own puppy Patch in 1965, although difficulties with finding and retaining a regular parrot meant that after the rapid succession of Joey and Barney, the tradition was not maintained.

Perhaps the most important addition arrived late in 1965. *Blue Peter* had gained a second weekly edition in September 1964, and it quickly became clear that they'd need a third presenter; in came John Noakes, a fresh-faced chipper Northerner who was more than happy to take on the more active location reports that Christopher Trace wasn't exactly keen on. Trace himself left during the summer of 1967, replaced by former *Doctor Who* assistant Peter Purves, and the first truly iconic *Blue Peter* team was complete. Not just the most famous faces on children's television but some of the most famous faces on television full stop, Pete, John and Val presided over an eccentric and eclectic variety of features ranging from trying their hands at riding both Penny Farthings and the newly launched Space Hopper to nervously assisting defected Soviet strongman Walter Cornelius with some jaw-dropping feats of physical endurance, and presiding over a 'Design A Monster For Doctor Who' competition; the winning entries, The Steel Octopus, The Akwaman and The Hypnotron, really do have to be seen to be believed. In an ongoing series of features, the team also followed the progress of a baby named Daniel, who displayed slightly more on-screen decorum than another baby who appeared on the show around the same time – Lulu, a visiting elephant calf from Chessington Zoo, who notoriously made something of a mess of proceedings.

In many ways, *Blue Peter* was the quintessential BBC show – good clean fun that challenged without being challenging, exposed the workings of television in an organised and professional way, and encouraged viewers to aspire towards their own sense of achievement and fulfilment in a manner that at the same time benefited everyone. It must hardly have seemed likely that the more entertainment-focused and commercially minded ITV would make any move towards trying to copy the format for themselves – but in 1968, that's exactly what they did.

Initially presented by Pete Brady, Susan Stranks and Tony Bastable, Thames Television's *Magpie* (ITV, 1968–80) – so named, as several former presenters have alleged, in a wry in-joke about the fact that the magpie is known as a thief – was to all intents and purposes *Blue Peter* for an entirely different audience. With a Hammond organ-led psychedelic pop theme by The Spencer Davis Group, masquerading as 'The Murgatroyd Band' in honour of the show's feathery mascot, *Magpie* sought to address viewers who it was felt might not be able to relate to the more refined and cultured world occupied by Val and company. Where *Blue Peter* might have featured school brass ensembles or juvenile juggling champions, *Magpie* profiled actual pop stars and big-screen pin-ups. Visits to see Puff the pony took the place of the in-studio pets, and the show did not confine itself to the minute degree of studio space it had been allocated, frequently spilling out into the corridors, reception and even outdoors of Teddington Lock, gamely pressing ahead regardless of the weather.

Perhaps most audaciously, in place of the badge that afforded you prestige in the eyes of the wider world, or at least the wider world that visited National Trust properties, *Magpie* appealed to the hoarding instinct of the audience with a whopping ten badges. The original *Magpie* badge was given out at individual presenters' discretion: One For Sorrow to anyone who wrote in and told them about how they had overcome a hardship; Two For Joy for anyone who shared a happy story; Three For A Girl And Four For A Boy for impressive artwork on strictly gender demarcated lines; Five For Silver to anyone who actually came up with an idea that got used in an edition of *Magpie*; Six For Gold for an impressive work of fiction; Seven For A Secret Never To Be Told as an anonymous nomination for a friend who you felt deserved one – which, as presenter Tommy Boyd pointed out, was somewhat negated by the telling; Eight For A Wish to all competition runners-up; Nine For A Kiss for anyone who has taken up a new hobby; and Ten Is A Bird You Must Not Miss for anyone who actually appeared on *Magpie*.

They even held their own annual charity appeals, albeit asking for money rather than everyday items, with the total counter up on a huge thermometer line snaking around the walls of Thames Television and usually running into the tens and hundreds of thousands. As subsequent presenter Mick Robertson put it, that's a lot of milk bottle tops.

It wasn't actually ITV's only *Blue Peter* rival, but Southern's *How* (ITV, 1966–81) generally kept its head down, minded its own business and got on with what it was there to do – explain things. Originally devised by presenter Jack Hargreaves as a late evening show aimed at resolving disputes and wagers that started in the pub, *How* eventually evolved into a children's show in which he and fellow presenters Bunty James, Fred Dinenage and Jon Miller revealed the facts and technology behind such everyday questions as how ships in bottles are constructed and how clay is shaped and hardened, with a deft combination of scholastic interest and cameraman-baiting wit.

Introduced by the presenters holding up one hand and exclaiming 'How!' in a manner that may not have travelled well in terms of cultural sensitivity, it was nonetheless hugely popular in its own quiet way and only came to an end when Southern lost its ITV franchise; indeed, it returned, with Dinenage joined by Carol Vorderman and Gareth 'Gaz Top' Jones, as *How 2* (ITV, 1990–2006).

Blue Peter and *Magpie*, however, became locked in an unspoken but intense and sustained rivalry, even if many of the presenters secretly wished they could all just be friends, which only intensified once the early seventies hit and *Magpie*'s stylish glam rock graphical design and trendy young presentational team of Mick Robertson, Douglas Rae and Jenny Hanley threw the inadvertent prim and properness of their BBC counterparts John, Pete and new recruit Lesley Judd into even sharper relief. Where *Blue Peter* might have retold the story of the Stone of Scone yet again, Mick and Susan would put on their woolly hats and head on out to present a report on an inner-city art project for disadvantaged kids; while the famous annual unveiling of the coat hanger, tinsel and candle-wrought *Blue Peter* Advent Crown – with the show's scheduling frequently necessitating the presenters to 'cheat' and light the fourth and final candle a couple of days early – was countered by the *Magpie* team joking around with bizarre historical festive facts and joining in with community carol singing.

There was no doubt that *Magpie* had the cool credibility, but *Blue Peter* had Biddy Baxter, who could not have cared less and simply thundered ahead improving and adapting her own show on its own terms. In 1971, the presenters won headlines by burying a 'time capsule' at Television Centre containing *Blue Peter*-related memorabilia and a set of newly minted decimal coins – and it won headlines again when it was excavated in 2000, and revealed live on air to be primarily full of rancid water – and the show even received royal assent also in 1971 when Princess Anne joined Val on safari in Kenya for the first ever *Blue Peter Special Assignment* (BBC, 1971–81).

Designed by renowned horticulturalist Percy Thrower, the meticulously tended *Blue Peter* Garden – which played host to many a firework display – was unveiled in 1974. 'Makes' for witch and wizard puppets, Easter cakes and homemade sledges prompted mailbags full of requests for the accompanying fact sheets, and significant studio guests like Anne Frank's father Otto and disabled author Joey Deacon had a more profound impact on young viewers than perhaps anyone had expected. Even the filmed reports could become national talking points, most infamously John Noakes' staggering ascent of Nelson's Column with a basic standard of equipment that nowadays would provoke a health-and-safety nightmare before anyone had even finished suggesting it. An incident in which a troop of Girl Guides stoically singing 'If You're Happy and You Know It Clap Your Hands' were momentarily menaced by an out-of-control campfire live in the studio, however, was slightly less planned for.

The spin-off series *Val Meets the VIPs* (BBC, 1973–74) saw Valerie chair a studio discussion between an audience of children and a heavyweight guest of the sort that they might not normally have an opportunity to converse with; during an unguarded moment, the controversial then-Secretary of State for Education and Science Margaret Thatcher confidently assured one juvenile inquisitor that there would not be a female Prime Minister within her lifetime. There was, however, just one name during this time that anyone and everyone would associate with *Blue Peter*.

Shep, a Border collie with vastly more energy than sense, made his first appearance in September 1971, and within minutes had tried both to bolt off to have a nose at the cameramen and nibble the presenters'

FACTUAL SHOWS

faces off before leaping into a puppy bed before the 'make' was even complete. Whether attempting to 'help' Roy Castle play the drums or challenging *Doctor Who*'s resident robot dog K9 to a scrap, Shep could be relied on to bring a note of unpredictable and scarcely controllable anarchy to proceedings, and formed an immediate bond with John Noakes, whose vain exhortations to 'get down, Shep!' quickly became a national catchphrase and inspired a song by comedy troupe The Barron Knights, albeit not one of their better efforts. John and Shep were so popular and inseparable as a double-act that they were even given their own series. Opening with a traffic light changing to green and a bracing brass band rendition of 'On Ilkla Moor Baht 'At', *Go with Noakes* (BBC, 1976–80) saw the unlikely duo travel the British Isles in search of outdoor pursuits, and although John later fell out with the BBC when contractual issues prevented them from working together on commercial television – famously he appeared in a Spillers dog food commercial with the nearly identical Skip – he later broke down in tears when informing viewers of Shep's recent death on the early evening BBC magazine show *Fax*.

With the even younger and trendier Tommy Boyd replacing Douglas in 1977, *Magpie* continued to corner the audience share that *Blue Peter* had virtually no interest in, famously running interviews with an up-and-coming singer-songwriter named Kate Bush and a bodybuilder turned actor trying his luck in London who went by the somewhat more Austrian name of Arnold Schwarzenegger. This might sound as though they were outmanoeuvring the opposition into irrelevance, but in its own small ways *Blue Peter* was still moving with the times, albeit usually quite slowly and often entirely by accident – and you could not find a better example of this than an update to the theme tune around the same time. Sidney Torch and The New City Orchestra's recording of Herbert Ashworth-Hope's hornpipe 'Barnacle Bill' and Wilfred Burns' library music cue sign-off 'Drums and Fife' had been in use since the very earliest days of *Blue Peter*; in 1979, both were given a makeover by Mike Oldfield, a rock musician with a keen interest in updating traditional-sounding tunes for the synthesiser age, and his arrangement of the *Blue Peter* theme became an unlikely top-twenty hit. It may have hardly been in line with the emergent New Romantic movement, but as the eighties approached, it certainly sounded a lot more contemporary than The Spencer Davis Group.

In fact, *Blue Peter* went from strength to strength in the eighties, just as many of its old contemporaries were being quietly retired on account of seeming a little past their time. A lot of this was down to the ever-judicious selection of presenters, who could always be relied on to set a fresh-faced good example without ever coming across as *too* square. John and Pete were replaced in 1978 by Christopher Wenner and Simon Groom, who won infamy – and a rebuke from Biddy Baxter – for their somewhat nuanced delivery of a scripted item about Durham Cathedral's antique door knockers. Children's BBC veteran Tina Heath replaced Lesley in 1979, only to leave a year later to have her daughter – with, in a fairly radical move at the time, her pregnancy followed in a series of features on the show, including a live ultrasound scan.

Tina's replacement, Sarah Greene – recruited after *Blue Peter* had run a feature on *The Swish of the Curtain* (BBC, 1980), a Children's BBC adaptation of Pamela Brown's tale of juvenile amateur dramatics derring-do she had recently starred in – set many an adolescent heart a-flutter with her dressed-down studenty image; as did that year's fellow new recruit – despite being landed with a green-and-white suit designed by a viewer – Christopher's replacement, Peter Duncan. Enormously popular and ideally suited to the format, Peter actually came back for a second stint after his ill-suited short-stay replacement, Michael Sundin, was quietly dropped after less than a year on air, and even fronted his own spin-off show. *Duncan Dares* (BBC, 1985–87) went further than *Go with Noakes* had ever dared go, pairing him up with firefighters, wilderness survival experts, mountaineers, long-distance hang-gliders and even on one occasion someone who claimed to be able to cross the Irish Sea in an old car.

Jigsaw's Janet Ellis took over from a *Saturday Superstore*-bound Sarah in 1983, bringing along the wry raised eyebrow smirk that had characterised her work with Jig and Perry, but also capable of taking matters seriously, notoriously when she had to break the news that the *Blue Peter* Garden had been vandalised in 1983. It has become a punchline since, but the live footage of her surveying the pointless damage – and the harm done to the fish – scarcely supports the idea that *Blue Peter* was all forced grins and jolly pursuits. It wasn't all bad news, though; redevelopment work at Television Centre meant that the original time capsule had to be excavated, and it was relocated – with a new one created by Simon, Janet and Peter – in the newly restored garden. Newer animal recruits included twin cats Jack and Jill, famed for their habit of darting off set the second that transmission started, and Simon Groom's inquisitive golden retriever Goldie, who soon wound up sharing screen time with her slightly more excitable daughter Bonnie. *Val Meets the VIPs* was reinvented as *In the Limelight with Lesley* (BBC, 1980), and the appeals continued to break fundraising records, especially after the introduction of the Bring-and-Buy Sales in 1979.

Poor old *Magpie*, however, had fallen victim to the inevitability that anything that moves with fashion will eventually find it has moved out of fashion, and amidst rumours of boardroom battles, it was cancelled almost without notice in 1980. Thames did try to maintain its momentum with a procession of reinvented magazine shows, but it was never quite the same. Possibly named by someone who didn't fully understand the audience they had inherited, *Ace Reports* (ITV, 1980–81), presented by Wayne Laryea and Brian Jacks with a huge roster of roving correspondents, adopted a more dynamic approach with particular emphasis on daredevil sports, but only really attracted much attention over an ill-advised spoof item suggesting that plugging a dustbin lid covered in tinfoil into your television as a makeshift 'satellite dish' would allow you to pick up international television.

Ostensibly broadcast on clandestine network 'Channel 14', *CBTV* (ITV, 1982–85) featured early alternative comedy stars Jim Sweeney and Steve Steen sneaking into Teddington Lock by outwitting hapless commissionaire Harry Fielder to broadcast their own illegal magazine show anchored by Anneka Rice, Mike Smith and Paul Henley. *Splash* (ITV, 1985–88) brought in experienced youth presenters Michael Groth, Victoria Studd and Nino Firetto in the hopes of fashioning a replacement with more teen appeal, but although they worked well as a team, the format itself – which lurched awkwardly between Culture Club video exclusives and features on how you can help conserve the caterpillar population – never quite landed and it found itself the open target of jokes on *Your Mother Wouldn't Like It*. It proved to be the last of its kind on ITV.

Blue Peter, however, had good reason to look to the nineties with optimism. By 1988 they had their youngest and most with-it presentation team yet – Caron Keating, Mark Curry and Yvette Fielding – along with an omnibus repeat of the week's highlights on a Sunday morning, and they were still capable of making headlines, such as Mark accidentally knocking the head off a Lego statue live

FACTUAL SHOWS

on air, and a summer expedition to the Soviet Union which took in a mud bath where Mark revealed more of himself than might have been expected from the venerable institution, and Caron appeared to enjoy a tough traditional massage a little *too* much. Lovestruck teenagers with their finger hovering over the Record button might have had good reason to be grateful for that particular week's Sunday repeat.

You could like it, you could pretend to hate it, but you just couldn't escape it – *Blue Peter* was always there and always trying to find something either interesting or charitable for you to do. Plus, if we're all being honest about it, everybody probably secretly wished that school could have been a bit more like *Blue Peter* too.

8

Variety and Game Shows

'It's Friday, it's five to five . . .'

Sitting up straight. Standing up straight. As kids, we all knew the drill of how you were supposed to behave and when. There was always one occasion, however, when no matter how much you may have been uncomfortably ordered into your smartest clothes and sternly told to be on your best behaviour, any pretence that maintaining law and order was a possibility was quickly discarded through sheer weight of force – and that was party time.

Whether it was your own birthday party, a parent's works Christmas do or even on a very rare occasion something at school that required celebration, it was an occasion when 'best behaviour' wasn't exactly either mandatory or encouraged. High on the sugar rush of formless slabs of green jelly wedged in next to an equally oddly shaped single scoop of vanilla ice cream, a small army of hyperactive terrors sporting elastic-secured plastic green and white striped hats and frantically blowing roll-out squeakers would pretty much run amok for two hours that, to the adults, must have felt like twelve. Games of pass the parcel, musical statues and musical chairs played out to the stop-start accompaniment of a jumping *Pinky and Perky* album sobbing for mercy in the corner, entertainers dropped by and asked for a volunteer that was never you, and everyone left with a bag full of both kinds of Refreshers and one of those cellophane fortune teller fish things that just folded into a shape entirely of their own invention and volition. It was a rare treat in a staid world of thank-you letters and continually changing rules over whether 'a few' legitimately constituted two or three — but it was one that you could secretly revisit every Friday at five to five.

Crackerjack! (BBC, 1955–84) — readers are invited to shout their own CRACKERJACK! in response, although you will never get as loud as the truly undisciplined studio audience — wasn't the first variety show for children, but it was the loudest and most raucous, and may well never have been exceeded on that front. The format may have been a simple one — children took part in a series of games interspersed by pop and variety acts before the presenters acted out a panto-styled sketch to close the show — but it was performed and watched at a truly staggering pace and volume, and it's a wonder that BBC Lime Grove wasn't shaken loose of its foundations with every single repetition of the show's title.

Initially hosted by Eammon Andrews — subsequent hosts included Leslie Crowther, Michael Aspel, Ed 'Stewpot' Stewart and Stu Francis of 'arm wrestle an Action Man' comedy boast fame — with a small army of supporting comics, the games included the infamous 'Double or Drop', in which contestants were loaded with armfuls of prizes, and cabbages if they got the wrong answer, with the last one still with their gargantuan haul in their hands being declared the winner; although if the studio audience's hysteria was to be believed, no prize was more sought after than a *Crackerjack!* pencil.

The cast got up to all manner of corny joke-driven silliness and nonsense song-driven high jinks, with long-serving regulars Don Maclean and Peter Glaze proving such a popular combination that they were eventually given their own series of silent slapstick shorts, *Don and Pete* (BBC, 1979), and the closing sketch invariably concluded on a current pop hit rewritten with comically appropriate lyrics. As these were adapted to fit the sketches rather than the other way around, this sometimes led to some unusual choices, and there can't have been many other shows presenting their own parody take on Sparks' 'Something for the Girl with Everything' or XTC's 'Making Plans for Nigel'; David Bowie's thoughts on their appropriation of 'Golden Years' sadly went unrecorded. Famed for everything from the much-loved *Doctor Who* send-up 'Hello My Dalek' to Don and Pete's groan-inducing overlong buildups to a dreadful pun ('MACLEAN!' – 'Yes, I had a bath this morning!') to Chas 'n' Dave's memorably bewildering theme song singing the praises of the 'lovely word' that was neither lumberjack, steeplejack nor Uncle Jack, *Crackerjack!* and its rallying call 'It's Friday, it's five to five . . .' reverberated through the decades, but like the parties it sought to emulate, it had its own picking-up time. A simple format that was starting to feel a little of date by the mid-eighties, *Crackerjack!* was cancelled as part of a round of cost-cutting aimed at funding the launch of the BBC's daytime service. Rumours that several executives were haunted at night by an echoing responding roar of 'CRACKERJACK!' sadly cannot be confirmed.

Crackerjack! may have been the loudest variety show on children's television, but it was far from the only one. Naughty schoolboy Wee Jimmy Krankie and his big brother Ian – better known to their friends and family as Janette Tough and her husband Ian – who were regulars during the later series of *Crackerjack!*, set a catapult-wielding bad example across *The Krankies Klub* (ITV, 1982–84), *The Krankies Electronic Komic* (BBC, 1985–87) and *K.T.V.* (ITV, 1989–91). Juvenile-skewed stage illusionists of the order of Ali Bongo, The Great Kovari and The Great Soprendo, did their close-up conjuring in *Magic Circle* (ITV, 1977), alongside Ray Alan and his fez-sporting puppet Ali Cat in the more clock-governed *Five Magic Minutes* (ITV, 1980–81).

Notably less anarchically and hosted by Colin Bennett in the guise of slippery brilliantined showbiz impresario 'Vince Purity', *You Should Be So Lucky!* (BBC, 1986–87) was doubtless made with the best of intentions but unfortunately proved to be a masterclass in alienating your audience. Not only were all of the clapometer-adjudged snakes and ladders board-traversing contestants drawn from stage schools and introduced as stars-in-waiting you'd be seeing more of very soon, there were also frequent interruptions from The Purettes, a leaping troupe of Shirley Temple-evoking girls and boys with old-fashioned hairstyles and outfits. There was at least an attempt to ameliorate for this by having Vince introduce them through unimpressed gritted teeth, but it was too little too late and, essentially, children will never willingly want to watch other children who are being promoted as more talented than them.

Meanwhile, club comic Bobby Bennett took to the stage at the Leeds City Varieties Theatre to compere *Junior Showtime* (ITV, 1969–74), a parade of singing and dancing juvenile talent that featured the genuinely talented pre-fame likes of Bonnie Langford, Joe Longthorne and Mark Curry alongside a small army of shrill foot-clattering youngsters who were possibly only ever considered talented by their parents, in addition to former *Opportunity Knocks* winner Glyn Poole, who managed to score a minor hit in 1973 with the chirruping ukulele-led 'Milly Molly Mandy'. The fact that this is its most tolerable legacy probably tells you all that you need to know about the show itself.

Cycling along a suspiciously similar path, Chris Harris toured the regions in a bicycle-towed 'crazy pink caravan' in *Hey Look, That's*

Me! (BBC, 1977–83), giving local youngsters with an interesting hobby an opportunity to display their skills on television in what was effectively an inverse version of *Why Don't You?* And Chris Kelly presided over what was almost a primitive precursor to *The X Factor* only with more shrill renditions of 'The Good Ship Lollipop' and impressions of Prince Charles that opened by announcing they were impressions of Prince Charles in *Anything You Can Do* (ITV, 1969–74).

More tolerably, Freddie Garrity – better known to sixties pop fans as frontman of Freddie and The Dreamers – hosted *Little Big Time* (ITV, 1968–73), an all-singing all-dancing light entertainment miscellany that incorporated 'Oliver in the Overworld', a deeply hallucinogenic running serial about a far-off enchanted land inhabited by anthropomorphic machines, and a quest to fix Freddie's grandfather clock and return the Royal Winding Up Key to the Clockwork King. Originally sung by a cog-depleted metronome, the song 'Gimme Dat Ding' became a hit for The Pipkins – nothing to do with Pig and company, no matter how much they might have sounded like Tortoise and Hartley – in 1970.

Play School illustrator Mike Amatt turned the house-roaming passive-aggressive live action larks of his real life cat Smiff and Old English Sheepdog Mop into the animated song-festooned show-within-a-show *Mop and Smiff* (BBC, 1985), with Prunella Scales and Timothy West on domestic pet voiceover duties; when a second run called for a seaside town-touring approach, feline practicalities saw to it that Smiff was left at home while Mike and Mop packed a guitar and headed off in a novelty car for *Mike, Mop and the Moke* (BBC, 1985).

For those who preferred to watch other children doing something less gratingly showbizzy and more intellectual, there were plenty of quiz shows that you could secretly aspire to be on yourself. Hosted in turn by Michael Rodd, Brian Trueman and Mark Curry, *Screen Test* (BBC, 1970–84) was based around teams of youngsters answering observation-based questions on clips from movies, a suspiciously large number of which were drawn from the Children's Film Foundation's extensive catalogue. As more or less the only place on television you could regularly get to see extracts from *Star Wars* or *Jaws*, it should have been essential viewing, but there was one unavoidable element that had viewers running for cover as soon as that percussive theme music started – the 'Young Filmmaker of the Year' contest.

On paper, giving talented teenagers with access to 16mm film three minutes of airtime was a tremendous idea; most of them, however, were less eager to become the next Pressburger and Powell than they were to be the new George A. Romero or David Lynch, with angular metal men crawling through ruined landscapes to screeching music, school corridors haunted by spectral sports teams and drug dabblers enduring migraine-inducing flashbacks to bad trips abounded. Most notoriously and nightmarishly, the infamous 'Ice Cream' spelled out in no uncertain terms what awaited anyone who accepted that lift with a friendly man in a big car. At least the certificates at the start of actual films gave you fair warning.

Variously presided over by Howard Stableford, Paul Jones and Bruno Brookes, *Beat the Teacher* (BBC, 1984–88) afforded clean-cut smartypants types the opportunity to get their own back on 'sir' by trouncing them at wry logic puzzle posers, in the hope of outdoing each other on an electronic noughts and crosses board. There was clearly an element of teacher-trouncing in the air during *So You Want to Be Top?* (BBC, 1983–85), in which Gary Wilmot led contestants through a procession of loosely 'school day' themed rounds where the objective was to get one over on authority, interrupted by spoof advertisements for dubious classroom dodge-facilitating products endorsed by one 'Arthur Loaf'. For the final run, for no obvious reason, the format was rejigged so that the 'pupils' were played by adult actors in entirely scripted exchanges, in a move that probably left viewers wishing they were actually back at school.

Essentially adapted from the board game Battleships but using co-ordinates based on the phonetic alphabet and chunky BBC Micro graphics so nobody would notice, *Finders Keepers* (BBC, 1981–85) had Richard Stilgoe refereeing as two teams from opposing schools strategically struck out to win 'pathetic prizes' – rarely more exciting than a show-branded lunchbox and flask – and also decorated the show with a ready supply of anagrams and a theme tune that, excitingly, he played live on air as the credits rolled. Gyles Brandreth and Bonnie Langford put 'The Bananas' and 'The Coconuts' through their problem-solving paces with a side order of gnu-themed whimsy in *Puzzle Party* (ITV, 1977), and their more voluble counterparts held forth on a chosen specialist subject as judged by a Chris Kelly-led celebrity panel in *Chatterbox* (ITV, 1977). Ever keen to represent the more cerebral corners of the Children's ITV audience, Tommy Boyd was the driving force behind *What's Happening?* (ITV, 1982–83), a live quiz show in which teams of current affairs-savvy youngsters recruited by their respective Independent Local Radio stations were grilled on the week's news and invited to spot deliberate mistakes in reports read by genuine ITN anchor Leonard Parkin.

Debbie Greenwood anchored high-tech 'video quiz' *First Class* (BBC, 1984–88), putting year-straddling teams from rival schools through their paces with general knowledge questions, the celeb-identifying 'spinning gold disc' and, daringly, a high score-chasing go on arcade games including Track and Field and Paperboy. It also boasted a surprising familiarity with current pop culture, although an observation round on pop videos notoriously came a cropper when a contestant replied that the game seen at the start of 'It's a Miracle' by Culture Club was a computerised rendition of Monopoly; 'I'm sorry,' replied Debbie, 'the answer is Computer Console.' Meanwhile, *Spytrap* (BBC, 1985) was quite simply one of the most bizarre quiz shows ever invented for any audience. Adopting a loose John le Carre-inflected Cold War espionage theme, Bill Homewood led the contestants through a series of surveillance and code breaking-based rounds before announcing it was time to 'swing by the Sweat Room for some punishment with Pertwee', whereupon they were barked at by Bill Pertwee to look lively with star jumps and squat thrusts.

Star Turn (BBC, 1976–81) roped two teams of children's television-adjacent celebrities into a series of improvisational parlour games refereed by Bernard Cribbins, culminating in a wild free-for-all mystery playlet in which Cribbins assumed the role of intrepid detective Ivor Notion who – with customary deerstalker rotation – invariably 'had a notion' about the solution. Graeme Garden took over the notion-having as the series evolved initially in parallel into *Star Turn Challenge* (BBC, 1978–81), in which the teams were drawn from a specific programme or performing troupe, treating viewers to edge-of-the-seat prop comedy showdowns between *Multi-Coloured Swap Shop* and The News.

More than possibly inspired by the cinematic success of Indiana Jones, *On Safari* (ITV, 1982–84) pitted child-and-parent teams against perilous swamps and prize-guarding Venus fly traps with a khaki-clad Christopher Biggins and Gillian Taylforth on hand to adjudge everything 'safari, so goody'. Opportunities to play along yourself at home were surprisingly few and far between, which is possibly why *Puzzle Trail* (BBC, 1980–84) proved such a sensation.

VARIETY AND GAME SHOWS

Presented in daily ten-minute instalments, *Puzzle Trail* – another superbly anticlockwise-logic invention from Clive Doig – challenged viewers to write in identifying the mystery object that the abstract clues and off-the-wall narrative was hinting towards, as variously hosted by Donna Reeve, Tommy Boyd, Howard Stableford, Kirsty Miller and ex-Monkee Davy Jones, invariably with the aid of enough visual effects to book up an editing suite for weeks.

If you wanted more anarchy with your questions about the name of the new film about a shark set in America, though, then *Runaround* (ITV, 1975–81) was essentially little more than an excuse for cockney comic Mike Reid to exhort teams of youngers to belt across a game board in a blur of flashing lights and sirens. *Hold Tight!* (ITV, 1982–87) took over the newly opened Alton Towers, and Bob Carolgees, Pauline Black and Sue Robbie guided contestants around a massive tower block-sized snakes and ladders board while pop acts like Shakin' Stevens and Bad Manners – who also provided the theme music – performed on and around the various rides and attractions.

A follow-on from *Tiswas* – or at least the final series iteration of it – in all but name, *How Dare You!* (ITV, 1984–87) was essentially little more than a gunge-flinging festival masquerading as a competition to win a trophy-mounted wellington boot and opportunities to raid the 'Goody Bin', barely kept under control by Clive Webb, Floella Benjamin and John Gorman, who also wrote and performed the high-speed ramshackle theme song. Floella was later replaced by Carrie Grant and Cheryl Baker, while the theme song gave way for the final series to a re-recorded version of Five Star's notably tamer recent hit 'Stay Out of My Life'; it stopped daring people not long afterwards. Their *Now That's What I Call Music* contemporary Sinitta had more luck as host of *The Wall Game* (ITV, 1985–86), ostensibly involving teams competing to stage improvised plays but primarily concerned with their ability to, as her theme song had it, 'take a wall, and knock it down, take a wall, and knock it to the ground'.

If you just wanted the pop music without the other kids showing off their knowledge, then you weren't exactly short of options. Possibly the glam rockiest that a television programme ever got, *Lift Off with Ayshea* (ITV, 1969–74) was fronted by model, actress and pop star with a massive 'A' pendant Ayshea Brough, who introduced everyone from Slade, Sweet and Mud to Black Sabbath, Cliff Richard and Roger Whittaker before singing a couple of songs of her own, and famously featured the first ever broadcast appearance of David Bowie's Ziggy Stardust persona. Short, simple and sensational, it was still very much a children's programme – Ayshea's co-hosts included puppets Fred Barker and Ollie Beak – but one that was to have a huge influence, and producer Muriel Young later repeated the format with follow-on series hosted by individual bands; The Bay City Rollers in *Shang-A-Lang* (ITV, 1975), second division glam rockers – who nonetheless wrote 'I Love Rock 'n' Roll' – in *Arrows* (ITV, 1976–77) and *Marc* (ITV, 1977), in which T-Rex frontman Marc Bolan capitalised on a resurgence of popularity with the punk rock crowd by introducing a couple of the more presentable acts. The final edition, recorded just before his tragic road accident, concluded with an attempt at an improvised duet with his old mate David Bowie, which collapsed into laughter when Marc somehow contrived to fall over.

Radio Luxembourg's rising star David 'Kid' Jensen hosted *Lift Off*'s direct replacement, *45* (ITV, 1974–75), which took a slightly more 'quality rock' approach, concentrating primarily on bands who could 'cut it' live and – slightly ironically given the show's title – the big-selling albums of the moment; perhaps to emphasise this, the show changed its name partway through to *Rock On with 45*. Critical of what he saw as the imaginatively threadbare and financially deficient nature of previous efforts, producer Mike Mansfield came up with an ingenious solution – he 'cued' *Supersonic* (ITV, 1975–77) himself from the production gallery, dispensing with the need for awkward presenter links and leaving the bands free to put on a show and the budget free to spend on props, effects and party trimmings. One of the very few ITV *Top of the Pops* rivals that actually warranted that description, *Supersonic* managed to attract big names and also had a knack of spotting what was about to become a hit – and Elton John and Kiki Dee used the studio to film their promo video for 'Don't Go Breakin' My Heart' – but by Mansfield's own admission the format was not really suited to the sudden arrival of punk and disco, and it was cancelled while it was still on a high. It takes someone who actually – for once – understood the pop industry enough to pull that off. Hosted by Alistair Pirrie with Lyn Spencer, Suzanne Dando and a pre-fame Lisa Stansfield, neon-hued *Razzmatazz* (ITV, 1981–87) scored by refusing to take itself too seriously while allowing the assorted new romantics and modish heartthrobs to take themselves as deeply seriously as they saw fit. It combined a postmodern theme song literally spelling out how difficult the title was to pronounce correctly, self-mocking inter-presenter witticisms and a bizarre competition where contestants had to say 'Peggy Babcock Babcock Peggy' three times in order to win an assortment of up-to-the-minute goodies like 'Into the Gap' by The Thompson Twins or a Grandstand Firefox game.

For many, though, there was only one name in pop on children's television. Bounding onto the set to a thumping riff-rocker so obviously modelled on 'Panic in Detroit' that David Bowie must surely have had a word with his lawyer, *Cheggers Plays Pop* (BBC, 1978–86) saw Keith Chegwin marshalling a thrillingly cacophonous audience while opposing teams, the Reds and the Yellows, battled for nothing more than points in a challenge to see whose encyclopaedic knowledge of the pop charts was matched by their ability to master ridiculous games involving inflatables and ball pools. Nobody really knew for certain what the rules were, and the end of each round was signalled by either a hooting four-note klaxon or a nose-thumbing lead guitar flourish. By not remotely attempting to be cool, *Cheggers Plays Pop* managed to become the most exciting pop show this side of *Top of the Pops*, with even the meanest and moodiest pop hopefuls happy to come on and plug their latest single.

In contrast, *Get It Together* (ITV, 1977–81) was an unsteady fusion of pop and game show, with the loose quiz element seeming secondary to an often-underwhelming collection of performances; the production team appeared to struggle to secure anyone within a reasonable distance of the top ten, and had to rely mainly on up-and-coming acts that never quite made the 'up' and the temporarily career-derailed likes of The Real Thing and Slade. In fact, there was something of an out-of-time air to proceedings in general, with hosts Roy North and Linda Fletcher called on to sing – and The Teri Scobie Dancers called on to dance to – a succession of hits of a year or two previously.

There was only ever really one true self-designated superstar in variety, pop music, game shows and general rule book-abandoning fun and games, however, and he was basically a one-rodent party all by himself. Created by David Claridge, the brashly self-assured Roland Rat and his known associates, practical and grounded Kevin the Gerbil and tedious tech whiz Errol the Hamster, had originally been engaged to introduce a daily cartoon slot on TV-am in 1983, possibly on account of being cheaper than hiring an actual human presenter. His somewhat unique form of audience interaction and rapport with the presenters and technical staff quickly caught on, and within weeks Roland's short inserts were actually turning the ailing station's fortunes around, leading a million columnists to believe that they had personally invented the all-too-obvious joke about a rat joining a sinking ship. None of them seemed quite so quick to notice that 1984 was both the Year of the Rat and the setting for George Orwell's classic dystopian novel, but while Big Roland may not have been watching you, viewers were certainly watching him in their millions as TV-am began to use the cast of rodents more and more.

Rat on the Road (ITV, 1983–84) took the trio out on day trips in the customised pink breakdown-prone Ford Anglia Ratmobile, followed by a visit to Switzerland for *Roland's Winter Wonderland* (ITV, 1983) and Japan – in the company of Roland's stowaway trouble-causer younger brother Little Reggie – in *Roland Goes East* (ITV, 1984). By now, they were also scoring hit records including the scratch-tastic 'Rat Rapping', Kevin's Roland-heckled rendition of 'Summer Holiday' and a bizarrely straight cover of 'Love Me Tender', and attempts were already being made to extend the brand further.

Operation FOGI (ITV, 1984) – 'Free Our Glenis Immediately' – revolved around a bid to rescue another new team member from the pets department at Harrods, which ended up requiring a little more ingenuity than Errol's suggestion that they disguise themselves as 'very rich leeks'. *Roland's Countdown to Christmas* (ITV, 1984) opened an advent calendar door each day in between much festive comic bickering, and *The Official Worldwide Roland Rat Appreciation Society Summer Spectacular* (ITV, 1985) – 'or OWRASS, for short!' as the choir of off-key children singing the theme song had it – took the form of an extended studio-based show that seemed to lack the gimmick-based charm of the earlier outings.

By this time, however, the superstar was already in talks with the BBC. Launched with an appearance on panel game show *Blankety Blank* — no, really — and the Christmas Day spectacular *Roland's Yuletide Binge* (BBC, 1985), which saw him march on BBC1 Controller Michael Grade's office demanding his own show, *Roland Rat – The Series* (BBC, 1986–88) and its theme song from hot new pop producers of the moment, Stock, Aitken and Waterman, was supposed to usher in a return to the BBC's all-conquering Saturday night schedules of the seventies. Instead, possibly hampered by too many new characters, including human agent D'Arcy D'Farcy, slightly dubious Scottish traditionalist Fergie the Ferret and Colin the Flea, and an eccentric booking policy that infamously saw angular American post-punk band Pere Ubu as the musical act one week, the nominal broadcast hijacks by the then non-existent 'BBC Three' failed to attract very much interest at all. Roland was very quickly shunted into early Saturday morning Formula 1-themed but otherwise entirely standard quiz show *Roland's Rat Race* (BBC, 1988–89), before moving on to superhero parody *Ratman* (BBC, 1988) and *Tales of the Rodent Sherlock Holmes* (BBC, 1990), which was honestly exactly what it sounds like.

By this time, though, the writing wasn't just on the wall for Roland. Perhaps aware that there was an untapped market in children's parties that went beyond the odd box of Disney-themed rice paper cake toppers, a whole industry had sprung up that ranged from ball pit-festooned activity centres to fast food restaurants offering their own burger-centric 'parties'. Even those blokes who showed extracts from *The Spaceman and King Arthur* on 16mm projectors — themselves once seen as an all too modern intrusion on a world of Simon

Says and balloons that burst without anyone touching them – found themselves in turn usurped by the most parental stress-avoidant option of them all: hiring and putting on 'a video'.

Video was a huge challenge if not an outright threat to the future of children's television, and it's hardly surprising that the reaction was to try to 'get with the times' in a big way. After all, the computer-generated post-Dungeons and Dragons stylings of *Knightmare* (ITV, 1987–94) and Pat Sharp's rampages around the indoor theme park chaos of *Fun House* (ITV, 1989–99) might seem a long way from Don and Pete annoying Ed with a gag about a-bomb-in-a-bull. Although when you think about it, there really isn't that much distance between one child failing to keep hold of a pile of board games – and cabbages – to the disdain of those watching at home, and another in a Virtual Reality helmet failing to adequately follow the fairly basic directions being frantically shouted out by their team-mates. It wasn't quite time to send everyone home with a party bag just yet. Although they wouldn't have minded if it had a *Crackerjack!* pencil in it.

(CRACKERJACK!)

'Help me help me if you can, space investigator man'

It may have taken a couple of years and the intervention of one Sir Clive Sinclair and his ZX80 to make the home computing boom a reality, but as the eighties dawned and every other magazine show had a breathlessly reported feature on the 'silicon chip', it was already obvious that before too long, there'd be a microcomputer in the corner of every living room, more than likely hooked up to the television that had complacently enjoyed corner-dominance for far too long already.

THE GOLDEN AGE OF CHILDREN'S TV

For once, the BBC was surprisingly quick off the mark in exploiting and exploring this new development in home entertainment technology. Their very own chunkily keyed educationally slanted 8-bit chipset pioneer the BBC Micro arrived in high street stores and thousands of schools in December 1981, accompanied by an array of programming-related programming. Radio 4's *The Chip Shop* explained the ins and outs of the OPENUP and OSCLI commands with a recordable and loadable bit of code at the end of the show, doubtless proving a nerve-soothing listen for businessmen stuck in commuter traffic, while BBC2's *Making the Most of the Micro* and *Micro Live* presented the latest news from the home computing world in a manner that very heavily implied that the BBC Micro was the only available retail option.

This drive towards floppy disc drives even began to inform slightly older varieties of home entertainment, with *Doctor Who* adopting a pronounced computational slant, complete with juvenile mathematical genius TARDIS traveller Adric on hand to help explain why the Master needed all those equations, and the crew of the *Challenger* in Radio 4's *EarthSearch* never exactly finding themselves short of need for an exchange about logic paths and chipset alignment. Elsewhere on Radio 4, Douglas Adams' magisterial *The Hitch-Hiker's Guide to the Galaxy* poked fun at the absurdity of the rise of technological evangelism almost as fast as they could rush out a new computer with an extra couple of kilobytes of memory. Meanwhile, throughout it all, a generation of teenagers more or less ignored all of the above and kept right on playing Horace Goes Skiing on their ZX Spectrums, Commodore 64s and to a lesser extent Amstrad CPCs.

Apart from, that is, the ones who preferred to don their metaphorical chainmail and head off in a more paper and dice-based direction, albeit one that they had little predictive control over.

VARIETY AND GAME SHOWS

Pioneering role-playing strategy game Dungeons and Dragons had arrived in the UK in the late seventies, inspiring small armies of tabletop warriors to take up pencil-based arms, an even larger army of do-gooders fretting about the liable orc-hallucinating effects on youngsters who had the temerity to play and enjoy a game without obtaining written permission first, and teachers who banished issues of *White Dwarf* from the classroom on the basis that role-playing had 'been in the news'. Despite their technological disparity, the two found conceptual common ground courtesy of the exciting art of the text-based Adventure Game. For those who enjoyed such pursuits, it was a fantastic time to be stuck in your bedroom. For those poor old teachers, it was just another reason to hold more assemblies.

Producer – and previously co-creator of *Vision On* – Patrick Dowling had all of the above very much in mind while he was devising *The Adventure Game* (BBC, 1980–86); in fact, he actually tried to engage Douglas Adams to work on the format with him, only to find that he was already developing *The Hitch-Hiker's Guide to the Galaxy* for television and unable to commit to yet another deadline he was likely to miss by several weeks at best. What he came up with, however, was simply so good and so original that he clearly didn't need any help with it.

The Adventure Game deposited a trio of contestants – two Children's BBC-adjacent actors or presenters such as Elizabeth Estensen, Fred Harris, Maggie Philbin, Graeme Garden, Madeline Smith, John Craven, Johnny Ball, Sarah Greene or Richard Stilgoe, alongside an expert in a related field, such as *Mastermind* winner Christopher Hughes or Rubik's Cube champion Nicholas Hammond – on the planet Arg, where they had to solve a series of puzzles in order to achieve a goal such as recovering a vital fuel crystal for their journey home. Aiding and abetting them, although even the aiding generally took the form of politely disdainful teasing, were resident local life form the Argonds, whose names were all anagrams of 'dragon'. This was somewhat handy considering that their natural form was a dragonlike appearance, with a more human look only reluctantly adopted to appease their visitors. Joining their bumbling uncle-like ruler Rangdo – played by Ian Messiter in humanlike form and Kenny Baker in his preferred trundling aspidistra guise – were butler Gandor (Chris Leaver), communications officer Darong (Moira Stewart), hostesses Gnoard (Charmain Gradwell) and Dorgan (Sarah Lam), backwards-talking Australian-accented Rongad (Bill Homewood) – who was always on hand to encourage the contestants with an exclamation of 'Doogy Rev!' – and Lesley Judd, who stayed behind after appearing as a contestant in the first series to become a 'mole', throwing in an extra element of confusion for, and some might argue betrayal of, her erstwhile colleagues.

The puzzles were enough to challenge even anyone who knew how to escape from the goblin's hall even if Thorin did insist on sitting down and starting singing about gold, taking in code-breaking with the aid of a sign reading 'Richard Of York Gave Battle In Vain', a complicated geometric puzzle based around the question 'How many Argonds are around the pond?', a computer-based maze game involving resident robot dog thing Dogran, and the intricate colour-coded electronic blippering floor-based exchange rate mechanism that fuelled local currency Drogna. The most fondly remembered, however, was the concluding challenge the Vortex, requiring the contestants to traverse an open-floored gantry while avoiding an invisible – although very much visible to viewers in the form of a scrolling assortment of BBC Micro vector graphics – opponent capable of 'vapourising' them, necessitating a long walk home against a starscape backdrop. Their only hope for locating it and attempting to predict its moves were the conveniently vapourisable green cheese rolls doled out as what appeared to be consolation prizes in earlier games. Needless to say, the Vortex became an instant popular choice for re-enacting on that bit of the playground where it suddenly went into alternately shaded paving stones for no readily apparent reason.

Introduced by an extract from Carulli's 'Duo in G' performed by Julian Bream and John Williams, *The Adventure Game* appeared on BBC1 early on Saturday mornings in 1980 – right after repeats of *The Banana Splits* – and immediately captured juvenile imaginations with its sleek calculator-age stylings and the feeling that, with presenters who were normally trying to 'educate' you reduced to baffled expressions at a riddle about a frog that was not a tree, you were almost playing along at home by proxy. For the second series, which temporarily saw the contestants transported to Arg via an intergalactic transporter situated in Patrick Dowling's house, with an equally temporary replacement use of Grieg's 'Norwegian Dance' as the theme music, it was relocated to early weekday evenings on BBC2, as it was simply too popular and had too wide an appeal to stay so far out of the way. Hardly surprising, given it was the closest that you could get to playing a computer game when you weren't allowed to use the computer. Although, oddly, the closest that *The Adventure Game* came to becoming an actual computer game was a lone Drogna-themed puzzle for – as you may have already guessed – the BBC Micro. It may also help to explain the latterday popularity of Escape Rooms amongst a generation of office workers with distant memories of Noel Edmonds and Fern Britton trying to fish a key out of a tube of water using a magnet on a rod.

A couple of light years away, *Captain Zep – Space Detective* (BBC, 1983–84) was taking an equally high-tech approach to solving puzzles all of his own. Captain of *Zep One* and lead investigator for the Space Office of Law Verification and Enquiry – or S.O.L.V.E., for short – Captain Zep and his assistants Jason Brown and Dr Spiro delved into their extensive casebook of interplanetary smuggling conspiracies and politically motivated framing for treason (on such exotically named worlds as Armagiddea, Delos, Sauria and Synope) as a training exercise for a studio audience full of youngsters in futuristic orange jumpsuits and slicked back hair, halting the reconstruction at a crucial point to ask them to record their own conclusions on who the guilty party was on a neon pink 'magic' slate. It didn't end there either – even after the in-studio reveal one crucial aspect of the cosmic crime was conspicuously left unresolved so that the Captain could turn to the camera and ask the audience at home, 'So who *was* the saboteur? Why *was* Grazarax in the Munitions Bay?' and – with an enthusiastic entreaty to 'Stay Alert!' – invite them to write in with their theories for a chance to win a S.O.L.V.E. badge of their very own.

Captain Zep's adventures didn't just have a good deal in common with the computer-age escapades seen in near-future sci-fi comics like *2000 AD* and *Eagle* – it actually looked like them too. Through the miracles of modern technology, the Captain and company were superimposed into minimally animated comic strip panel renderings of their past investigations by Paul Birkbeck, with slick transportation shuttles, off-coloured icy yet boiling landscapes and obfuscating aliens in visored helmets. Appropriately, it also came with its own synth-heavy New Wave-styled theme song memorably reassuring everyone that 'across the stars he's on his way, it's Captain Zep to save the day', performed by tail-end punk outfit The Banned under the more appropriate pseudonym 'The Spacewalkers'.

VARIETY AND GAME SHOWS

Although aimed at a Children's BBC audience, *Captain Zep – Space Detective* was very much of a piece with post-BBC Micro sci-fi serials for a family audience, like *The Tripods* and early eighties *Doctor Who*, and in fact even managed to emulate the latter more closely than expected with a surprise change of lead actor. Indicating that Captain Zep was a title rather than a name, Richard Morant took over the lead role from Paul Greenwood partway through the show's run, leading to a heated exchange of opinions about their relative merits on viewer correspondence show *Take Two*.

Surprisingly, despite their ad breaks being full of promotions for Commodore 64 'family starter packs' – in other words, they came bundled with a business spreadsheet application, an Adrian Mole game and a joystick that could be used with precisely neither – it took ITV quite some time to get in on the space puzzle-solving action, and when they did they somehow managed to both copy it too closely and at the same time get it very wrong indeed. With Roger Sloman and later Jim Carter assuming the role of the intergalactic sage from Ulphrates III, and Sylvester McCoy as team-marshalling henchman Wart, *Starstrider* (ITV, 1984–85) took the form of a moodily lit neon and glitter-edged dry ice-swamped intelligence test leading up to a competitive ride on space insect-slanted bucking bronco the Grunderhunter, and guiding a blindfolded team-mate across a multi-shaded grid. *Starstrider* clearly aspired to be mentioned in the same breath as *The Adventure Game* and *Captain Zep – Space Detective*, but it made the mistake of simply replacing the originality and interactivity of both with a handful of suitably outlandish if not altogether convincing alien names. More successfully, Kate Copstick in the guise of modishly Sigue Sigue Sputnik-like cyberpunk rapping android Whizz (BBC1, 1985) and her puppet sidekick Bug enlisted viewers to help them figure out BBC Micro-derived graphical posers. Meanwhile, very much in the same style but utterly discarding the interactive element, *The Galactic Garden* (BBC, 1984) deposited Andrew Sachs and Sarah Neville's visiting miniaturised space travellers around the back of a suburban house for a nose at the native flora and fauna, with plenty of moralising about the ecological thoughtlessness of modern gardeners along the way.

By the late eighties, regardless of whether or not you'd managed to use yours to calculate how to avoid the Vortex, stay balanced on the Grunderhunter or indeed deduce why Grazarax was in the Munitions Bay, it's fair to say that everyone really had made the most of the micro and were looking in bigger and better – and ironically physically smaller – directions. The hot new Christmas presents were the Commodore Amiga and the Atari ST and their new generation of souped-up point-and-click adventure games, secure in the knowledge that there was no way they would be obliged to upgrade to a brand-new dedicated gaming console eighteen months later and then again and again and again every eighteen months after that. Dungeons and Dragons, meanwhile, had somehow shaken off the initial warlock-averse 'satanic panic' to become a huge commercial prospect, even to the extent of inspiring a Hanna-Barbera cartoon series that thanks to the BBC somehow once again became even more popular over here than it was in America. Little dates as quickly as the latest cutting-edge technology, but even so, it'd be nice to see anyone who can finish Sonic the Hedgehog trying to figure out the correct sequence in the Drogna game.

Interlude 2
Look Out for Look-In

Aside from the ever so slightly crucial detail of confirming what programmes were on and when, there was never really that much for younger viewers in either listings magazine. *TV Times* tried out a handful of columns, including the *Magpie*-skewed 'Message from Murgatroyd', but it hardly amounted to essential reading. Meanwhile, *Radio Times* may have afforded slightly more space to John Craven's 'Back Pages', but his profiles on Children's BBC stars and explanations of technical feats were so tightly packed in that you were constantly worried he was going to be cut off mid-sentence.

The year 1971, however, saw the launch of 'Junior *TV Times*', *Look-In*, a feature and pin-up-packed magazine full of strips based on top ITV shows, from *Follyfoot* and *The Tomorrow People* to *Man About the House* and *Mind Your Language*, with huge starstruck features on new and returning series, audience-appropriate pop and sport coverage and eyecatching covers from movie poster artist Arnaldo Putzu. What was more, it also included a two-page scourable grid of child-friendly programming across the ITV regions, leading to widespread curiosity over such tantalisingly localised delights as *Gus Honeybun's Magic Birthdays*, and seething resentment at the fact that everyone else seemed to be getting *Stingray* and you weren't.

Amazingly, it took the BBC until 1985 to get in on the action. *Beeb* was more or less a direct copy of *Look-In*, only with BBC-centric strips, including the confusingly off-script *Grange Hill*, *The Tripods* and *The Family Ness* – not to mention the dull zoo vet-based adult drama *One by One* – rarely exciting cover stars and a faintly out-of-touch *Blue Peter* feel to its attempts at pop and fashion features. It only lasted from January to June.

By the mid-eighties, the writing was on the wall. *Look-In* shifted to a greater emphasis on pop and movie stars before eventually looking out for good in 1994, while in 1989 the BBC launched *Fast Forward* with a series of sense-assaulting adverts led by a multi-million decibel sung repetition of the title and breathless voiceovers from Sophie Aldred. It was more *Going Live!* than *Saturday Superstore* in its approach and, crucially, more like a regular teen magazine with a mild BBC-favouring slant. The days of the junior listings magazine were long gone, but they still live on for anyone who ever wondered what on Earth went on in *Puffin's Pla(i)ce*.

9

Drama

'I want to help you, Ro-land'

Before the 'invention' of 'the teenager', as the old adage famously has it, children were generally dressed as slightly smaller-sized versions of their parents. And as they sat down in their sensible shoes, sleeveless pullovers and frilly pinafore dresses to watch what few examples of drama there were on children's television, they were effectively watching a cut-down version of what their parents would have been watching too. Just as the knock-on effects of rationing had still yet to fully stand back and let your local grocery fill up with all manner of exciting consumer fare, there was correspondingly little money or inclination available to inspire much in the way of child-friendly serials, and much of what little there was simply adapted existing tried and tested literary favourites like *Little Women* (BBC, 1951), *Heidi* (BBC, 1953–59) and *The Silver Sword* (BBC, 1957) using costumes and sets left over from adult productions.

Rare original serials included stranded Martian Biladophorous' E.T.-anticipating bid to avoid detection before he could return home in *Stranger from Space* (BBC1, 1951–52) and the cosmic homework enlivened by animations from *Captain Pugwash* creator John Ryan of *Space School* (BBC, 1956). There was also the uneventful and decidedly non-boisterous family exploits of *The Appleyards*

(BBC, 1952–60), young Lucy's violin-facilitated trips back to incidents of historical family tree chicanery in *The Silver Swan* (BBC, 1953), and the knowing wink-to-camera antics of radio serial star who solved crimes in his spare time *Captain Moonlight – Man Of Mystery* (BBC, 1958–60), but there was barely enough of that to keep younger viewers seen and not heard.

As the sixties approached, however, they were very definitely being seen and heard, with their homemade tea-chest basses and the closest to quiffs that they could get away with short of a fringe-levelling clip round the ear from their 'elders'. The rock'n'roll boom had given a whole generation if not purchase power then certainly pester – and indeed pest – power. What was more, ITV was up and running and although it took a while, and it concentrated its teenager-baiting energies elsewhere, the commercial station still realised that there was money to be made from juvenile obsessions and giving the audience more of what they wanted after seeing it on the big screen, and so everything changed courtesy of a series of Sunday afternoon serials with a dash of Cold War paranoia and a blast of jet fuel.

Leading rocket scientist Professor Norman Wedgewood and his family made their edge-of-the-seat cliffhanging debut when incurably nosey youngest son Jimmy accidentally found himself on board an experimental Moon mission in *Target Luna* (ITV, 1960). During the tense ordeal, the family struck up a close rapport with investigative journalist Conway Henderson, who looked after matters back at ground control while they made a lunar landing and found to their surprise that they hadn't been the first in *Pathfinders in Space* (ITV, 1960), then found themselves diverted in a desperate search for water after a spot of sabotage by delusional scientist Harcourt Brown in *Pathfinders to Mars* (ITV, 1960), and encountered friendly Kiki and her primitive people while trying to rescue a stranded astronaut in *Pathfinders to Venus* (ITV, 1961).

Effectively a junior counterpart to the BBC's massively popular *Quatermass* serials — which were proudly introduced on air as not being 'suitable for children or for viewers of a nervous disposition' — it's difficult to comprehend from this distance just how massive the *Pathfinders* were, but you can get a sense of just how huge the serials were from two programmes that followed in their wake. Conway Henderson's colleague Mark Bannerman got his own spin-off serials, firstly investigating what appeared to be non-human attacks on a nuclear power station in *Plateau of Fear* (ITV, 1961), followed by asking unwelcome questions about events at an underwater research station in *City Beneath the Sea* (ITV, 1962) and *Secret Beneath the Sea* (ITV, 1963). Over at the BBC, several of the *Pathfinders* production team were brought in to work on a new family series about a mysterious time traveller in a police box.

When it came to actual children's drama, however, the BBC may have been spurred into making more of it but preferred to stay very much down to Earth and stick to what they knew, leaving ITV to win the huge audiences and even on occasion headlines with a string of serials that gave younger audiences a very different kind of cut-down version of what their parents were watching. Originally conceived as an adult series, *Object Z* (ITV, 1965) and *Object Z Returns* (ITV, 1966) concerned disagreement-stricken international attempts to deal with a meteorite on a periously close trajectory towards Earth, while *Sierra Nine* (ITV, 1963) followed the titular scientific watchdog task force as they searched for the source of a mind-control signal affecting leading scientists and the truth behind a purported longevity drug.

Captain W.E. Johns' wartime flying ace found himself solving crimes at the behest of Scotland Yard in *Biggles* (ITV, 1960), with Neville Whiting as the newly demobbed James Bigglesworth and 'Johnny Remember Me' chart-topper John Leyton as his sidekick Ginger. Laurence Payne combined walking his bloodhound with well-mannered fisticuffs in a revival of weekly paper private detective *Sexton Blake* (ITV, 1967–71). Youngsters Betsy and Tim set up a 'hotel' for local wild animals in *Badger's Bend* (ITV, 1963–64); and – possibly influenced by *Batman* as much as by *The Famous Five* – Mini, Speedy, Sniffer, Big Bill and the unnicknamed Philippa, collectively known as *The Queen Street Gang* (ITV, 1968), rescued scientists and retrieved inventions from deliberately over-the-top comic strip-style villains.

The Master (ITV, 1966) saw holidaying teenagers Nicky and Paul marooned on a remote Scottish island which doubled as the hideout of a centuries-old telepathic megalomaniac bent on global domination, while most bizarrely of all, *Orlando* (ITV, 1965–68) starred Sam Kydd as a tough part-time criminal, who he had previously played in the primetime adult smuggling drama *Crane*, now fighting the nasty pieces of work he once did 'odd jobs' for with the aid of teenage detectives Steve and Jenny Morgan and 'The Gizzmo', a talisman with apparently genuine magical powers.

Nothing ever quite came as close to replicating the thrills and spills of big-screen action, however, as *Freewheelers* (ITV, 1968–73). Between leaping on and off helicopters and covering their ears from controlled explosions, the rotating trio of modishly mop-haired teenagers and their dynamic Carnaby Street-evoking theme tune acted as the street-level eyes and ears of Ronald Leigh-Hunt's Colonel Buchan. They sought to shield politically sensitive defectors, prevent leftover Nazis from blackmailing the government with weather control devices, and investigate the theft of politically sensitive gold bullion from a cross-channel ferry. It was like a juvenile cross between *Funeral in Berlin* and *Department S* and was, it has to be said, quite some distance from Enid Blyton.

In fairness, the BBC were experimenting with some innovative and in some cases daring ideas. *Paradise Walk* (BBC, 1961) followed West Indian immigrant Sammy as he strove to avoid the temptations of London street crime; and a group of white kids with a penchant for risky daredevil stunts and petty theft had to put their dubious skills to better use exposing the 'real' villains in *A Handful of Thieves* (BBC, 1969). Setting slightly more of a better example, 'four boys, a girl and a printing press' did their bit in unmasking post office swindlers and alerting the authorities to the presence of unexploded wartime bombs in *Adventure Weekly* (BBC, 1968–69).

Meanwhile, ITV was not exactly above doing the odd costume drama such as century-straddling epic *The Flaxton Boys* (ITV, 1969–71), evacuee woe chronicle *Tom Grattan's War* (ITV, 1968–70) and the first of many suitably grim Leon Garfield adaptations in *Devil-In-The-Fog* (ITV, 1968) and *Smith* (ITV, 1970). But despite their budgetary advantage the BBC still managed to routinely trounce them in this area; notably, *The Railway Children* (BBC, 1968), which provided the inspiration for Lionel Jeffries' celebrated 1970 big screen adaptation. A decade is a long time in youth culture, though, and as the seventies burst into colour, ITV was about to take everything into a more spookily post-psychedelic direction.

The Tyrant King (ITV, 1968) wasn't the first children's drama serial to be made entirely in colour — that honour went to adolescent canal boat-delivery travelogue *Flower of Gloster* (ITV, 1967) — but it was the first to wear its kaleidoscopic visuals on its sleeve, complete with a soundtrack dripping with the early prog-rock likes of Pink Floyd, The Moody Blues and The Nice. Adapted from a novel intended to get youngsters interested in using the London Underground to visit museums and other tourist attractions, it drew eye-assaultingly overdressed teenagers Charlotte, Peter and Bill into a web of stolen and smuggled artefacts headed by 'Uncle' Gerry, played with sinisterly camp relish by Murray Melvin, and across a murky landscape of abandoned locks and dilapidated warehouses; it may come as little surprise that director Mike Hodges went on to helm *Get Carter* in 1971.

Hot on its heels came *The Owl Service* (ITV, 1969), based on Alan Garner's 1968 novel about three teenagers who find themselves up against local superstitions and superstitious locals when they stumble across a set of oddly decorated antique plates while holidaying in a remote Welsh village. Shot in eerie rural locations in a quick-cut refractive lens-festooned style that would not have looked out of place in any big-screen freakout of the day – in fact it starred Gillian Hills, no stranger to the artform herself thanks to appearances in the likes of *Blow-Up* (1966) – and decorated with a soundtrack that veered between delicate harp twinkling and roaring motorbike effects, *The Owl Service* was very much intended as a children's serial but was very much windingly rooted in what can only be described a 'folk horror'.

It's certainly a term that could be applied to the legendarily far-out *Ace of Wands* (ITV, 1970–72), a thumpingly psych pop-theme equipped series starring Michael Mackenzie as Tarot, a mysterious snakeskin-jacketed Jim Morrison-alike stage illusionist who solved crimes in his spare time with the aid of his manager Sam, stage assistant Lulli, bookseller friend Mr Sweet and brother and sister photographer and model duo Chas and Mikki. Calling them 'crimes', however, is a little too reductive – their adversaries included Wiccan arms dealer Madame Midnight, embittered telepath Mr Peacock, unhinged doll collector Mama Doc, a troupe of playing card-themed children's entertainers and their schoolkid-hypnotising dummy The Joker, and cadaverous sharp-suited sorcerer Mr Stabs, all of whom seemed more intent on creating mischief for their own personal gain than any grand plans of financial or political power.

Ace of Wands' place in the schedules was later assumed by *The Tomorrow People* (ITV, 1973–79), a proudly glam rock-influenced melange of video age visuals and swooping portamento synth music about the next step in evolutionary progress – a scattering of flare-sporting teenagers with telepathic and telekinetic powers and the ability to teleport, or 'jaunt' as they had it. Working with their sentient computer TIM out of a disused Underground station, in association with the largely unseen Galactic Trig, the 'Homo Superior' had to fend off constant existential threats, including aliens who derived power from dividing humans into warring Blue and Green factions, an intergalactic criminal with an ecology-threatening spaceship about to blast out from beneath a funfair, ill-intended fashion craze 'living skins' and, on one notorious occasion, well-known alien slug Adolf Hitler. Employing a constantly revolving regular cast reflecting the increasingly multicultural makeup of Britain, it perhaps most famously featured Mike Holoway, drummer with teenpop outfit Flintlock, who in one story somehow managed to raise the Devil with their music. Delving back to the actual ancient myths and superstitions themselves, *The Feathered Serpent* (ITV, 1976–78) followed young Tozo's attempts to outwit the murderous progress of power-hungry high priest Nasca in ancient Mexico with dialogue and chicanery straight out of a complex adult thriller.

This conflation of nightmarish visions of the far future, the superstitious past and the decaying present was all over ITV's children's output in the early seventies. Catherine Storr's famously teenage girl-spooking novel *Marianne Dreams* formed the basis for *Escape into Night* (ITV, 1972), the story of an ill girl who finds that her crude and unfinished drawings have a sinister 'existence' in a dreamworld, while sixth-former Martin accidentally tuned in to coded messages from 'The Voice of Truth' plotting to sabotage a nearby airbase in *Tightrope* (ITV, 1972), and teenage potholer Terry stumbled across a murderously sought-after secret formula in *The Jensen Code* (ITV, 1973).

Early ecological plea *Timeslip* (ITV, 1970) adopted a more futuristic approach – albeit a fairly grim one – with chronologically displaced secondary school starters Simon and Liz propelled backwards and forwards through their family history to witness the potentially drought- and ice age-causing effects of miraculous technological innovations and a world overrun by 'useful' clones that nobody could now tell apart from the originals. Perhaps most terrifyingly of all, *The Intruder* (ITV, 1972) focused on an unassuming teenager in a coastal town whose world is suddenly thrown upside down by the arrival of a mysterious stranger claiming to be him, threatening to rob him of his entire identity and family. Played out against a backdrop of a town left behind by modernity and nightmarishly visualised threats of retribution, it does not exactly make for reassuring viewing. On a lighter note, *Jamie* (ITV, 1971) actually got to enjoy whimsical adventures courtesy of a magic carpet he had found in a junk shop, though even he had the disturbingly 'unusual' Mr Zed to contend with.

None of these, however, ever quite managed to come close to a run of deeply strange serials produced by HTV. *Arthur of the Britons* (ITV, 1972–73), starring Oliver Tobias as a grittily historically realistic iteration of King Arthur as a tribal chieftain trying to unite his local rivals – played by such acting heavyweights as Tom Baker and Brian Blessed – was divertingly odd enough even with its pronounced emphasis on sword with no sorcery, but it looked positively traditional compared to what came next. *Doctor Who* writers Bob Baker and Dave Martin, who had contributed some of Arthur's adventures, scored a deeply disturbing hit with *Sky* (ITV, 1974), the saga of a boyish alien entity who had been sent to Earth to assist with its geographical evolution but accidentally arrived in the wrong time zone, causing the elements to try and repel him with extreme force.

Jill Lauriemore's *The Georgian House* (ITV, 1976) propelled two teenage tour guides at an ancestral hall back to the eighteenth century, where they became involved with house servant Ngo, who is relatively well treated but ultimately still a slave. Baker and Martin's *King of the Castle* (ITV, 1977) saw Roland, a public-school boy forced by reduced circumstances into living in a tower block, stumble across a dungeon in the basement where he has to outwit grotesque representations of his real-world bullies to escape; the finished serial was considered so frightening that it was moved to a Sunday afternoon slot in the belief that children were more likely to watch it with their parents then.

Considered by many to be a high watermark in children's television, Jeremy Burnham and Trevor Ray's *Children of the Stones* (ITV, 1977) followed astrophysicist Adam Brake and his teenage son Matthew to Milbury, a small village within a megalithic stone circle, where they find out more about the reports of historically recurring events than anyone had bargained for. Burnham and Ray also created *Raven* (ITV, 1977) for ATV, starring Phil Daniels as a borstal inmate sent to assist with an archaeological excavation of a site earmarked for nuclear waste disposal, discovering a historic personal obligation to save it from destruction.

Broadcaster and prolific writer about 'real life' paranormal phenomena Daniel Farson was responsible for *The Clifton House Mystery* (ITV, 1979), an ingenious serial about a family living in a haunted house that suddenly evolves into a sensationalist television 'mockumentary' partway through. Concluding the tradition in fine style, Bob Baker's hugely popular *Into the Labyrinth* (ITV, 1980–82) plunged teenagers Phil, Helen and Terry into the time-hopping feud between good sorcerer Rothgo and evil sorceress Belor for control of elusive magical power source the Nidus.

You'd think on this evidence that the bar for spooky children's dramas had been set maybe slightly higher than it ought to have been, but surprisingly, there were limits – P.J. Hammond's saga of mysterious element-coded agents repairing damage to the fabric of time, *Sapphire and Steel* (ITV, 1979–82), had been conceived with a similar children's slot in mind, but was very quickly repositioned as an early evening adult serial. Not that it stopped a huge audience of children from watching and then refusing to have their photograph taken after the one with 'The Shape'.

Further post-school scares came with *Come Back Lucy* (ITV, 1978), a chiller about a Victorian phantom with an eye on swapping existence with the present-day girl she had 'befriended'. There was also historical vision-plagued *Echoes of Louisa* (ITV, 1981), and an adaptation of John Wyndham's novel about a boy with an alien 'living' in his mind, *Chocky* (ITV, 1984); it played on more modern paranoias than the original book and led to newly written sequels *Chocky's Children* (ITV, 1985) and *Chocky's Challenge* (ITV, 1987).

Supernaturally themed anthology *Shadows* (ITV, 1975–78), featured a litany of disaster-averting visions from the future, school-work-conveyed messages from Holy Grail-seeking knights, and fixations on bottles rumoured to have once belonged to witches. For those who could make it past the opening titles of weirdly misshapen images, *Shadows* boasted a number of remarkable instalments, including the celebrated 'And For My Next Trick ...', in which Clive Swift's children's entertainer finds that his newly discovered actual magical abilities come at a cost; 'Dutch Schlitz's Shoes', which saw *Ace of Wands* antagonist Mr Stabs run up against a mobster's possessed footwear; and Arthurian origin story which became a series in its own right, *The Boy Merlin* (ITV, 1979) – and it would have an even more significant legacy for Children's ITV as a whole.

What was effectively a further run of *Shadows* – including the infamous 'The Exorcism of Amy', starring Lucy Benjamin as a girl who swaps places with her malevolently obsequious imaginary friend who 'never promised you a happy ending' – ended up becoming the first series of *Dramarama* (ITV, 1983–89), an anthology series made up of a one-off plays in different genres and often with distinct local flavours contributed by every ITV regional broadcaster. Opening with the show's logo shimmering across a theatrical curtain and a spectral vocodered 'sting', *Dramarama* is often remembering for its more horror-aligned entries, such as 1989's mirror universe excursion 'Back to Front' and 1984 time-twin confrontation 'Josephine Jo', not to mention hard-hitting entries like young offender fugitive thriller 'Night on the Narrow Boats' in 1984.

But *Dramarama* could be as funny, as silly, as serious, as satirical and as just plain strange as it wanted. Whether it was spoof superhero farce with 'Mighty Mum and the Petnappers' (1983), rough regional comedy in 'Vencie' (1983), light-hearted fifties nostalgia in 'Rip It Up' (1983), fame industry satire in 'Purple Passion Video' (1985), an exposé of life behind the scenes in television drama production written by a disgruntled *Doctor Who* writer in 'The Comeuppance of Captain Katt' (1986), or the bizarre saga of an ordinary boy finding himself on trial by an assortment of eccentric character actors in 'The Young Person's Guide to Getting Their Ball Back' (1983) and 'The Young Person's Guide to Going Backwards in the World' (1985), you never quite knew what you were going to get with *Dramarama*. And it regularly featured up-and-coming acting talent too – famously, both Peter Capaldi and David Tennant made early appearances in the final run of the show.

Yet another attempt at shoehorning *Mr Stabs* (1984) into his own series sadly came to nothing, but 1984 foster home drama *Dodger, Bonzo and the Rest* (ITV, 1985–86) – often mistakenly referred to as 'Our House' on account of the cast singing the Madness hit as the theme tune – and Bill Oddie's 1988 slab of oddness about a reformed 'meanie' toymaker *The Bubblegum Brigade* (ITV, 1989) both graduated to a full run, while 1988's notably less optimistic 'Blackbird Singing in the Dead of Night' provided the template for the long-running *Children's Ward* (ITV, 1989–2000).

If you were a delicate flower who preferred stories that were often even actually about delicate flowers, you could always find far more reassuring fare in the likes of Bonnie Prince Charlie's historical defender *Redgauntlet* (ITV, 1970); juvenile survivalist expedition *Grasshopper Island* (ITV, 1971); Catherine Cookson's horse-helping *Joe and the Gladiator* (BBC, 1971); birdwatching-themed kidnap mystery *The Long Chase* (ITV, 1972); and Monmouth Rebellion-set attempt at unseating James II *Pretenders* (ITV, 1972).

Then there was the swashbuckling poor-defending exploits of Robert Louis Stevenson's *Black Arrow* (ITV, 1972–75); nineteenth-century riches-to-rags saga *Boy Dominic* (ITV, 1974–76); the light-hearted lives and loves and accusations of spying levelled at the inhabitants of *Rogue's Rock* (ITV, 1974–76); genteel adaptations of *The Secret Garden* (BBC, 1975) and *Ballet Shoes* (BBC, 1975); mill workers' rights protest chronicle *Midnight Is a Place* (BBC, 1977); colour-in-cheeks occasioning seabound secret weapon theft saga *The Doombolt Chase* (ITV, 1978); and the more sedate chronologically displaced stories of the Mary Queen of Scots-aiding *A Traveller in Time* (BBC, 1978).

Inevitably, on account of the enduring myth that all girls are obsessed with horses, there were also plenty of equine-themed dramas, from *The Adventures of Black Beauty* (ITV, 1972–73) – which, in fairness, did make a lone excursion into spooky territory with a much-playground mythologised episode about some lost treasure and a ghostly monk – to the almost inadvertently comically implausible *Horse in the House* (ITV, 1977–79). Although there was one series that made the jump over the well-hooved norm: *Follyfoot* (ITV, 1971–73) followed tousle-haired wayward teenager Dora as she was sent to help out on her uncle's prestigious stud farm, famed for its 'lightning tree' that kept growing after being sizzled in a storm. The aim was for her to straighten out her prog rock and motorcycle-admiring ways, and she found more in common with her co-workers – class-disgruntled miner's son Steve, shadily connected biker Ron and bluff veteran 'Slugger' – than she had in her privileged family background. Introduced by The Settlers' gallopingly dramatic hit theme song 'Lightning Tree', *Follyfoot* dealt subtly but unflinchingly with social and political issues of the day, including early retorts to the entitled behaviour of monied ruralists and advocating for animal rights. For 'boys', *The Flockton Flyer* (ITV, 1977–78) recorded the Carter family's attempts to gain permission to reopen a local steam railway line, and *God's Wonderful Railway* (BBC, 1980) followed several generations of a railway-working family very slowly from the line's construction in the Victorian era to its temporary wartime closure. Heartwarming and nostalgic it may have been – well, apart from the episode where an evacuee was taken ill after eating a 'fungus thing' – but there were also harsher realities out there, and some of the audience clearly wanted to see them reflected.

In amongst numerous grittier offerings, *The Runaway Summer* (BBC, 1971) involved children secretly sheltering an illegal immigrant from Kenya, while *Striker* (BBC, 1975–76) revolved around a talented footballer from a single-parent family whose father forbade him from playing, and *Kizzy* (BBC, 1976) tackled prejudice against a Romani girl who relocates to a smalltown community. The hard as nails *Rocky O'Rourke* (BBC, 1976) took place in a dockland world of street crime and frayed flared trouser cuffs, and *The Kids from 47a* (ITV, 1973–74) learned to fend for themselves when their mother was taken into hospital. Local council corruption and intimidation spurred a gang of teenagers who'd had enough into mounting *The Siege of Golden Hill* (ITV, 1975); a tough Mancunian boy and a misfit Czech refugee witnessed a murder in *Soldier and Me* (ITV, 1974); and *Westway* (ITV, 1976) focused on the experiences of the younger members of a post-hippiedom commune.

Enid Blyton's square-jawed do-gooders *The Famous Five* (ITV, 1978–79) were brought daringly up to date in a world of cagoules, tracksuit tops and dropped aitches for a hugely popular series of lavish filmed adventures. Julian, Dick and Anne, George and Timmy the dog even had their own rowdy cast-sung stomping pop theme, and it would have continued for longer but when they had adapted all of the original novels, the Blyton estate declined to allow the producers to come up with their own further adventures.

Most strikingly, *The Changes* (BBC, 1976), with a chugging German synth band-inspired soundtrack, was ostensibly a thriller about the population experiencing an unexplained compulsion to destroy machines, but the equally inexplicably immune heroine Nicky found herself joining forces with a similarly unaffected Sikh family, whose culture and religion were depicted both as a default background detail and in a subtle and positive light.

All of these shows, however, were honestly just clearing the path for a children's television drama that divided children and parents like no other. Created by *The Kids from 47a*'s writer Phil Redmond, *Grange Hill* (BBC, 1978–2008) was set in a tough North London comprehensive school, with a thoroughly realistic ethnically diverse assortment of pupils ranging from academically promising go-getters to those whose parents couldn't afford a uniform, and teachers ranging from strict traditionalist disciplinarians to trendy modern Open University types, with the odd sadistic P.E.-teaching bully boy thrown in for good measure – and that's where its problems started.

In no mood to do anything other than accurately reflect the schoolday-to-schoolday experiences of a huge proportion of the audience, Redmond fought to show the ups and downs of school life in as simultaneously a dramatic and dull manner as he could possibly get away with, which made *Grange Hill* an instant flashpoint for complaints and concerns about taste and decency. Endless column inches were devoted to either side of the argument, and the show was more than once very nearly taken off after the volume of objections became too great to ignore, and all the while the audience kept watching in their millions – or at least some of them did. It was not unusual when visiting a friend's house to be grilled on whether you were 'allowed' to watch *Grange Hill* at home.

The ingenuity of *Grange Hill*'s format was that the cast literally grew up with the viewers, allowing the characters to deal with maturing emotional and social concerns as they moved up a year while also opening the door to a new younger incoming audience as a fresh register of first years was taken. Well-intentioned mischief maker Tucker Jenkins and his gang Alan Humphries, Tommy Watson and Benny Green, and their rivalry with mouthy Trisha Yates and wannabe gangster Michael Doyle, taunting of weedy sap Justin Bennett and attempts to evade corridor-roaming 'nutjob' Booga Benson would progress up the educational ladder – with some difficulty in some cases – to make way for future favourites. These included wheeler-dealers Pogo Patterson, Gonch Gardener and Freddie Mainwaring; school heartthrobs Stewpot Stewart, Claire Scott, Annette Firman and Ant Jones; rule-flouting rebels Suzanne Ross and Danny Kendall; public-spirited wide boy Banksie Banks; good girls tempted by bad behaviour Fay Lucas, Julie Merchant, Cally Donnington, Laura Regan and Julia Glover; scouse joker Ziggy Greaves; and many more favourites than it would be possible to list here.

Meanwhile, no-nonsense headmistress Mrs McCluskey presided over an often-irreconcilable roster of staff, ranging from strong-armed firm but fair P.E. teacher 'Bullet' Baxter to dishevelled left-wing modern schoolmaster 'Scruffy' McGuffy and the legendary Mr Bronson, an anachronistic leftover from a merger with local private school Rodney Bennett, whose furious shouts of 'KEN-DALL!' reverberate to this day. Bronson did, however, go out of his way to encourage pupils he felt had potential even if nobody else could see it, including passionate political activist Ronnie Birtles and overweight target for bullies Roland Browning, whose shy inarticulacy as he was pursued around the playground by constantly rebuffed would-be friend Janet St Clair, who endearingly called him 'Ro-land', masked a genuine gift for the French language.

Another reason why *Grange Hill* and complaints were never far away from each other came with its willingness to tackle hard-hitting and often shocking and brutal issues. Whether it was violent abuse meted out in the classroom by sadistic Mr Hicks, a shoplifting contest attracting the attentions of the police, Antony Karamanopolis' fall from a high wall after a dare, Jeremy Irving coming a cropper while showing off in the swimming pool, a grim encounter with a man on the common after a bus conductor refused to allow any *Grange Hill* pupils on board, or – most famously – a contentious but thoroughly necessary storyline in which previously innocent mischief-maker Zammo Maguire was discovered to be using heroin, the show continually pushed past the line of acceptability with the purpose of opening up important points of debate.

Unrepentant racist bully Gripper Stebson found that while some pupils were intimidated by him, others including Randir Singh, Precious Matthews and Glenroy Glenroy were more than prepared to physically stand up to him, leading to some surprisingly violent scenes. In contrast, Imelda Davies' all-girl gang – Georgina Hayes, Helen Kelly and Sharon Burton – were initially introduced as a straightforward squadron of bullies, but it soon became clear that Imelda had deeper issues stemming from her neglected home life and was beyond reason or control. This culminated in the gang turning on her when they felt she had gone too far even for them, Imelda being sent to a school for children with psychological needs, and on a more positive note Helen emerging as an aspirant engineer arguing that she should be allowed to do work experience that had been reserved for boys.

Grange Hill may have traumatised some viewers, but it did so with the best of intentions and in any case, there were always more than enough humorous interludes to compensate for it, from Gonch getting one over on would-be bully Trevor Cleaver with his 'walled-up ghost' hoax to Freddie Mainwaring on a school trip being reduced to wearing an Aran sweater and wellies after one mud-bound tumble in flashy clothes too many. Whether politicians and parents liked it or not, *Grange Hill* was all things to all viewers, and while the writing wasn't exactly on Danny Kendall's 'Speaking Wall' for traditional drama, it was certainly emblematic of a pronounced change and a willingness to go much darker.

Around the same time as *Grange Hill* first opened its gates, the Kraftwerk-soundtracked *Out of Bounds* (BBC, 1977) saw two teenage gymnastic champions caught up in a plot to hush up an armed robbery; Lesley Manville and Jamie Foreman starred as sixth formers who started a school newspaper with an emphasis on investigative journalism in *A Bunch of Fives* (ITV, 1977–78); and *Noah's Castle* (ITV, 1979) tapped into contemporary paranoia with an ordinary family uprooted into a life of heavily fortified self-sufficiency ahead of the economic breakdown their father was convinced was coming.

The Latchkey Children (ITV, 1980) plotted to prevent the council from replacing the one tree on their estate with a sculpture; eleven-year-old Patsy went on the run from her abusive stepfather in *Break in the Sun* (BBC, 1981) penned by novelist Bernard Ashley; Billy Staynton took a slightly less traumatic journey across Europe in search of his real parents in *Barriers* (ITV, 1981); real-life chart star Hazel O'Connor played schoolgirl club singer Joanne in *Jangles* (ITV, 1982); and fifteen-year-old Bella enlisted her creative friends to turn about the fortunes of *The All-Electric Amusement Arcade* (ITV, 1983).

With a theme song from local art-rock heroes Renaissance, Gog, Baz, Ian, J.G. and fiercely feminist paper lass Sam wrestled mid-round with everything from being asked to move furniture for old ladies to interrupting a burglar, being mugged for their subs money and the machinations of 'evil' paper boy Neville *in The Paper Lads* (ITV, 1977–79), while *Murphy's Mob* (ITV, 1982–85) charted the efforts of third division-dwelling Dunmore United's manager Mac Murphy to keep the team's teenage fans, who he felt responsible for, on the straight and narrow. The constant cliffhangers involving barking guard dogs, the snarly prospectlessness-decrying punk theme song ('Everywhere you go, everything you see, someone's saying no – it's a tragedy!') by Gary Holton, and the graffiti-strewn walls in the closing titles – astonishingly blithely including swastikas and a naked woman – probably indicate how much of a struggle he had on his hands. On a lighter seafront-based note, teenager Sandy and her sardonic younger brother George moved with their parents to run Blackpool guest house *Seaview* (BBC, 1983–85), striking up an unlikely close friendship with local ne'er-do-well James as they sought to adjust to their new surroundings via a string of money-making schemes taking in Saturday jobs, non-starting pop groups and political protests, all of which invariably collapsed into farce. Unusually, their parents were not depicted as stern authority figures who didn't 'get' it, but as still young enough to understand – if not sympathise with – their children's obsessions, as well as causing a fair few local headaches of their own.

There was of course still lighter fare around if you preferred, courtesy of the seemingly unending saga of a trio of brothers living in the 'wilds' in the grounds of *Brendon Chase* (ITV, 1980); displaced turn-of-the-century pit community boy turned rural ingénue *Andy Robson* (ITV, 1982–83), with its misleadingly dynamic theme song from B.A. Robertson and Barbara Dickson; Peter Bowles in a new take on the original body-swap comedy *Vice Versa* (ITV, 1981); lavish historical drama *Moonfleet* (BBC, 1984); and a charming and much-loved adaptation of Clive King's 1963 novel *Stig of the Dump*

(ITV, 1981), with an affectingly comic turn from Keith Jayne as the caveboy flung forward in time.

Blitz Spirit high jinks led to a moral dilemma over how to morally deal with a downed German pilot in *The Machine Gunners* (BBC, 1983), and *The Baker Street Boys* (BBC, 1983) looked to Sherlock Holmes' oft-overlooked network of street-urchin informants to investigate the mysteries of the Winged Scarab and the Disappearing Dispatch Case, much to the consternation of Inspector Lestrade. Deaf and dumb mining community orphan *Our John Willie* (BBC, 1980) and Welsh wartime evacuee *Joni Jones* (BBC, 1982) both found themselves pelted with language barrier-facilitated insults by unfriendly locals, using terms that while not exactly explicit, certainly would not have been used within earshot of a teacher, but there was little in them to cause much in the way of real consternation.

Otherwise, however, something had definitely shifted in a more down-to-earth direction. Wheelchair-user *Letty* (ITV, 1984) fancied herself as an amateur detective in the fashion of a recent spate of down-at-heel television private eyes, and *The Boy Who Won the Pools* (ITV, 1983) – sixteen-year-old Rodney Baverstock – had to learn how to temper his compulsion to go on a spending spree with a desire to help out his friends, promising soul singer Sami and electronics genius with a dream of becoming 'bionic' Thornton. The decidedly odd *Running Loose* (ITV, 1986–88) was a semi-scripted drama about inner city kids on an outward-bound holiday presented as a mock fly-on-the-wall reality show, while the light tone of stolen gargoyle runaround *The Witches and Grinnygog* (ITV, 1983) masked a dark tale of historical retribution for religious persecution.

Presented as 'files' rather than episodes, *Dead Entry* (BBC, 1987) tied the home computing boom into a Cold War-instigated assassination plot, while Jeannie Tanner withstood her father's fury at her aspirations to live like 'the city tart' in *White Peak Farm* (BBC, 1988), and prim and proper middle-class schoolgirl Kate had her spoilt rotten status thrown into upheaval by the return of her abducted-as-a-baby older sister Rosie, now a surly punk with a tendency towards East End vulgarities, in *The Cuckoo Sister* (BBC, 1986). *Running Scared* (BBC, 1986) was a Kate Bush-soundtracked thriller about two girls who know more about a local villain's mid-crime mislaid glasses – or 'bins', which the Broom Cupboard presenters had to explain to confused viewers – than was good for their health. And unlikely geographically displaced friends-in-need Alex and Afis formed a united bond against local trouble-causers in *Sticks and Stones* (BBC, 1986). Both refused to shy away from having their racist characters use racist terminology.

Thankfully, comic respite could be found in *Wonders in Letterland* (ITV, 1985), a quirky serial about a young girl called Jenny trapped inside a board game in a dusty old toy shop, which introduced viewers to Elizabeth Estensen as time-hopping pettily motivated sorceress Tabatha Bag – or T-Bag for short. Part alternative comedy, part panto and part interactive puzzle solving, their escapades were an immediate hit and, with the less than reliable assistance of her reluctant sidekick T-Shirt, who usually ended up siding with Jenny and later her replacement Sally, T-Bag continued her quest for long-lost mystical artefacts that could increase her magic abilities across *T-Bag Strikes Again* (ITV, 1986), *T-Bag Bounces Back* (ITV, 1987), *Turn-On to T-Bag* (ITV, 1988), *T-Bag's Christmas Cracker* (ITV, 1988), *T-Bag and the Revenge of the T-Set* (ITV, 1989) and *T-Bag's Christmas Carol* (ITV, 1989).

Georgina Hale took over as her sister Talulah Bag for *T-Bag and the Pearls of Wisdom* (ITV, 1990), *T-Bag's Christmas Ding-Dong* (ITV, 1990), *T-Bag and the Rings of Olympus* (ITV, 1991), *T-Bag's*

Christmas Turkey (ITV, 1991), *T-Bag and the Sunstones of Montezuma* (ITV, 1992) and *Take Off with T-Bag* (ITV, 1992), and doubtless would have continued with her gloriously futile quest if Thames Television had not lost their franchise.

Similarly comedic supernatural adventure with an absurdist twist could be found in *C.A.B.* (ITV, 1986–89), in which aspirant schoolkid secret agents Colin and Franny delved into a world of coded messages and stolen ancient Egyptian artefacts. *Jossy's Giants* (BBC, 1986–87) followed the fortunes of retired footballing hero Jossy Blair as he takes over as manager of local youth team the Glipton Grasshoppers, a rag-tag assortment of yobs, wheeler-dealers and aspirant punks needing a push in the right direction, which invariably came through implausible comic mishaps that Victor Meldrew would have found difficult to credit. Introduced by a terrace chant theme song declaring that 'football's just a branch of science', it was a remarkable series that managed to combine the age-old saga of triumph over adversity with the otherwise overlooked shared absurdity that bonds youth teams and organisations together and some believable footballing action. Hardly surprisingly, it was hugely popular, and it was probably only the advancing ages of the frankly irreplaceable cast that prevented it from continuing further.

In fact, children's television drama in the eighties wasn't quite as far removed from the Wedgewood family's black-and-white alarmed stares at something conveniently off-camera as it might have appeared at first glance. The young audience still had the same need to be entertained and enthralled as they had always done, and arguably it was now being catered for more effectively and prolifically than ever, with a huge number of serials making a correspondingly huge impact with deft use of modern broadcast technology. Arguably none of them made quite as much of an impression as an adaptation of Helen Creswell's *Moondial* (BBC, 1988), awkwardly broadcast in close proximity to another adaptation of her almost identical if somewhat lighter *The Secret World of Polly Flint* (ITV, 1987). Starring Siri Neal as Araminta Kane, a well-to-do girl left to her own devices when being looked after by relatives while her mother was ill, and finding herself having to 'fix' damage to time, against the express wishes of the sinister and apparently time-averse Miss Raven – a chilling turn from Hammer veteran Jacqueline Pearce – it seemed to strike as much of a chord for its early digital effects and disturbing atmosphere as for its actual dramatic content; so, even only a couple of years after *The Box of Delights*, it became a new benchmark to measure children's drama by. Though it didn't stay one for long.

Inspired by the freewheeling dialogue and offbeat mystery-solving of the current big adult hit drama show *Moonlighting*, a schoolteacher named Steven Moffat created a series based around a junior local newspaper staffed by 'problem' pupils from the nearby school. Driven by the dynamic interplay between Julia Sawalha as the bossy and bullying editor Lynda Day and Dexter Fletcher as disruptive hoodlum turned reporter Spike Thomson, *Press Gang* (ITV, 1989–93) didn't have any flashy proto-CGI effects, and it handled even its most hard-hitting storylines in a less brutal yet more effective manner than *Grange Hill*, but it had something that children's television drama had never quite really had before but would have a good deal more of in the future – it was better than pretty much anything their parents were watching.

'In my box of such delights'

What every youngster secretly wants from a gripping adventure serial is a central figure they can relate to – and they used to be in shorter supply in children's television than you might think. Adult characters you can aspire towards being, but it's that much harder to actually put yourself in their adult-sized shoes, especially when you don't share a hidden past with a secret organisation who want you back for just one last little job. Children, on the other hand, pose problems entirely of their own. They would in theory be so much easier to relate to, but that theoretical conclusion doesn't account for their tendency to be inconsistently acted, ridicule-invitingly posh, kitted out in the sort of clothes you'd have nightmares about being made to wear, and frustratingly prone to hanging around in ornamental gardens hoping for something to happen. It's small wonder that so many found themselves instead taken with American action serials about retired detectives with every conceivable variety of talking vehicle.

There was one serial, however, in which the nominal hero was a well-spoken and well-to-do boy crowbarred into an old-fashioned and uncomfortable-looking school uniform and did more than his fair share of standing around in the grounds of grand buildings, but it was smart, sceptical, rational and practical, poked fun at his own outdated vernacular idioms – even if our hero did consider more or less any minor inconvenience to be 'the purple pim' – and was brilliantly acted as well. It was equally brilliantly written and directed, and boasted state-of-the-art visual effects and music, and later came to be routinely cited as one of the best television shows ever made. The hero was Kay Harker, and this was *The Box of Delights*.

A sequel to his 1927 children's novel *The Midnight Folk*, John Masefield's tale of festive sorcery and clandestine scrobbling plots *The Box of Delights* was first published in 1935. The BBC first adapted it as a six-part serial in the Home Service's 'Children's Hour' in the run-up to Christmas in 1943, with Robert Holland's scripts given a freshly seasonal re-performance in both 1948 and 1955. It was then adapted by John Keir Cross in 1966 — and repeated in 1968, 1969 and 1977 — for a Christmas Eve edition of *Saturday Night Theatre*, with a new adaptation by Howard Jones following in 1974, by which time the Home Service had become Radio 4, in a festive edition of the children's show *4th Dimension*. As much as all of this may have confirmed that *The Box of Delights* was already a firm favourite with audiences and with the BBC, it also suggested that children's radio was not really moving with changing times. Over on children's television, though, it was a different story, and new faces and new innovations were already taking their drama output in a very different direction.

Director Renny Rye had joined the BBC in the mid-seventies, originally working on location shoots for *Rentaghost* and filmed inserts for *Blue Peter* before taking over as the latter's producer and later assistant editor while continuing to direct adult dramas, including an adaptation of H.E. Bates' *A Moment in Time* in 1979, early eighties RAF-based serial *Squadron*, and BBC2's early evening teen drama *Maggie*.

Paul Stone, meanwhile, had been working as an artist on *Jackanory* since the late sixties, but in 1971 he was given the opportunity to direct a serial that certainly gave ITV's outlandishly spooky contemporaneous offerings a run for their money. Adapted from Peter Dickinson's recently released novel, and with music from the BBC Radiophonic Workshop's John Baker, *Mandog* (BBC, 1972) concerned a group of children who stumble across a refugee from the future who has accidentally transferred his consciousness into their family dog. A good deal more serious and sinister than that might make it sound, with the unlikely allies — one of whom, unusually for the time, was a wheelchair user — pursued across run-down urban locations, *Mandog* was followed by the slightly lighter adventures of *Lizzie Dripping* (BBC, 1973–75), and in 1974 by one of the sort of literary adaptations that the BBC truly excelled at. Nina Bawden's 1973 story of wartime evacuees caught up in rumours of a curse on a Welsh village, *Carrie's War* (BBC, 1974), became a compellingly intimate and eerie serial driven by an affecting performance from Juliet Waley, and it was so widely acclaimed that the tie-in paperback cover remained in place well into the nineties. It was around this time that Paul Stone first began to have aspirations towards making a children's drama serial to better all others, and there was only ever one book he had in mind for this – *The Box of Delights*.

That anyone working in the BBC Children's department around this time should have harboured such grand ambitions should hardly come as a surprise. Each major production seemed to edge ever further forward whether in terms of visual or dramatic innovation, and in 1976 they had begun an unofficial tradition of a serial in the lead-up to Christmas with a supernatural or science-fiction slant or a leaning towards gritty realism tempered by triumph over the odds – and even on occasion all three. *The Phoenix and the Carpet* (BBC, 1976) took E. Nesbit's genteel 1904 tale of good deeds performed with the aid of a mythical bird and a flying carpet and gave it an unexpected abrasive edge by adding garish flame effects, archaically formal and often atonal music and a politely spoken but far from adorable puppet Phoenix, scoring a huge success and setting an impressive template for what followed.

King Cinder (BBC, 1977) pitted juvenile leads Peter Duncan and Lesley Manville against local heavies in a grim tale of corruption on the speedway circuit, incorporating literally gritty motorcycle races and chases and a crunching heavy-ish metal soundtrack. Sarah Sutton took the lead in *The Moon Stallion* (BBC, 1978), a deeply allegorical tale of a blind girl able to sense the presence of a spectral horse on the Wiltshire moors and finds herself a conduit for pagan deities warning about the advance of technology over nature. *The Enchanted Castle* (BBC, 1979) took an even more refined and undramatic E. Nesbit tale of reality-hopping children and added a surreal feel more in tune with *Blue Peter* 'makes' than cutting-edge visual trickery, with the cardboard plate-faced Ugly-Wuglies causing many a sleepless night for easily unsettled viewers.

L.T. Meade's Victorian status-swap tale of a lost fifty-pound note accidentally stitched inside a dress, *A Little Silver Trumpet* (BBC, 1980), had been out of print for several decades and was virtually forgotten, until a viewer who had enjoyed *The Moon Stallion* wrote in to suggest it for a similar serial. *Codename Icarus* (BBC, 1981) recruited an awkward teenage maths prodigy into a school for 'gifted' children covertly operating as a development scheme for new weapons technology intended to provide leverage in the Cold War, posing numerous questions about who the real villains were along the way. *Break Point* (BBC, 1982) opted for a more positive culture-clash comedy of manners about aspirant teenage tennis aces; the cast were actually selected on the basis of their personality while whacking a couple of balls around on a local court, with novice Jane Pearson going on to win a few tournaments herself. In 1983, though, there was a repeat of *Carrie's War* in lieu of a new serial – and it turned out that there was good reason for this.

Back when *Carrie's War* was actually in production, the rights to *The Box of Delights* had been tied up in a proposed movie version that ultimately never happened, and it took the best part of a decade to extricate and renegotiate them. In the meantime, Paul Stone had continued directing other literary adaptations, including an ambitious full-size staging of Roald Dahl's *James and the Giant Peach*

THE GOLDEN AGE OF CHILDREN'S TV

(BBC, 1976), Nina Bawden's rural porcine farce *The Peppermint Pig* (BBC, 1977) and Leon Garfield's inappropriately jaunty tale of two Victorian boys who decided to see if a baby really can be raised by wolves, *The Strange Affair of Adelaide Harris* (BBC, 1979), before becoming a producer – and one of his first projects marked his first direct collaboration with Renny Rye.

Since 1968, the BBC had been running a series of acclaimed and suitably chilling and macabre literary adaptations under the banner 'A Ghost Story for Christmas'; these were intended for an adult audience who were assuredly not of a nervous disposition, and very much fuel for vain begging to be allowed to 'stay up', but in the early eighties Children's BBC had a go at presenting a couple of not altogether that much less spooky seasonal plays of their own. Adapted from Penelope Lively's novel about the theft of a chalice that supposedly protected a village from the bubonic plague, *The Bells of Astercote* (BBC, 1980) was produced by Anna Home and directed by Marilyn Fox. But Paul Stone took over as producer for Leon Garfield's tale of a runaway Victorian boy searching the back streets of London for the truth about his father's fate, *John Diamond* (BBC, 1981), and was joined by Renny Rye for Edward Chitham's *Ghost in the Water* (BBC, 1982), a superbly chilling and gloomy – and wet – story of a Victorian girl trying to clear her name from an officially recorded suicide verdict via spectral contact with a present-day teenager. Not long after its New Year's Eve broadcast, the call that Paul Stone had been hoping for finally came through.

It was at Children's department Head Edward Barnes' suggestion that Renny Rye was brought in to direct *The Box of Delights*, but when he first read Alan Seymour's adaptation of Kay Harker's efforts to protect a magic box entrusted to him by Punch and Judy man Cole Hawlings – which allowed the holder to 'go swift' or 'go small' – from the sinister attentions of possibly inauthentic clergyman Abner Brown, his reaction was mild terror at the thought of having to recreate the elaborate imagery in any sort of convincing form, especially as much of it involved live animals. Fortunately, everyone involved was determined to do the novel justice, and an enormous amount of time, money and patience for a children's programme was afforded to the serial.

The production team resolved to assemble a cast that was both heavyweight and entirely suited to the tone of the piece, with everyone perfectly suited to their part, from Patrick Troughton's warm and twinkly turn as Cole Hawlings, Robert Stephens – who agreed to take the part after a post-panto 'audition' with Rye in a theatre bar – imbuing Abner Brown with a sense of genuine menace and measured fury, and Patricia Quinn's deliriously cacklingly villainous Sylvia Daisy Pouncer, all the way to Joanna Dukes as gangster-fixated tomboy Maria Jones, Bill Wallis' cocky and snivelling Rat, and Geoffrey Larder and Jonathan Stephens as creepy yet cowardly henchmen Foxy-Faced Charles and Chubby Joe. Devin Stanfield, recently seen in a key supporting role in *Chocky*, won the part of Kay Harker largely on account of his ability to react convincingly to the unseen during production wonders within the box, but he proved every bit as good an actor as the more experienced adult leads, playing Kay as assured and cool-headed but aware that the grown-ups were not going to take him seriously, thus giving the young audience someone that they could strongly relate to.

A similar amount of care and attention was devoted to the visual effects, carefully blending traditional theatrical illusions with drawn animation and inventive use of Quantel, a video manipulation system mainly used by the Current Affairs department but which could also be adapted to create convincing flight and miniaturisation effects.

Everyone concerned later reflected that if the rights had become available even just a couple of years earlier, it would simply not have been possible to create such a powerfully effective visual realisation – although even they had to admit defeat when it came to the novel's depiction of flaming spectral horses and a passage where Kay crosses the ocean on the back of a pack of dolphins. Even so, production was not without its problems, and projected location filming in Aberdeen ran into problems when the expected heavy snowfall failed to materialise. At considerable expense, arrangements were made for the BBC's artificial snow-making machine to be brought to Scotland, only for it to find itself halted en route by a blizzard.

There was one other crucial element that helped to elevate *The Box of Delights* even above the high standards set by BBC drama as a whole. Roger Limb had been with the BBC Radiophonic Workshop since 1972 and been contributing regularly to children's programmes ever since, including the foreboding combination of synth drones and cello that accompanied *Ghost in the Water*. For *The Box of Delights*, he used a similar if more upbeat combination of modern electronica and traditional baroque and early music instrumentation and influences with many of the musical motifs based on traditional Christmas carols.

For the theme music, the production team selected an existing recording that had as good as been hanging around in the Children's department looking for its moment. Conductor Barry Rose and the Pro Arte Orchestra's 1966 HMV recording of Victor Hely-Hutchinson's 'The Carol Symphony' – a collection of orchestral elaborations on traditional festive tunes, itself originally composed for a 1927 BBC Radio broadcast – was rapturously received on its original release and became a much-requested seasonal favourite with Radio 3 listeners. It also clearly had its fans within the Children's department, as extracts – more often than not from the section based around 'The First Nowell' – could be heard in the background of children's programmes throughout the seventies, including in editions of *Play School*, *Jackanory*, *Blue Peter* and *Think of a Number*. A different recording had also been used for the 1943 BBC Radio adaptation of *The Box of Delights*, and for this new version, Roger Limb made some minor modifications to bring it more in line with the tone of the production, and added effective opening and closing flourishes to emphasise the cliffhangers and recaps. Combined with the opening titles showing various characters shimmering in and out of view against a starry wintery night sky, it was little short of a triumph, and when it was released as a single – albeit without Limb's embellishments – it went on to become one of BBC Records and Tapes' biggest ever sellers.

Broadcast on Wednesdays from 21 November, with the final instalment going out on Christmas Eve just as the assembled characters raced to Midnight Mass to foil Abner Brown's last desperate plot, *The Box of Delights* was an instant smash and drew in a much larger audience than might have been expected for the timeslot. It was considered a prestige production and very much treated as one, with a barrage of publicity that ranged from an almost unprecedented *Radio Times* cover to an in-character Devin Stanfield 'flying' on to the *Blue Peter* set on wires, where he was joined by the ordinarily publicity-averse Patrick Troughton, who was clearly proud enough of the results to sidestep his reclusive tendency on this occasion.

It wasn't quite perfect – there were points, notably a lengthy animated sequence where Kay joins Herne the Hunter in a changing series of animal forms, that seemed to have been included as a spectacle rather than because they in any way advanced the narrative; a lengthy scene in which the local police inspector outlines how to make the 'posset' he believes will rid Kay of his fanciful delusions may be much loved now but simply appeared ridiculous to its target audience at the time; and the sudden appearance of characters like the bronze Head and the fortune-telling boy pegged under a waterfall who were given more background in *The Midnight Folk*; not to mention the lack of context for Kay's enmity with Sylvia Daisy Pouncer, can prove baffling – but frankly being perfect would have been to its detriment. *The Box of Delights* was intended from the outset as a high watermark for BBC children's drama, and to avoid its usual quirks and eccentricities would have denied it much of the charm, ambition and willingness to try even if the results didn't always work. It is difficult to imagine *The Box of Delights* being so spellbinding and so effectively evocative of the thrill leading up to Christmas if it didn't have a character entirely of its own.

It was nonetheless sufficiently perfect, however, to win BAFTAs for Best Children's Programme, Best Videotape Editor and Best Lighting, as well as nominations in the Video Cameraman and Graphics categories, and a Royal Television Society award for Technique.

With an overhaul of Children's BBC's output in progress – and everyone involved probably needing a bit of a breather – there was no new serial in the traditional slot in 1985, replaced instead by Depression-era Australian drama *Colour in the Creek*. In 1986, however, they came very close to matching *The Box of Delights*. Adapted from Lucy M. Boston's 1954 novel, *The Children of Green Knowe* told the gentle story of Toseland 'Tolly' Oldknow, a schoolboy obliged to spend the Christmas holidays at the family manor house with a great grandmother he has never met; 'Granny' Oldknow proves to be just as young in spirit as he is, and they take great delight in a shared secret – they can see, and communicate with, a trio of children who grew up in the house during the Restoration. They are not so much ghosts as a collision of echoes through time, and other than Tolly's superstitious wariness of Green Noah, a bent and knotted 'demon tree' in the grounds, there is little in the way of high drama or peril, but it triumphs on the strength of its atmosphere and warmth and the winning performances of Alec Christie and Daphne Oxenford in the lead roles.

Aliens in the Family (BBC, 1987) intentionally went in a very different direction with the cliffhanging saga of a young alien named Bond, sent to Earth on a training mission with the sinister sunken-faced 'Wirdegens' on his trail and with only his sister Solita's voice intermittently issuing from a radio to help them. Adopting the form of a teenage girls' magazine-friendly model – after rejecting those of Daley Thompson, Morten Harket and Michael Jackson – he stumbles across a family of recently shunted together step-siblings who elect to help him when they can find time between shouting at each other; indeed, in one notorious exchange very much in line with the baffling trend for including 'shock' moments in Children's BBC drama, a very restrained catfight between girly girl Dora and psychobilly cowgirl Jake culminates in the retort, 'At least I don't daub myself with Gro-Bust!'

Packed with slightly more relatable teenage references and name-checks for pop and movie stars ('Solita?' – 'Nah, mate, it's Kim Wilde!'), *Aliens in the Family* was very much an indication of the direction that Children's BBC was aiming to move in. *The Watch House* (BBC, 1988) covered more traditional ground with the tale of fifteen-year-old Anne, whose helping out at the local lighthouse to take her mind off her parents' divorce leads her to unravelling an age-old mystery and fighting for historical justice for spectral seadogs Henry 'The Old Feller' Cookson and Scobie Hague. Far less traditional, *Billy's Christmas Angels* (BBC, 1988) did manage to avoid both profanity and outright threats of violence, but given that it concerned a boy bargaining with local criminals to recover his older brother's pawned electric guitar, and who was guided on his quest by acapella troupe The Mint Juleps singing Bruce Springsteen songs, it was still very much in step with everything else that was going on, and in some ways suggested that the days of the spooky advent-straddling serial were literally numbered. The following year, ongoing youth club drama *Byker Grove* – a show that Dora and Jake could probably have just about agreed on – arrived, and that was pretty much that.

Renny Rye and Paul Stone worked together again on *The December Rose* (BBC, 1986), a suitably grim Leon Garfield adaptation about chimney sweep Barnacle Brown stumbling across a conspiracy amongst the rich and powerful in Victorian London – complete with the standard-for-the-time complaint-engendering inclusion of graphic violence, including a weighted body being dropped in the Thames, and Barnacle exclaiming to no obvious narrative benefit that he's fallen in "'orse shit!', which was a little much considering how sharply Kay had been told off for complaining that he hadn't a tosser to his kick.

After that, Rye directed Paula Milne's tale of estranged psychically linked adolescent twins Lee and Leah, *The Gemini Factor* (ITV, 1987), and Stone fulfilled another long-held ambition with an atmospheric adaptation of Philippa Pearce's *Tom's Midnight Garden* (BBC, 1989), but even then ambitions to outdo *The Box of Delights* were already well underway. Beginning in November 1988, *The Chronicles of Narnia* (BBC, 1988–90) – which itself pretty much did for the traditional Sunday Classics slot – adapted all of C.S. Lewis' Aslan-adjacent novels with the exception of the slight

The Horse and his Boy and *The Magician's Nephew* and the unfilmable *The Final Battle*, using many of the production techniques that had been perfected for *The Box of Delights* but harnessing even newer and more digitally exciting animatronic technology. Paul Stone was justifiably heaped with acclaim and awards and, suddenly, *The Box of Delights* came to be regarded almost as a footnote in the build-up towards this latest innovation in children's drama.

In fact, despite a repeat in 1986, there was a time when *The Box of Delights* genuinely felt like just another children's drama serial. Despite the acclaim, it had been and gone as quickly as *A Little Silver Trumpet*, and for quite some time – the odd expensive home video release aside – it was little-seen and near-forgotten, only really retaining a strong presence in the memories of those who had seen and been captivated by it at the time. Those memories and that affection were just too powerful for this to remain the case, however, and gradually *The Box of Delights* came to be regarded and celebrated as a classic example of small-screen drama.

More importantly, however, it also led viewers of all ages to stage their own annual rewatches on the exact date and time of the original broadcasts, hunt down original copies of *Christmas Music from Guildford Cathedral*, and stage their own attempts at making a 'posset', presumably followed by spitting it out immediately, which was certainly closer to Cole Hawlings' 'old' magic than anything that *Byker Grove* ever managed. It may have marked a turning point and a high watermark for children's television, but it also retained a sense of wonder and tradition and proved that the old and new can work together to superlatively atmospheric effect. A little like Kay Harker staring wistfully out of a train window on his way to new adventures and unexpectedly catching sight of reminders of his past ones. It was most definitely *not* the purple pim.

10

Imports

'Flippin' like a pancake, poppin' like a cork'

If the past was a foreign country, then what did that make actual foreign countries in the past? They were – and largely through sheer ignorance and naivety rather than intolerance and fear – simultaneously regarded with suspicion and aspiration, somehow at the exact same time viewed with the same sort of apprehension and unease embodied by the Major from *Fawlty Towers* and the same sort of ravenous glee as a child who had seen such exotic fare as hamburgers and milkshakes depicted as everyday luxuries in comic strips.

They thrust politicians with implausibly comical names onto the world stage, assassinated dissidents with poison-tipped umbrellas in broad daylight, saddled the Eurovision Song Contest with men in oddly hued satin jackets, and made declarations about stuff to do with currencies that you didn't understand but which made your parents shake their head with pitying disdain. They also promised a small artillery of scarcely imaginable ice cream flavours, inspired lurid rumours of game shows where the contestants stripped off, set hopeful hearts racing with third-hand tales of holiday romance, and allowed children to become momentary playground celebrities each September by waving around seemingly infinite blister pack strips of shockingly sour-tasting sweets or baseball cards bearing the images and game statistics of unknown and unknowable but evidently very famous players.

Like Rigsby in *Rising Damp*, we pretended to find them comical and disquieting at the same time as not especially secretly really, really wanting a bit of whatever it was they were having. It's small wonder, then, that — with the exception of big-budget glossy American soap operas about people way richer than you could ever dream of being, family-living-with-animal-or-robot sitcoms with two and a half jokes between them if you were lucky or action series inevitably about a prematurely retired cop teamed up with some amazing yet utterly unremarked on technological crime-fighting marvel aside — we got so little of their television.

Except, that is, when it came to children's television, where you just couldn't move for imports. There was often so little money to go round, and so many hours to fill, that the international broadcasters offering endless series of seven or eight dozen episodes apiece to be bought in bulk were more than just a viable option. Handled carefully, they could indeed educate, entertain and inform, and some of them were not only more successful over here than they ever were with the audiences that they were originally intended for; they as good as became honorary BBC and ITV programmes in their own right, and you just can't tell the story of children's television without them.

In some cases, this was because the BBC in particular tried to reshape the shows in their own image. Back when *The Monkees* (1966–68) were actually riding high in the charts, Mike, Micky, Davy and Peter's Beatles-gone-wild speeded-up slapstick invention-testing antics were pulling in huge BBC audiences on Saturday evenings. As they faded from the pop scene, however, the series slipped into the children's schedules to become a Saturday and holiday mornings staple, albeit edited – often very crudely – to remove countercultural references, subconscious-shaking subliminal cutaways, entire songs and even one or two entire episodes that were considered that bit too far out for younger viewers.

A similar stellar trajectory awaited the BBC's similarly hacked-about prints of *Star Trek* (1966–69), which in the days before it reinvented itself as a fan-centric franchise was left adrift as more or less a children's programme in all but original intent. ITV didn't tamper with the original versions of *Batman* (1966–68) too much, but they still went on to shoehorn it into more obscure child-friendly corners that would certainly have left Robin declaiming the Holy Scheduling Relegation.

When it came to BBC edits, however, there was only one hastily amended name in the alley. When Hanna-Barbera's feline scam festival *Top Cat* (1961) was broadcast, Britain's supermarkets were full of tins of a cat food brand of the same name, and on account of strict advertising rules the BBC could not risk showing it under its proper name for fear of a visit from Officer Dibble. Their solution was to cut awkwardly in the middle of the opening titles to a wonky blue title card with the emergency stand-in title 'Boss Cat'; the end credits simply took a great big pair of scissors to the original prints to remove a mention, with a corresponding jump cut in the theme song and lurch in T.C.'s bedtime routine. Although *Top Cat* itself had long since been rebranded, the BBC continued to use the confusion-engendering edited prints well into the nineties.

Although some Hanna-Barbera efforts, like *The Impossibles* (1966) and *The New Shmoo* (1979), came and went as quickly as they had done in America, others – often split off into individual cartoons from larger package shows – just seemed a better fit over here and were still hovering around the children's schedules long after their tie-in hardback comic books were gathering dust in dime-store bargain bins. 'International Sneaky Service' codebreaking Cold War analogy *Secret Squirrel* (1965–67), chimp-copiloted intergalactic law enforcement *Space Ghost* (1966), contraption-festooned vehicular showdown *Wacky Races* (1968) – and its wartime spin-off urging all and sundry to nab him, jab him, tab him, grab him and generally stop that pigeon now, *Dastardly and Muttley in Their Flying Machines* (1969) – all became synonymous with Saturday mornings in a way that they never quite managed to in America.

As did all-girl guitar band on the road high jinks *Josie and the Pussycats* (1970–72); zoo-based quasi-stoner food-nabbing indolence *Help! It's the Hair Bear Bunch!* (1971); mildly dubious pulp detective revival with added shape-changing van *The Amazing Chan and the Chan Clan* (1972); canine martial arts ineptitude *Hong Kong Phooey* (1974); down-at-heel sub-*Columbo* snickering dog private eye *Mumbly* (1976); canine cyborg heroics *Dynomutt, Dog Wonder* (1976–77), prehistory and scream queen teamup *Captain Caveman and the Teen Angels* (1977–80); teenage classic horror progeny versus the Organization of Generally Rotten Enterprises *Drak Pack* (1980); and the almighty Hanna-Barbera universe team-up *Scooby's All-Star Laff-A-Lympics* (1977).

Very much originally intended as a primetime adult sitcom, Harry Boyle's hippy-plagued quest to make an honest buck for his useless children in Nixon-era America *Wait Till Your Father Gets Home* (1972–74) became an unlikely favourite with younger viewers on both channels, while teen-and-dog ghostbusting phenomenon *Scooby-Doo, Where Are You!* (1969–70) was scarcely ever out of the schedules, leading to much confusion when later differently configured revivals *The New Scooby-Doo Mysteries* (1972) and *Scooby-Doo and Scrappy-Doo* (1979) showed up alongside it.

IMPORTS

Scooby-Doo's creators Joe Ruby and Ken Spears set up their own would-be rival animation house, making a strong debut with ITV Saturday morning-hogging comedy werewolf saga *Fangface* (1977), but never seeming to hit upon the right licensed properties with know-all cat and clumsy dog showcases *Heathcliff and Dingbat* (1980) – which the BBC famously cut the entire 'Dingbat and the Creeps' segments despite the fact that they still confusingly appeared in the closing titles – and *Heathcliff and Marmaduke* (1981), tenuous video game tie-in *Pac-Man* (1983) and the frankly ridiculous Mister T (1983–85), in which the strong-armed star of *The A-Team* was recast as a crime-solving gymnastics coach, with the real Mr T turning up on film at the end to deliver a moral. Thankfully, UK viewers were spared the truly baffling *Rubik, the Amazing Cube* (1983).

A more effective challenge came from Filmation, whose clue-in-the-name mini-action movie sophistication took in Pavel Chekov-deficient but purring Lieutenant M'Ress-bolstered *Star Trek* (1974) and the 'lost city'-prone *Tarzan, Lord of the Jungle* (1976–77), with added easily imitable melodic yell and hyperintelligent simian sidekick N'Kima. There was also the disco soundtracked and suited galaxy-saving teenage avatars of Hercules, Mercury and Astrea who, with maintenance robot MO and giant floating head Sentinel One, made up the *Space Sentinels* (1977); darkly hued team-up with Bat-Girl and interdimensional comedy sprite Bat-Mite, *The New Adventures of Batman* (1977); unlikely cinematic Western serial revival *The Lone Ranger* (1980–81); and FIFA public relations mascot turned intergalactic fair play-enforcer with magic size-changing bag *Sport Billy* (1980).

Most memorably of all, there was Prince Adam of Eternia and his 'fearless friend' Cringer defending Castle Grayskull from the evil forces of Skeletor in unashamed show-length toy advert *He-Man and the Masters of the Universe* (1983–85) and his close relative *She-Ra: Princess Of Power* (1985–87). Throughout it all, the noted gentleman, scholar and acrobat star of *The Pink Panther Show* (1969–78) just kept on rearranging that man with the triangular nose's construction plans, whether accompanied by 'The Inspector', 'The Ant and the Aardvark' or 'Crazy-Legs Crane', before hurtling off after that boy's racing car secure in the knowledge that its school holidays-dominating gravity-defying quiet subversion was what viewers were really looking for.

For sheer mind-frazzling impact on BBC viewers, however, nothing could match the escapades of human-in-cartoony-animal-costume psychedelic pop group *The Banana Splits* (1968–70). Meeting in their shaking-prone club house, guitarist Fleegle the dog, bassist Drooper the lion, organist Snorky the elephant and drummer Bingo the ape presided over the cartoon heroics of 'The Three Musketeers' with their annoying juvenile sidekick Tulee and the Arabian Knights – Prince Turhan, Princess Nida, Fariik the Magician, Raseem the Strong, Bez the Beast – who could shapeshift into any animal by declaring himself to be the 'siiiiiiiize' of it. Zazuum the donkey was generally placid until he had his tail yanked by unsuspecting palace guards, upon which he would become an unhaltable whirlwind of kicks. Into the mix went live-action sci-fi shipwreck mystery 'Danger Island', sub-Monkees songs performed in theme parks, corny gags, Banana Buggy races, surprise attacks from their go-go dancing rivals The Sour Grapes Bunch, and generally just rebounding around the set crashing into each other. It's likely that an entire generation is haunted by echoes of their jaunty yet somehow weirdly nightmarish theme song whenever the existence of Saturday morning is mentioned.

'Danger Island' wasn't the only one of its kind, however – over in Australia, television had stumbled across a suspiciously similar off-the-map community. Set up in unnecessary detail in the lengthy Scott Walker-soundalike theme song – which even featured an additional verse over the end credits – *The Lost Islands* (1976) was an edge-of-the-seat fantasy thriller about five child prodigies on a round-the-world voyage on *The United World* in the name of international harmony. They get swept overboard in a storm and washed up on an uncharted Pacific Island, Tambu, which unfortunately for them is populated by a society of quasi-medieval manual workers and their mysterious hooded glowing seaweed-powered master The Q, who fears the dangerous notions of intellect and freedom presented by Australian Tony, English Mark, American David, German Anna and Chinese Su-Yin and perpetually schemes to throw them to the island's colony of man-eating crabs.

Introduced by a rewrite of 'Waltzing Matilda' setting out a blueprint for global harmony, fellow ITV import *Secret Valley* (1980) was set in an abandoned holiday camp transformed into a rope bridge walkway-festooned mini-civilisation and beacon of self-sufficient social cohesion by a gang of local kids apparently entirely made up of future stars of *Home and Away*. They constantly have to fend off the unwanted attentions of banished ne'er-do-well Spider McGurk and his gang, and land-hungry local developer William Woppa, with a barrage from their flourbomb-stocked battlements. *Secret Valley* also acted as the setting for the decidedly odd *Professor Poopsnagle's Steam Zeppelin* (1986), in which the kids set off to rescue an inventor held hostage by kidnappers intent on discovering the secrets of his neo-steam age technology.

The whistly theme-introduced *Falcon Island* (1981) followed the mixed flotsam and jetsam-scavenging fortunes of a pair of coastal siblings, while *The Henderson Kids* (1985–87) and their overwrought soft-rock vow to 'carry on, together, every step of the way' in fighting a local businessman's crooked redevelopment plans turned up on Channel 4 later in the decade, by which time many of the cast – including one Kylie Minogue – could be seen looking slightly older and significantly more famous in *Home and Away* and *Neighbours*. Her on- and off-screen beau Jason Donovan, meanwhile, could be sighted in nineteenth-century fortune-seeking immigration drama *Golden Pennies* (1985), turn-of-the-century triumph over disability-related adversity *I Can Jump Puddles* (1981) and bluntly named children's home high jinks *Home* (1983). There was a sense by then, though, that the well – or indeed the puddle – was long since run dry, and when the BBC picked up the decade-old *Top Mates* (1979) to show over the school holidays, nobody was really convinced.

Over in New Zealand, the well-mannered if answering back-prone *Children of Fire Mountain* (1979) deployed a combination of pranks and sarcasm to foil plots to build supermarkets on sacred land and disrupt shady councillor Doomy Dwyer's plans to sell outlawed 'grog' to the Māoris, while *Children of the Dog Star* (1984) tied Māori heritage to modish theories on ancient intergalactic travellers sent to 'educate' the earliest humans. With its feet more securely on the ground – or at least on the floor of an automobile – *The Flying Kiwi* (1979–81) joined a newly arrived English family on their adventures in the titular vintage car which was, sadly, not what its nickname implied.

Juvenile Los Angeles-based crime-solvers *The Red Hand Gang* (1977) – Frankie, J.R., Joanne, L'il Bill and Doc – enjoyed one single series of skateboard and catcher's mitt-fuelled adventures, with their investigations into a jewel thief posing as a sports star and a plot to train a chimp to steal valuable artworks going largely ignored in

IMPORTS

America. As if to add insult to injury, it was their canine sidekick who got his own roaming odd job spin-off show, *Here's Boomer* (1979–82). When the BBC bought it in 1979, however, something about their rampages along sidewalks and through subways in pursuit of a good old-fashioned mystery – not to mention the naggingly insistent cast-on-trampoline-sung theme song – caught on in a big way and it was shown no fewer than six times. ITV – which might normally have seemed a more natural fit for the show – tried to get in on the action by buying *Here's Boomer*, but it just didn't take off in the same way, suggesting that it was maybe the novelty of seeing the BBC taking an unlikely show and making it 'theirs' that made it work.

Tabitha (1977), a spin-off from legendary sitcom *Bewitched*, following Darrin and Samantha's half-witch teenage daughter as she attempted to make it in the broadcast industry without recourse to using her magical powers and 'cheating', and *Big John, Little John* (1976), a wild comedy about a hapless high school teacher who found himself saddled with a propensity to turn into his twelve-year-old self at inopportune moments after inadvertently taking a swig from the Fountain of Youth – as memorably outlined at considerable length in the opening theme – became similarly enduring hits on the BBC while remembered as little more than a footnote in the US. *The Hardy Boys/Nancy Drew Mysteries* (1977–79) paired two sets of teen detective sensations in alternating disco-era casebook entries of the week, with blow wave-sporting eye candy duo Parker Stevenson and Shaun Cassidy as Frank and Joe, and Pamela Sue Martin doing her best big-eyed stopping running then looking around then starting running again acting as Nancy, very much dividing their potential audience, albeit provoking a mass scramble for the front room whenever they teamed up. Most surprisingly of all, putative must-watch sensation *California Fever* (1979) came and went without proving anything of the sort. At least in America, where the feverish Californian lifestyle was all too everyday a prospect; when the BBC started showing it, however, viewers just couldn't get enough of Ross, Vince and Laurie and their beach-hogging run-ins with hot rod hoodlums, police-baiting pirate radio stations and roller disco showdowns, interspersed with convergence on Zen-dispensing coffee shop Rick's Place, to the extent that it was – daringly – shown apparently untampered with during the school Christmas holiday mornings, 'racy' storylines and all.

Elsewhere in the world, not everyone was enjoying as much freedom to catch waves, catch criminals and catch your boss dropping litter onto the floor and propelling it back into his hand by wiggling your nose, and some of the grimmer realities of life in the shadow of the Iron Curtain found their way into a series of BBC-bought children's shows that would have kept grown adults up at night, drenched in arty camerawork and art-rock soundtracks. Shot in saturated primary tones that Dario Argento might have considered a bit much, Spain's *Oscar, Kina and the Laser* (1978) sent an academically prodigious boy, his pet goose and a sentient beam of concentrated light – which could also make them 'invisible' for reasons that may have become lost in translation – to rescue the kidnapped son of a scientist. West Germany weighed in with *The Legend of Tim Tyler* (1979), the saga of a boy who sold his infectious laugh to wealthy but lonely and unfulfilled industrialist the Baron, who found that the one thing money could not buy was a right good chortle. Based on a Jules Verne story, Czechoslovakia's *The Secret of Steel City* (1979) chronicled a standoff between two steampunk-styled nations divided by their similarities over an eerily anachronistic arms race. It won numerous international awards, but it is probably safe to assume that one for allegorical subtlety was not amongst them.

IMPORTS

You could, however, still count on Europe for more BBC-bought traditional tales that seemed to last for an entire year. Denmark's *The Children of Totem Town* (1970) rejected the imperatives of 'the man' and built a countercultural wigwam-based community in the playground between their tower blocks, provoking outrage when they prevailed upon a more urbane boy to smoke a 'peace pipe'. Norway's *The Boy from Lapland* (1976) found that tennis racquet shoes were frowned on at 'normal' school, while Belgium offered the Bert Kaempfert-soundtracked *Captain Zeppos* (1964–68), an aristocrat turned self-starting secret agent with an uncanny knack for stumbling across conspiracies in his home town of Belden.

A co-production between various British, German and Austrian broadcasters, *Kim & Co* (BBC, 1975) starred teen pin-up and aspirant pop star Simon Fisher Turner as a jet-setting junior journalist chasing conspiracies and mysteries across a Europe thronged with very seventies haircuts. Swiss-German co-production *Heidi* (1978) stayed true to the original novel but tried to liven matters up with an irritatingly insistent flutey theme tune and the juvenile lead's shockingly dense mop of curls, while West Germany went it alone with *Silas* (1981), a much more dynamic effort with appropriately swashbuckling music about a nineteenth-century runaway circus boy who teams up with clumsy local oaf Godik to rescue a kidnapped girl from 'The Shrew' and her gang of smugglers. *Silas* actor Patrick Bach also starred in *Jack Holborn* (1982), another saga of a nineteenth-century runaway shown by ITV almost concurrently with *Silas*, which was not in any way confusing whatsoever.

Canada stood in for nineteenth-century Mississippi when several of Mark Twain's novels were conflated in *Huckleberry Finn and his Friends* (1979), a convincing straw hat and paddle-steamer rendering of Huck and Tom's adventures with a wistfully nostalgic theme song helpfully confirming 'that's where they came from, the time that they came from'. Coming from another time entirely, *Benji, Zax and the Alien Prince* (1983) enlisted the enduring cinematic canine to help protect stranded Antarian Prince Yubi and his wonky-eyed flying yellow robot guardian from a suspiciously Darth Vader-like constitutional rival.

Champion the Wonder Horse (1955) – still being shown by the BBC into the early nineties – paired Gene Autrey's screen steed and twelve-year-old Ricky for a series of range-riding adventures heralded by a speaker-rattling theme song boasting that 'you'll hear about him ever'where you go'. 'Greensleeves'-accompanied rescue-initiating rough collie *Lassie* (1954–73) bounded across endless expanses of rolling hills to alert the authorities to collapsing buildings, while *The Littlest Hobo* (1979–85) roamed from town to Canadian town doing more or less exactly the same, distinguished only by a melancholy country-and-western theme song extolling the virtues of a rootless lifestyle. Somehow, his fellow Canadians *The Kids of Degrassi Street* (1979–86) managed to be even more mawkish in a series of interconnected morality plays about the travails of pre-adolescence, much of which appeared to revolve around reiterating that if you cheat at school you're only cheating yourself. More excitement could be found in *Degrassi Junior High* (1987–89), which followed joker Joey Jeremiah 'Esquire', punk girl Spike and boys- and booze-hungry Steph through more relatable teenage angst, fuelling legends of 'banned' episodes that later turned up in a conveniently out-of-the-way late-evening slot on BBC2.

On a more directly educational and indeed more European slant, retelling key moments in history through the eyes of a chimp, an old man with a long beard and a sort of floating robot calendar, *Once Upon A Time . . . Man* (1979) opened with an ominous overcranked blast of Bach's 'Toccata and Fugue' and titles that purported to depict the entire evolution of humankind from the big bang through to the solar burnout-occasioned destruction of the Earth, leaving many viewers too terrified to watch any further. Others were left baffled by – on account of it being made by the same production team – an unexplained cameo by Barnaby amongst the cosmic swirls and boiling lava slowly forming into a planetary structure. Similar French existential angst could be found in *Shadoks* (1968–74), a race of angular birds who found their home planet just that bit too angular and aspired towards a new life on Earth. Perhaps the floating robot calendar should have had a word.

Italy's *The Fantastic Adventures of Mr Rossi* (1984) pitted the relentlessly optimistic everyman and his more realistic dog Harold against the relentless ennui of modern life, with even the downtempo yodelling samba theme song pleading with him to 'believe in happiness' seeming to conspire against him. Often mistaken for an import, European folk tale anthology *Storybook International* (ITV, 1981–87) was actually made in the UK in association with international broadcasters, although it is chiefly remembered now for the lengthy opening titles in which a minstrel identifying himself as 'The Storyteller' recounts how he is variously known as Ivan, Yan, Johann and John in different territories. Similarly, *Under the Same Sky* (ITV, 1984) gathered together European-made mini-dramas with new narration from Terry Jones and Tom Baker, provoking a few troubled memories with an Austrian drama about a girl who fell into a hole while bullying her sister. Meanwhile, French animal-skewed reinterpretations of Alexandre Dumas in *Dogtanian and the Three Muskehounds* (1985) and Jules Verne in *Around the World with Willy Fog* (1987), not to mention Aztec legend with a sci-fi twist *The Mysterious Cities Of Gold* (1986), which originally included educational segments that proved too much even for the BBC who abruptly edited them out, were famed for their irritatingly catchy theme songs but as actual programmes seemed to stretch into infinity without anything much ever really happening. More straightforward historical fun came from Germany's *Vicky the Viking* (1974–76), a Norse youngster who solved oafish villagers and pillagers' problems with a much-imitated nose-rubbing 'thinking' gesture and two separate flagon-hoisting theme songs that alternated on a seemingly random basis.

Japan's visually wild world of dizziness-inducing strobing colours, men in robot and alien suits fighting in mid-air with the aid of all too visible wires, and heroes that suddenly went 'up' for no reason was, in those pre-anime days, possibly a little too extreme for Western audiences to tolerate. The odd stray dubbed effort like intrepid ocean floor explorer *Marine Boy* (1966) did make it across and dazzle audiences with their luridly unfamiliar style, but it wasn't really until the late seventies and the race to discover the next big space craze after *Star Wars* that British viewers really got their first, albeit diluted, taste of the full-on anime experience.

Very much an adult animation in its original form, *Science Ninja Team Gatchaman* became *Battle of the Planets* (1978) when Sandy Frank Entertainment extensively recut it for international distribution. Bird-themed Earth-protecting space agents Mark, Jason, Princess, Tiny and Keyop may well have had adventures in the Phoenix – or, in its blazing transmutated form, Firey Phoenix – that were liable to appeal to fans of Chewbacca and company, but there were also a lot of what can only be described as rough edges that had to be removed first; futuristic bird-shaped throwing stars, grubby 'naughty' visuals and, most jarringly of all, primary antagonist Zoltar's propensity for switching gender, with their excision creating more than a few plot holes. In came comedy plot-recapping robots 7-Zark-7 and 1-Rover-1 at Centre Neptune, and convenient references to Zoltar's 'sister' to account for the long hair and lipstick. This didn't always quite smooth over matters – 'The Fierce Flowers' and their predisposition to consume women rather than men posed more questions than it answered, and even in the opening titles, a mid-air display of space-diving acrobatics concentrated a little too closely on Princess' tumbling pants – but, especially once older brother-sourced rumours about the forbidden original version began to circulate, the excitingly new experience kickstarted a curiosity about Japanese animation that inspired a massive boom a decade later.

Star Fleet (1982) deployed a mix of marionettes and 'suitmation' for the epic saga of young space pilots Shiro Hagan, Jon Lee and Barry Hercules ferrying Princess Lamia and her ape-like bodyguard Kirara and irritating hovering android PPA in a bid to protect the mysterious 'F-Zero-1' from the attentions of the Imperial Master and his ocular implant-assisted operatives Commander Makara and Captain Orion. What really made *Star Fleet* stand out were the frequent occasions on which X-Bomber's three fighter craft docked to form gigantic red robot Dai-X for spectacular space cruiser-walloping action sequences. Amongst those admiring Dai-X was Queen guitarist Brian May, who promptly roped in a load of heavy metal legends to record a squiggly guitar solo-festooned excursion on *Star Fleet*'s catchy soft-rock theme song. French co-production *Ulysses 31* (1981) shifted the ancient Greek legend of the *Odyssey* to the thirty-first century, 'soaring through all the galaxies' with the assistance of his son Telemachus, blue-skinned alien girl rescued from the clutches of the Cyclops Yumi, and bolt-scoffing robot assistant Nono.

So what of Ireland, so geographically, culturally and in many cases familially close that it didn't seem 'overseas' at all? It has its own long and rich history of children's programming, although perhaps on account of that geographical and cultural proximity, very little of it found its way on to the BBC, ITV or even Channel 4. With one notable exception. Possibly more than a little 'influenced' by a certain pair of cinematic androids but devoid of their wit and charm, scrap-hewn robots *CP and Qwikstitch* (1982) – effectively a vacuum cleaner and a sewing machine respectively – enjoyed, if that's the right word, adventures amongst the human electronic and mechanical detritus dumped on Junkus Minor, resolutely delivering the exact same moral every single time. The BBC regularly screened their minimally animated exploits at the conclusion of the school holiday morning schedules, and during those five minutes time actually appeared to stand still. It was a more compelling argument for just switching off your television set and going out and doing something less boring instead than the actual show that purported to do that.

'I must have the singing ringing tree!'

Once upon a time, a prince journeyed many miles and for many days to seek the hand of a beautiful princess in a far-off land. Considering that she was privileged, entitled, spoiled and by her own designation 'beautiful', she wasn't especially interested and sent him away to prove his worth by securing the one thing she didn't own – a legendary musical tree. He found himself transformed into a bear by the tree's malevolent custodian for his efforts, and shortly afterwards she was transformed into a crooked-nose green-haired witch for pretty much the same reasons. Despite having lightning-heralded spells, extreme weather conditions and every trick camera effect in the book thrown at them, they managed to find each other and the tree and lived happily ever after, although it's not certain that many of the children watching from behind the sofa — presumably having checked that there wasn't a giant talking fish there first — did. Meanwhile, behind the Iron Curtain, an iron-willed lady from the BBC set about an officious KGB inspector with her handbag — and that's the story of how *The Singing Ringing Tree* (BBC, 1964) came to simultaneously enrapture and terrify a generation.

Loosely adapted from the Brothers Grimm's *Hurleburlebutz, Das Singende, Klingende Bäumchen* — the movie that became *The Singing Ringing Tree* — was made by East Germany's state-owned studio DEFA in 1957. Although it operated under significantly fewer restrictions than other studios elsewhere in the Eastern Bloc, DEFA was still expected — and that's putting it politely — to make films that encouraged and depicted what were considered to be desirable values, and to present East Germany in a favourable light to the wider world. As long as the results reflected good social and political ideals — if not necessarily socialism per se — everyone was happy.

Director Francesco Stefani and the majority of the cast and crew were already DEFA regulars, but Stefani was keen to find newer talent for the two leads. Already something of a teen heartthrob, up-and-coming television star Eckart Dux was a natural choice for the Prince, while Christel Bodenstein was a student at the State Ballet School in East Berlin who had little interest in acting but was persuaded to audition regardless. They were cast as much for their looks as their acting ability — on the basis that their transformations would be thrown into even sharper relief for the viewing audience — but they also shared a dynamic and abrasive chemistry that made their portrayals all the more believable. Coming from a modest background and being shy and unassuming by nature, Bodenstein particularly relished the opportunity to play an entitled brat, suggesting character details of her own invention such as the Princess putting on her crown before getting out of bed, and this fuelled a truly magnetic performance that made her comeuppance and change of heart all the more effective.

Shot entirely in DEFA's main soundstage Marlene Dietrich Hall – previously host to Fritz Lang's 1927 science fiction classic *Metropolis* and many of Dietrich's own films – *Das Singende, Klingende Bäumchen* was filmed across two months late in 1957, an experience that Bodenstein and Dux later recalled as having been more like fun than work. They may, however, have been conveniently neglecting to recall the inevitable trials and tribulations of a production featuring so many live animals; on one occasion, the sound of the clapperboard startled some birds who flew up into the studio rafters and could not be coaxed down; while during the snowdrift scene, a normally placid horse bolted and the studio doors had to be very hurriedly opened to allow it to charge outside.

Das Singende, Klingende Bäumchen was released on 13 December 1957 and was a modest success – albeit enough of one for Bodenstein to be recognised in the street – although it later met with far greater popularity through television showings. It was less popular, however, with state-sponsored critics, who afforded it largely dismissive reviews that criticised the romantic subplot and its conclusion as an endorsement of bourgeois ideals and a celebration of monarchic orthodoxy. Herself no advocate of rampant unencumbered capitalism, Bodenstein found these reactions even more irritating than being asked for her autograph while socialising, and she went to great lengths in interviews to emphasise the Princess' dawning humility and sense of social responsibility, which she felt were enough of an embodiment of the positive values of socialism in themselves. The only problem was that whoever was right about it presenting East Germany in a favourable light, it wasn't really getting much opportunity to do so to the wider world. Fortunately, there was one broadcaster that was only too happy to show it.

Peggy Miller, a formidable figure who gave even Soviet border guards cause to quake in fear, had served as a translator during the Second World War, a role that had brought her into regular contact with the BBC's European Service. On returning to civilian life, Peggy joined the BBC in a role that involved booking and licensing internationally produced films, and in 1964 she joined the Family department as a producer with a responsibility for adapting imported shows for BBC audiences. She continued in this role right through to the mid-eighties, personally supervising all aspects of preparing bought-in children's programmes for broadcast, from sourcing the films – which often necessitated travelling to negotiate with the distributors and in some cases the authorities directly – editing and dubbing, arranging publicity and frequently writing tie-in novels for BBC Books. With one eye – or rather ear – on attracting the audience's attention, and the other on balancing the books by avoiding music licensing costs, she also commissioned new orchestral scores and pop-influenced themes. Many much-loved imported shows owe their exposure to UK audiences entirely to her imagination and determination, but arguably her most significant legacy came with *Tales from Europe* (BBC, 1964–69).

Commencing with DEFA's 1959 production of Hans Christian Andersen's *The Tinderbox* in October 1964, *Tales from Europe* showcased short serials bought in from across the burgeoning European Economic Community and beyond, filling out the afternoon schedules while saving on costs without compromising on educational or entertainment value. Although there were plenty of French, Swedish, Norwegian, Dutch, Danish and Swiss contributions, the overwhelming majority came from Eastern Bloc nations and for entirely practical reasons – heavily subsidised by the authorities, they were able to make fantasy serials at greater expense and in a much greater volume than the BBC could even dream of. Thus it was that British viewers got to thrill to Poland's *The Scouts and the Motor Car*, in which some scouts somehow contrive to become lost at sea after finding a broken-down vintage car on a railway track; Yugoslavia's trek to Moscow by *The Boy and the Pelican*; and Russia's *The Secret of the Grey Gull*, in which a boy sets sail in a ship of the same name to clear his family's reputation of a false smuggling accusation. At a time when international television and indeed international culture in general – even that which was practically on their own doorstep – was an exotic mystery to most British viewers, the opportunity to see such outlandishly different entertainment must have been a mind-opening experience, but even they had nothing on *The Singing Ringing Tree*.

First shown by BBC1 between 19 November and 3 December 1964, *The Singing Ringing Tree* featured sets, costumes and wildly disorientating effects that were beyond the technical and financial reach of the BBC or even ITV, and looked even in black and white like it had been shot through a haze of Christmas decorations and sweet wrappers. Closer to a nightmare than a fairytale, it looked like an abstract expressionist film that might otherwise only have been seen late at night on BBC2, and sounded like an avuncular lecture on how the spoils of the bourgeois social framework will only lead to rack and ruin, yet even the overt political undertones – it was, after all, made at a time when Germany was literally divided into two separate countries – seemed like light relief next to the alarming shrieking light-flashing interludes.

Frightening enough to traumatise some and visually arresting enough to fascinate others, it also benefited from an unusual role reversal as the Prince, while both brave and loyal, was revealed to be idealistic and ineffectual whereas the Princess, despite being spoiled and high-handed, was also haughtily resourceful and fearless and more than willing to roll up her ornate sleeves and face down their demonic tormentor. At a time when it was unusual enough to see a children's series where a character lived in a block of flats, this was a mind-bending experience indeed.

Peggy Miller edited the original German language version of *Das Singende, Klingende Bäumchen* into three episodes of roughly twenty-three minutes duration each, adding new title cards and closing captions and a brief recap to the opening of the second and third instalments – and, in the process and by a fortunate quirk of timing, created two nightmarish cliffhangers almost entirely by chance. Patched directly over the top of the subtly faded original German soundtrack, a new English narration was recorded at De Lane Lea, a specialist dubbing studio on London's Dean Street, by BBC2 arts presenter Tony Bilbow, who could often be found analysing similarly out-there European films on *Late Night Line-Up*. This was his first association with *Tales from Europe* but he later returned to narrate *The Secret of the Grey Gull* as well as Netherlands-sourced story of a boy in danger of missing his emigrating family's boat, *The Last Passenger*; Poland's tale of twins who plan to harness the 'gold' from the night sky in a bid to become joint Prime Ministers, *The Boy Who Sold the Moon*; Czechoslovakia's reptile-minding antics *Katya and the Crocodile*; and Sweden's *Here Comes Peter*, about a boy who went on holiday and that was pretty much that. To be fair to Peter, however, he would have been hard pushed to find anything to do that would have had as much impact as *The Singing Ringing Tree*. It was quite simply the darkest and most twisted – and certainly the most disorientating and eye-assaulting – fairytale that most children would ever have witnessed. After that first instalment went out at half past five on that unassuming Thursday evening in November, children's television would never be quite the same again.

Although the other *Tales from Europe* soon faded into hazy if densely symbolic memories about a pelican's triumphant arrival in Red Square, *The Singing Ringing Tree* seemed to strike a chord with viewers – doubtless a very similar one to the discordant 'sting' that heralded the diminutive villain's blasts of malevolent magic – and it continued to be regularly repeated way beyond the conclusion of *Tales from Europe* itself. It was first shown in colour in November 1969, presumably providing fresh trauma for anyone who thought they had managed to conquer their fear of the black-and-white version, and it reappeared, often in the school holiday mornings, right through to August 1980; poetically, the final showing of the final episode took place a couple of days before Poland's ruling Communist Party signed a landmark accord permitting the formation of the trade union Solidarity. The world was beginning to change, but the memory of a blur of loud colours, loud noises and loud shudders from the audience would very much remain.

It was the success of *The Singing Ringing Tree* that convinced the Children's department of the potential of longer-form serials from overseas broadcasters, and while they may have featured significantly less in the way of head-spinning proto-psychedelic visuals and blunt political discourse-driven narratives, four in particular had very nearly as powerful an impact and as enduring a legacy for successive generations of younger viewers.

The 1964 French-German co-production *Les Aventures de Robinson Crusoë* became *The Adventures of Robinson Crusoe* (BBC, 1965), starring Robert Hoffmann in a faithful and gripping adaptation of Daniel Defoe's 1719 novel, juxtaposing Crusoe's memories of his privileged but unhappy life pre-shipwreck with his struggles to find food and firewood. Already haunting and atmospheric, it was further enhanced by a beat boom-influenced score from Robert Mellin and Gian Piero Reverberi, notably the sweeping yet desolate theme tune which went on to have a profound influence on a number of electronic ambient musical artists. Perhaps underlining just how different a place the world was at that time, Hoffmann had no idea the series had even been shown in the UK until he was recognised in London many years later, and he was taken aback to discover that the theme music — which he had similarly never heard — meant so much to so many people.

Actually made before it was adapted into Cécile Aubry's novel of the same name, 1965 French serial *Belle et Sebastien* starred the writer's son Medhi as a young boy in an Alpine village trying to protect a dog who has been falsely scapegoated over destructive and antisocial behaviour. Wistful yet bleak, the slow-moving but involving storyline in picturesque surroundings fuelled more cerebral imaginations as *Belle and Sebastian* (BBC, 1967), along with its follow-up *Sebastien Parmi Les Hommes* — 'Sebastian Amongst Men', or as the BBC had it *Belle, Sebastian and the Horses* (BBC, 1968) — although they didn't bother dubbing 1970's *Sebastian et La Mary-Morgan*. As well as being remade several times in different forms, including a lengthy Japanese animated serial that became a Children's BBC favourite in the early nineties, *Belle and Sebastian* also lent its name to a nineties indie pop band, who did their best to live up to the wistful monochrome aesthetic of the serial and its plaintive theme song.

The German-Yugoslavian *Počitnice v Lipici* of 1966 — 'Holidays in Livica' — starred Helga Anders as Julia, a teenager on the trail of the horsenapped *The White Horses* (BBC, 1968), complete with a wistful trotting lavishly arranged mid-paced theme song by Jackie Lee that vaulted into the top ten when released as a single.

François, Chevalier de Recci's Robert Etcheverry-portrayed plot to liberate a strategically vital French castle from Spanish troops in 1967's *Le Chevalier Tempête*, better known to UK audiences who might not have quite been able to figure out what a 'Storm Knight' was as *The Flashing Blade* (BBC, 1969), came equipped with a thunderingly dramatic theme song and a mystery all of its own; owing to a technical fault with the English language print, the twelfth and final episode suffered a broadcast breakdown during several attempts by the BBC to show it. Eventually, given that the twelfth concluded on a resolution of sorts, they just dropped the finale, although the lack of a coda left viewers wondering what had had become of his loyal sidekick Guiliot and whether the long-hoped for reunion with Isabelle de Sospel ever came about. It also enjoyed a peculiar coda entirely of its own – in the late eighties, looking for ideas for his new Saturday morning show *On the Waterfront*, Russell T. Davies wrote a new narration for *The Flashing Blade* that did not exactly emphasise the serious side of his swashbuckling escapades. Meanwhile, although it never managed to have the same sort of lasting impact, mention must also be made of the covert ops of French flying aces *The Aeronauts* (BBC, 1972), primarily on account of Rick Jones' deep funk theme song singing the praises of their 'cutting the clouds in a fury of sound'.

By the time that Russell was coming up with jokes about battle maps being used for weather forecasts, seismic changes were already in motion across Europe, and DEFA, having literally served its purpose, was dissolved in 1992, although the actual studios – now renamed Babelsberg Studio – remain in higher demand than ever. Made in simpler times and with simpler technology, the conclusion of

IMPORTS

The Singing Ringing Tree sees the Prince and the Princess reunited, safely restored to their usual photogenic selves and headed for that promised happily ever after, electing to leave the plant that had caused them such torment behind 'so that if anyone else found it, it would bring happiness to them as well'. How much happiness *The Singing Ringing Tree* brought to anyone who had found it while innocently waiting for *Blue Peter* is another question entirely.

11

That's Not a Children's Programme

'Goodies are coming for you and you and you'

There used to be such a clear delineation between what was 'for' children and what wasn't. You could stare with horrified curiosity at the covers of *Don't Answer the Phone* and *The Bogey Man* in your local video shop, try to read the blurb on the cover of that lurid paperback with a revolver, a tumbler of whiskey and a photograph of a naked woman on that carousel in the newsagents without anyone noticing which direction your eyes were moving in, or dawdle very slowly past the posters for *Kentucky Fried Movie* and *The Funhouse* on your way out from seeing *The Water Babies*, but it was no use. Anything for adults was off limits and an unspoken social contract meant that you knew it and didn't dare challenge it.

    Television, and the very fact that it was right there in your front room, struck a harder bargain, but there was still no shifting your parents or guardians. You could beg and plead to be allowed to watch *Arthur Hailey's Hotel*, *The Day of the Triffids*, *Blott on the Landscape* or *Kelly Monteith*, even if they didn't actually involve 'staying up', but to little avail. You knew where the children's programmes were – they even identified themselves as such – and that's where you had to confine yourself to. Being terrified by stray glimpses of *The Nine O'Clock News* was fine; being amused by stray glimpses of *Not the Nine O'Clock News* was not. There were hazier lines around the schedules, though, when children would still be watching whether by accident or design; and while little of it was actually intended as children's programming in any way, shape or form, you could have fooled any of the furtive captive audience.

For starters, it wasn't only children watching in the daytime. Something had to be available for the comparatively small adult audience, and while in the days before a full daytime service it was obvious that neither much in the way of thought or money had gone into it, this also inadvertently made the shows that little bit more appealing to any child with one eye on their Palitoy Family Tree House and the other on the television. Provided you were deft enough at averting your attention to avoid catching Leonard Parkin and some scary green hands typing in *News After Noon*, there were a large quantity of under-the-counter delights to be found either side of 'your' lunchtime programmes.

Jauntily themed Canadian comedy-drama about a feuding pair of riverside loggers *The Beachcombers* (1972–90) and Australian wartime snapshot and cap-pullage bookended family drama *The Sullivans* (1976–83) – featuring early glimpses of the likes of Kylie Minogue and Russell Crowe – enjoyed a lengthy parent-placating midday residency, while Grace Mulligan and Dorothy Sleightholm's hearty serving suggestions in *Farmhouse Kitchen* (ITV, 1971–90) and Nancy Kominski's self-animating palette knife watercolour showcase *Paint Along with Nancy* (ITV, 1974–78) came equipped with impossibly exotic theme tunes – a jazzily competing vibraphone, flute and organ smackdown and nimble-fingered cruise ship samba respectively. A more foreboding fanfare called *Crown Court* (ITV, 1972–84) to order, with Judge William Mervyn and QC Richard Wilson presiding as a procession of character actors presented a case – which could be anything from compensation claims arising from inconveniently sited conveniences at a retirement home to a local clairvoyant accused of 'cursing' a client – ahead of the bittersweet orchestral closing theme, with a jury of genuine members of the public delivering their verdict at the end of the week. Having to go back to school before the final instalment was a crime in and of itself.

Meanwhile, and bafflingly, a handful of long-forgotten mid-sixties animations found their way into a mid-morning slot on ITV apparently for the benefit of absolutely nobody in particular whatsoever, including the gridlock-heralded radio contact-enabled comic strip crime-busting efforts of Hemlock Bones, Joe Jitsu and *Dick Tracy* (1961), mod-attired antagonist of Hurricane Harry and Dr Madcap *Cool McCool* (1966), rhyme-spouting science-fiction pixie from a strange atomic race *DoDo, The Kid from Outer Space* (1965) and the fab gear animated larks of *The Beatles* (1965–67). Much beloved of the Fab Four themselves, the gleefully ludicrous plots were always based on an individual song – such as foiling a plot to 'rob' Penny Lane – and you do have to wonder how many later fans of John, Paul, George and Ringo first discovered them through catching one of those repeats on a day off school. Although the less said about Ringo's dustbin lid-facilitated subterfuge in the opening titles, the better.

Over on the BBC, magazine show *Pebble Mill at One* (BBC, 1972–86) installed presenters in the foyer of the BBC's Pebble Mill Studios in Birmingham, conducting off-the-cuff interviews with whichever celebrities happened to be loitering around that day, interspersed with gentle comedy from Hinge and Bracket-level wits and musical contributions from the conveniently non-space taking up singer-songwriter likes of Roger Whittaker and Barbara Dickson. It may have been compelling viewing, but it was about as cheerfully subdued as television ever got – which made it all the more peculiar that it was introduced initially by a dynamic brass-led theme that sounded more like it belonged to an action movie, accompanied by clips of people waterskiing through reception and Spike Milligan causing 'mayhem', and later by a moody slab of vocodered synthpop straight out of the Blitz Club.

After *Pebble Mill* and after one, however, you approached the afternoon schedules at your own risk. On the BBC, you might find an ageing comedy movie like *A Yank in Ermine* or *Please Don't Eat the Daisies*, or even a mildly naughty 'farce' like *Not Now, Comrade*, or you might find a regionally made documentary on crumbly film about the harsh living conditions of fourteenth-century monks or tugboat captains lamenting how they don't make these new-fangled fishing nets like they used to. On ITV, you might stumble across showbizzy daytime chat on *Afternoon Plus*, or Derek Batey guiding talented mutts through a sausage temptation-strewn assault course in *That's My Dog*, or you might find a glossily murky American TV movie full of sinister international smuggling rings, phials of scorpion venom and orphans who knew their foster father was 'a murderer' but weren't able to convince anyone, which were just that bit too menacing – and too badly acted – not to be terrifying; notoriously, ITV once contrived to show unspeakably sleazy late-night shocker *Bad Ronald* uncut in the middle of an ordinary weekday afternoon.

Earlier in the day, however, there were the schools' programmes, and if you happened to be off with a bunged-up nose and a bottle of Lucozade, then it was pretty much expected that you would watch them in the hope of compensating for your missed daily dose of education. Some, like the grainy film stock and tersely narrated scientific demonstrations with occasional closeups on scary 'hazard' notices of *Experiment* (1969–86), the abstract deconstructionist destruction of narrative form in *Middle English* (1981–2001) and the sheer other language-ness of *The French Programme* (1979–97), were sufficiently unnerving to made you wish you were actually *at* school. Others, however, existed in a whole secret universe of hidden television that you might not have got to explore otherwise, brimming with mysteriously named delights waiting to be discovered through a catarrh-blurred haze.

Frequently plugged directly after the BBC's lunchtime shows, *You and Me* (BBC, 1974–92) took a look at the world around us for the benefit of the under-fives, with a catchy theme song – as later 'borrowed' by Oasis – from Charlie, Karl and Julian and a procession of child-alarming puppet presenters: jerkily lumbering stop-motion cawing corvid and simpering hamster Crow and Alice, clacky-mouthed Duncan the Dragon, and socially aware market stall-manning indefinable puppets Cosmo and Dibs, whose message-driven arguments came accompanied by UB40's overhaul of the theme. Variously presented by bookshop-dwelling Henry Woolf and Vicky Ireland with obstinate superimposed foam rubber puppet man 'Charlie', *Words and Pictures* (BBC, 1970–96) explored the alphabet with the aid of self-propelled Magic Pencil and syllable-emphasising stop-motion animations featuring prehistoric grump Grandpa Gripe and the celebratedly spooky Witches of Halloween.

Factual documentary strand *Watch* (BBC, 1967–2009) saw fashionably coiffured Louise Hall-Taylor and James Earl Adair, and a plasticine-backed burst of sprightly flutey swinged-up Bach, striving to explain everything from evolution to the postal system with a smattering of songs and animations, along with running serials that were effectively miniature rock operas, including the stories of 'David and Goliath', 'Robinson Crusoe' and – most memorably of all – 'The Nativity', with Louise looking into the historical reality and plausibility on location in the Holy Land and James back in the studio retelling the biblical version of events with the aid of stylised conical paper puppets. If you watched *Watch* at school, this clear indication that the Christmas holidays were coming could not have been more welcome.

A similar de facto alternative Advent calendar could be found in *Music Time* (BBC, 1970–91), which interspersed Kathryn Harries and Peter Combe's earnest renditions of world music favourites annotated by dimly lit notes on a musical stave with fantasy-meets-slapstick serialised stop-motion animated adaptations of ballets including *Coppélia*, *The Nutcracker* and *Lieutenant Kijé*. More bizarrely, *Maths in a Box* (BBC, 1980), written by folk singer Alex Glasgow and apparently 'as easy as one-two-three', concerned trigonometry-fixated stranded alien Powka who travelled in and out of his computational cube with a chant of 'tikki-tikki-tox'. When you returned to school, it really did take some doing to convince everyone that you weren't just making it up.

Over on ITV, *Seeing and Doing* (ITV, 1967–92) covered similar ground to *Watch* courtesy of presenters Toni Arthur and Atarah Ben-Tovim, with a rocked-up power-pop theme song that replaced the original choice of Herbert Chappell's 'The Gonk' – as notoriously heard in *Dawn of the Dead* – and was replaced in turn by dull session guitarist noodling accompanying turning blocks depicting craft activities. *Good Health* (ITV, 1974–88) emphasised the value of personal hygiene and regular exercise through such child-acted comedy ludicrousness as a local news report on a superhero who fought germs, campy *Snow White*-riffing horror lampoonery with a witch proffering wicker baskets full of liquorice allsorts, and the legendary cautionary tale of foot-knackering fashion craze Blockaboots.

THAT'S NOT A CHILDREN'S PROGRAMME

Chris Tarrant narrated crumbly film documentaries about parking meters and bin lorries in *Stop, Look, Listen* (ITV, 1971–93), and Fred Harris, Shelagh Gilbey and Anni Domingo jumpsuitedly solved basic mathematical problems in a haze of ambient electronica and syllable-scattered 'futurespeak', while Sylvester McCoy found himself overwhelmed by their real-life application, in *Leapfrog* (ITV, 1978). *Reading with Lenny* (ITV, 1977–79) saw ventriloquist Terry Hall and his puppet Lenny the Lion trace a furry finger across the storybook exploits of Kevin the Kitten; when it was decided a little more oomph was needed, a certain fox rocked up complete with audience-mocking theme song to trade puns with 'Mr Howard' in *Let's Read with Basil Brush* (ITV, 1982–84). Somewhat less comfortingly, Alan Rothwell dispassionately introduced weird abstract short films in *Picture Box* (ITV, 1966–93); and if they weren't quite troubling enough, the opening titles depicted blurry footage of a rotating ornate velvet-mounted jewellery case accompanied by an eerie fairground-esque waltz played by avant-garde sound sculptors Lasry-Baschet on instruments fashioned from bone.

Later on, you could always put whatever you had ostensibly learned from schools' television to the test in the various quiz shows that sat in a sort of brainteasing no-man's-land between children's television and the proper evening schedules. Marking out its highbrow nature with atypical opening titles – initially a deck of optical illusion-festooned playing cards backed by jerky sitar-led jazz, later giving way to stentorian Eastern Bloc balalaika-strumming accompanied by a rotating slot machine fairground attraction decorated with an odd-looking Victorian family unit – *Ask the Family* (BBC, 1967–84) saw Robert Robinson challenge father and youngest son only to identify a 10,000-times magnified DIY component and deduce the current time if you flew directly from Edinburgh to Helsinki with a three-hour stopover in Valletta.

With desk-teetering novelty mascots and The Sundays T-shirts very much to the fore, a pair of students took on a braver individual going it alone in a hexagonally aligning race across the *Blockbusters* (ITV, 1983–93) game board in the hope of making it through to the coveted Gold Run. Nobody was ever sure why it had opening titles depicting the Elgin Marbles zooming through a futuristic cityscape and theme music that sounded more like it belonged to a sci-fi movie, but somehow the contrast between that and host Bob Holness' calm yet excited demeanour fitted together. Its regular Sue Robbie-helmed summer replacement, *Connections* (ITV, 1985–90), a more straightforward exercise in abstract clues and link-spotting, could only dream of such lasting infamy. Years ahead of its time, Angela Rippon's *Masterteam* (BBC, 1985–87) simply challenged a league table of teams of quizzers to outdo each other at solving fiendishly difficult puzzles and answering quickfire general knowledge questions, including in the exotically named 'Pot Pourri' round.

Masterteam was just one of several shows deployed to fill an inconvenient gap when the BBC's evening news bulletin moved from 5.40 p.m. to become *The Six O'Clock News* in 1984. Others included Gyles Brandreth's conversational challenge *The Railway Carriage Game* (BBC, 1985), bland American family sitcoms *Gloria* and *Charles in Charge*, hectoring keep-fit showcase *Go for It!* (BBC, 1986–88) – which awkwardly juxtaposed shaming tobacco-addicted patriarchs with unwitty witticisms like a photofit of junk food 'pusher' Sir Walter Raleigh – and *Fax* (BBC, 1986–88), a viewer correspondence show in which Bill Oddie, Debbie Rix, Billy Butler and Wendy Leavesley sought to answer troubling trivia ponderables such as what was on 'Watch with Mother' on Mondays and what happened to sixties TV star Richard Bradford, once landing themselves in hot water when Oddie demonstrated the workings of a cashpoint using what appeared to be an audience member's PIN. Their fun was curtailed all too soon by the rise of *Neighbours*, and while *Go for It!* and *Fax* struggled on in Sunday afternoon slots, poor old *Masterteam* – so very clearly headed for cult status – had to call it a day in favour of Henry Ramsay driving off with a cake on the roof of his car.

After that, it was time to turn over for a similar BBC2 slot; only because this was the 'arts' channel, it was generally filled with more cerebral and esoteric fare, with the odd teen drama thrown in for good measure. Technically a prequel to earlier cult hit *The Water Margin*, and even more confusingly a Japanese series based on ancient Chinese mythology, free-wheeling fast-talking *Monkey* (BBC, 1979–81) starred sixties pop star Masaaki Sakai as the titular simian deity, cast out of heaven after relieving himself in far too close proximity to Buddha's fingers, and banished to Earth to serve out his redemption by joining boy priest – played by a woman – Tripitaka, pig demon Pigsy and fish spirit Sandy on their quest to find holy scriptures reputedly in the lost region of Ghandara. Rewritten by David Weir, who added *Radio Times* reader-baitingly ridiculous titles like 'Pigsy Woos a Widow' and 'What Monkey Calls the Dog-Woman', with a voice cast including Miriam Margolyes, Burt Kwouk and Andrew Sachs and dynamic music from the Japanese rock band Godiego, *Monkey* became a massive cult favourite, and playgrounds were immediately full of children trying to 'kung fu' each other while yelling 'MONKAAAAAAAH!' and trying to summon his flying pink cloud with the nearest thing to a staff that was to hand.

Tucker's Luck (BBC, 1983–85) saw *Grange Hill*'s former tearaway defying all of Bullet Baxter's predictions that he would never amount to anything by throwing himself into adult education and youth training schemes while chasing girls, with threats of thumpings from older brothers never far away. His new life drove a wedge between him and the increasingly indolent and prospectless Alan and the increasingly criminal Tommy, but he forged new friendships with misunderstood local skinhead Ralph Passmore and his former classroom arch-enemy Trisha Yates. Set in a world of orange-logoed Job Centres – a point hammered home by the hilarious opening titles shot of Alan forlornly rifling through a handful of coins while dreaming of affording some chips – officious potential bosses and hair-raising railing-vaulting chases across supermarket car parks, it was a hugely underappreciated series that showed hope and possibility while never shying away from the harsh realities of Britain in the early eighties.

With B.A. Robertson's wistful theme song confirming that she won't work in a factory though her parents think she should, academically inclined Glaswegian schoolgirl *Maggie* (BBC, 1981–82) stood her ground and pursued her dream of attending university in a world of Postcard Records and *Gregory's Girl*. B.A. also turned up as one of the cast of performers in *Dear Heart* (BBC, 1982–83), set in the offices and within the pages of a teen magazine run by 'Superadviceperson' Toyah Willcox, punctuated by sketches about acne cream and rainbow-mohicanned punks disregarding 'Keep Off the Grass' signs, with a spiky post-punk edge that ensured a constant stream of outraged letters to *Points of View*.

Professor Heinz Wolff judged the efficacy of contestants' studio-traversing constructions in the blippery-themed *The Great Egg Race* (BBC, 1979–86), Bernard Falk challenged rival teams holed up in puzzle-festooned Eastnor Castle to *Now Get Out of That* (BBC, 1981–84), and Jeremy Beadle investigated the trade secrets behind history's greatest hoodwinkers in *The Deceivers* (BBC, 1981). Guitarist Deirdre Cartwright, bassist Henry Thomas and drummer Geoff Nicholls took you through the fundamentals of EQ levels and downstrokes in *Rockschool* (BBC, 1983–87), junior canoeing hopefuls took to the water in *Paddles Up!* (BBC, 1984–93) and Peter Purves commentated on squelchily themed motocross rally *Kick Start* (BBC, 1979–82).

Fame! (1982–85) found its way over from BBC1 once it went back on its promise to learn how to fly, and a few hardy souls pledged allegiance to *Harold Lloyd's World of Comedy* (1980), little more than a collection of classic silent comedy clips with a new over-explaining alliteration-crazed narration from Henry Corden and the Jimmy Joyce Singers urging all and sundry to 'laugh a while, dig that style – a pair of glasses and a smile'. If you were after straight-up pop thrills, however, Jenny Powell and Tony Baker hit the B-roads for fast-moving video-driven roadshow *No Limits* (BBC, 1985–87), and the more sophisto-pop orientated *Juice* (BBC, 1986) allowed vox-popped fans in designer gear to relate how much cleverer they were than you for liking 'Sweet Love' by Anita Baker. Ironically, it was the success of both of those shows that led to the tradition finally being upended in 1988, with the launch of dedicated youth slot *Def II*.

Channel 4, of course, did not want to limit itself or its audience by doing anything so restrictive and reductive as designating anything as a 'children's programme'. Misanthropic cartoon misery-guts *Murun Buchstansangur* (Channel 4, 1982–89) – a huge pale green head who lived in a crack under the kitchen sink – pursued his feckless lack of aspirations at the expense of anyone else's hopes and dreams, and while Gerry Anderson's pun-governed android P.I. *Dick Spanner* (Channel 4, 1987) might have started off as an insert in controversial high-speed Sunday lunchtime youth show *Network 7*, his adventures were later compiled into omnibus form, doubtless occasioning him to have to scoot out of the way of an omnibus with an advert plugging them on the side, for late afternoon outings. Presented by a dust-caked John Hurt and an alarmingly convincing animatronic dog, Jim Henson's *The StoryTeller* (Channel 4, 1987) ostensibly retold classic children's folk tales using technologically advanced puppets interacting with the likes of Sean Bean, Dawn French and Jennifer Saunders, but simultaneously had its eye on every award imaginable, most of which it deservedly went on to win. *S.W.A.L.K.* (Channel 4, 1982) starred Nicola Cowper as lovelorn schoolgirl Amanda, guided through her turbulent teenage emotions by Prunella Scales as photostory problem page masthead Aunt Patti, complete with a theme song that would not have sounded out of place on an Altered Images album.

The jury will probably always be out on whether *Doctor Who* (BBC 1963–89, 2005–) is actually a children's programme or not, although few could deny the thrills the TARDIS and the Daleks held for younger viewers, especially during Tom Baker's long-scarfed tenure. Both the BBC and ITV have always otherwise filled its traditional Saturday afternoon slot with American action serials, from the well-loved likes of *The A-Team* and *The New Adventures of Wonder Woman* to the probably best-forgotten likes of *Automan*, though there have been some notable exceptions.

Quick Before They Catch Us (BBC, 1966) thrust sharply dressed gadget-loving teenage Mods Kate, Johnny and Mark into a Swinging London full of spies and art theft, with a theme song from Beatle associate Klaus Voorman that was probably as close as you could get to a Lennon-McCartney original by that point. Richard Carpenter's lavishly filmed Clannad-soundtracked *Robin of Sherwood* (ITV, 1984–86) focused on the otherwise overlooked mythological aspects of the legend; this allowed a seamless transition when Michael Praed left after two rapturously received series as 'The Hooded Man' Robin of Loxley, to be replaced by Jason Connery as Robin of Huntingdon. The show also introduced the idea of the Merry Men including a Saracen – written in at short notice as an initially non-speaking character when extra Mark Ryan proved such a good fit on set – which has since been adopted pretty much en masse by all subsequent adaptations.

For sheer vaingloriousness, however, few could match the epic saga of *The Tripods* (BBC, 1984–85). Based on John Christopher's trilogy of novels, Will, Henry and Beanpole's desperate flight on foot to evade the mind-controlling 'capping' enforced by less than benevolent alien interlopers featured dazzling and exciting effects work. But with a huge amount of international co-funding and a corresponding volume of episodes to fill, they also notoriously enjoyed a stopover at a French château learning how to make wine; it's safe to say the audience didn't enjoy it quite as much. A second series saw them infiltrate the Tripods' home city and ended on a staggering cliffhanger, upon which the funding was pulled and that third and final series never came.

In amongst the mirth-free political discussion that dominated Sunday lunchtimes, there were numerous 'factutainment' shows like Chris Serle's themed rifle through the archives *Windmill* (BBC, 1985–88), its pacier pop music and computer graphics-driven compatriot *Boxpops* (BBC, 1988–92) and a young Carol Vorderman advising why you should *Take Nobody's Word for It* (BBC, 1987–89) – or indeed 'Taken Obody Sword Forit' – on widely held scientific assumptions. Later on in the day you could find the BBC's 'Sunday Classics', home to robust literary adaptations of everything from

Little Lord Fauntleroy (1976), *Great Expectations* (1981), *Gulliver in Lilliput* (1982) and *Vanity Fair* (1987) to *Sexton Blake and the Demon God* (1978), *Beau Geste* (1982), Tom Baker's turn as the great detective in *The Hound of the Baskervilles* (1982), *The Diary of Anne Frank* (1986) and *Brat Farrar* (1987). It is, however, primarily remembered for one reason and one reason alone – *Pinocchio* (1978), which adhered all too closely to the dark and twisted tone of the original novel, with a screechy splintery tantrum-throwing puppet wandering about amongst human actors and scratchily rendered 'sets' and prone to leaping in the air shouting 'WHEEEEE' for no clear reason. Most younger viewers were too terrified to keep watching for long.

ITV did make a couple of attempts at luring viewers away from the 'Sunday Classics', but their choices were eccentric, to say the least. *The Further Adventures of Oliver Twist* (ITV, 1980) and *Alice in Wonderland* (ITV, 1986) arguably showed that they would struggle to beat the BBC at their own game. And while *The Honey Siege* (ITV, 1987) succeeded as an original costume drama and *A Little Princess* (ITV, 1987) was a decent enough adaptation of Frances Hodgson Burnett's novel, it was always with the quirkier offerings that they scored actual hits. *Young Sherlock* (ITV, 1982) imagined Guy Henry as a school-age Holmes foiling a conspiracy to assassinate Queen Victoria to a backdrop of wax cylinders and coaches screeching to a halt on gravel in 'The Mystery of the Manor House'; it was to its great misfortune that it wound up overshadowed by Stephen Spielberg's less imaginative big-screen exploration of the same idea. *Seal Morning* (ITV, 1986) starred a young Holly Aird as a teenage girl who discovers life and love while looking after a washed-up seal pup in 1930s Scotland, and *Knights of God* (ITV, 1987) – actually held back by almost two years due to an unfortunate coincidence with

THAT'S NOT A CHILDREN'S PROGRAMME

news events – was set in a totalitarian near-future full of militarised vehicle chases that would have put an Arnold Schwarzenegger film to shame as Welsh teenager Gervais Edwards wrestled with a prophecy that he would restore law and order. *Shadow of the Stone* (ITV, 1987) introduced Shirley Henderson as a modern-day Glaswegian teenager with a psychic link to a seventeenth-century suspected witch, and the scarcely describable *Stookie* (ITV, 1985) revolved around a Glaswegian punk, who according to the theme song was 'always ready to take a chance' if 'always a victim of circumstance', foiling an art theft plot. Their only real enduring Sunday afternoon success, however, came with the James Galway-heralded Lilliputian further adventures of *The Return of the Antelope* (ITV, 1986–88).

Perhaps wisely, ITV also largely opted to leave the import-favouring Saturday afternoon well alone – with a couple of truly staggering exceptions. Opening with a dramatic orchestral flourish as he galloped determinedly past a gallows, Richard O'Sullivan's turn as historical highwayman *Dick Turpin* (ITV, 1979–82), reinvented as a righter of wrongs in cahoots with his juvenile sidekick Swiftnick, was massive in a *TV Times*-hogging manner that makes its subsequent disappearance all the more difficult to understand.

One of Philip Pullman's earliest novels formed the basis of *How to Be Cool* (ITV, 1988), a staggering tour de force with state-of-the-art visual effects inspired by *A Clockwork Orange* and *The Prisoner*, about a gang of image-obsessed teenagers who discover that 'fashion' is created and controlled by a sinister government department headed by Roger Daltrey as the vindictive Mr Cashman. Unfortunately, the less welcome presence of a certain other rock veteran lower down the cast list means that it is unlikely to enjoy any further exposure now. In an audacious move, *How to Be Cool* was preceded by a similarly computer-generated arresting setting – albeit with a curiously low-key theme tune – of Jenny Nimmo's similarly modern novel of *The Owl Service*-aligned Welsh mythology *The Snow Spider* (ITV, 1988), followed by adaptations of the follow-on novels *Emlyn's Moon* (ITV, 1990) and *The Chestnut Soldier* (ITV, 1991). It's not clear exactly how many viewers were watching either show, but they certainly made contrasting impressions on those who did.

ITV's daily broadcasts of Big Bird and company introducing sarsaparilla-referencing pre-school education, brought to you by the letters 'A' and 'G' and the number '3', made it that bit harder for your parents to refuse to allow you to stay up to watch their close associates in *The Muppet Show* (ITV, 1976–81). In fact, whether it was a consciously overplayed revival of radio detective *Dick Barton: Special Agent* (ITV, 1979) in serialised weekday instalments, elaborate festive rock musical spectaculars like wooden horse-legend reinterpretation *Great Big Groovy Horse* (BBC, 1975) and suspiciously *Watch* 'Nativity'-resembling *Follow the Star* (BBC, 1979) or the Alpine smuggler-thwarting and bomb-defusing derring-do of *Skiboy* (ITV, 1974), there were programmes that weren't for children but also sort of were everywhere you looked – although, no matter how much you may have loved Kenny Everett, using that as a basis to be allowed to watch his gleefully outrageous ITV sketch show was an argument few could win.

Probably no single programme epitomised this better, though, than *The Goodies* (BBC 1970–81, ITV 1982). Bill Oddie, Graeme Garden and Tim Brooke-Taylor's promise that their agency of mayhem-makers for hire would do 'anything anytime' was more than fulfilled by their long series of comic rampages through extreme exaggerated versions of topical concerns from energy shortages to disco mania, all of it crammed with silly jokes, over-the-top stunts, speeded-up slapstick and funked-up pop songs. Initially conceived as a late-night show for a countercultural audience, its comic strip-like qualities nudged it ever further forward in the schedules and nudged them ever higher up the pop charts, causing hysterics as they tried to capture a giant kitten menacing London, fled a 'puppet government' in the form of a similarly enlarged Dougal from *The Magic Roundabout*, and came face to face with a not remotely giant Giant at the top of a beanstalk. They enthusiastically embraced their new younger audience, and were always happy to put in a promotional appearance on *Blue Peter* or *Crackerjack!*, but never forgot their alternative roots, meaning that it was still always full of 'naughty' gags that were just about tame enough to avoid you being packed off to bed.

Of course, there was one slot at the very end of the week that you wished could be 'for' you but absolutely was not by any measurable standard, and was even more verboten than Kenny Everett. ITV's late Sunday night edgy comedy slot, home to such Monday morning playground chatter, included *Clive James on Television*, *Agony*, *Hot Metal* and, most notoriously of all, *Spitting Image*. Sometimes, you had to accept that you were lucky to even be allowed to watch *Paint Along with Nancy*.

'Space goes on forever'

Unless you were the most beyond hope of teacher's pets, the most exciting part of the school week – the bell at the end of a Friday notwithstanding – was when you got to watch television *at school*. Sitting cross-legged in front of that big TV on a stand with shutters on it, for reasons nobody could ever quite figure out, and pretending to shoot the 'dots' on the pre-programme countdown clock to the accompaniment of faintly disapproving looks from your teacher, you could pretend for that crucial twenty-odd minutes that you weren't actually in school at all. As you sat enthralled by *My World* (ITV, 1969–88) and *W.A.L.R.U.S.* (BBC, 1981–90), or just tried to avoid catching a glimpse of the hurtling zoom-in-and-out opening titles of *Near and Far* (BBC, 1975–88), your teacher also got twenty-odd minutes to pretend that they were pretty much anywhere else in the world. It was a welcome moment of escapism in a week of rulers and prefect badges, but it was also a false economy. You could imagine that you were at home watching television all you liked, but there was one inconvenient and unavoidable truth — the programmes didn't look like anything you would have seen at home.

Invariably a year or two out of date visually, with make-do-and-mend 'that'll do' sets and graphics, and a presentational style that suggested you had simply happened to stumble across them minding their own business in the corner of a television studio, schools' programmes were literally in a class of their own. There were a handful that looked just that little bit closer to 'proper' television, though.

Intended to provoke heated discussions in double social studies, *Scene* (BBC, 1968–2002) presented a series of miniature social realist plays that frequently brought sex and drugs — or at least kissing and furtive cigarettes — into the classroom under the pretence of opening up 'debate'. *How We Used to Live* (ITV, 1968–1988) followed various iterations of the Selby family from the late Victorian era to post-Woodstock social upheaval, contrasting harrowing episodes charting familial lack of fortune, through everything from the Somme to hallucinogen dependency, with chipper conversations about this new paper called the *Radio Times* that tells you what's on the wireless and when.

THAT'S NOT A CHILDREN'S PROGRAMME

None, however, came quite as close as *Look and Read* (BBC, 1967–2004), a series of cliffhanging serials that were generally more exciting and far-flung than pretty much anything you would get to watch at home, with only the minor inconvenience of a couple of songs about alliterative vowels to remind you that you were still sitting on the floor in the assembly hall.

Look and Read had its origins in another BBC schools' show, multi-disciplinary miscellany *Merry-Go-Round* (BBC, 1963–83). Producer Claire Chovil had experimented with running serials interspersed with teaching segments and limited to the first two hundred basic words of the English language aimed at improving literacy in two mid-sixties modules – Frank and Helen's angling-occasioned discovery of snatched wages 'Fishing for Fivers' (1965) and boy, girl and dog beachfront stolen medal retrieval 'Tom, Pat and Friday' (1966). The response to these was so overwhelmingly positive that the following year, rival duo Bob and Carol became the stars of the first ever *Look and Read* serial. Divided into two separate stories written by 'Tom, Pat and Friday' writer Joy Thwaytes – 'The Lost Treasure' and 'The Stolen Treasure' – 'Bob and Carol Look for Treasure '(1967) starred Veronica Purnell and Stephen Leigh as inquisitive youngsters on the trail of pilfered ancient artefacts, solving the mystery by way of a series of word-related puzzles that viewers were invited to crack too before they did. It was all very fresh-faced and clean-cut – albeit with certain references and allusions that would not have sat well even only a couple of years later – but the next serial took *Look and Read* off in a very different direction.

Written by Leonard Kingston, 'Len and the River Mob' (1968) starred George Layton as Len Tanner, a dock worker who stumbles across a gang smuggling goods stolen from struggling local businesses and finds himself framed for the robberies when he tries to expose crooked Mr Moon and Captain Grenko to the authorities. Filmed in a menacingly shabby dockland setting, packed with suspense and menace, including a jump to safety from a high window and even finding room for a boat chase – and, in a neat touch, having his landlady Mrs Green present the teaching segments for the episode in which Len is held captive – 'Len and the River Mob' could easily have been mistaken for a grittier adult drama by inattentive viewers. It even led to a sequel, 'Roy and the Danelli Job' (1971), which followed the fortunes of Kenneth Gardiner's calypso-singing dockhand, in viewer contribution-sourced multimedia primer *Television Club* (BBC, 1962–79).

'The Boy from Space' (1971) returned to the boy-and-girl format with Sylvestra Le Touzel and Stephen Garlick as Helen and Dan, two astronomy-fixated youngsters who come to the aid of a stranded alien boy they name 'Peep-Peep', in reference to his garbled bleeping speech patterns, helping to shield him from Aubrey Morris' sinister big-hatted 'Thin Man', a fugitive from his race intent on extracting information for malevolent purposes. Very much in the folk horror-aligned sci-fi style of the time, with the combination of a small cast, sparse locations and a storyline that hinged on an inability to communicate warnings of imminent danger – a sense of cosmic meets countryside unease that the teaching segments presented by Charles Collingwood in an observatory only served to highlight – 'The Boy from Space' brought an unexpected note of edge-of-the-seat terror into the mundanity of the school day. So, it's hardly surprising that so many erstwhile pupils panicking over Helen and Dan's obliviousness to the causes of Peep-Peep's alarm remember it so vividly while often not being able to recall what it was called.

It also marked two significant introductions to the *Look and Read* universe – scriptwriter Richard Carpenter and music from the BBC Radiophonic Workshop courtesy of John Baker, as well as the earliest glimpses of word-forming songs and animations that punctuated future serials, including the 'Magic E' wizard, word-wall building Bill the Brickie and the consonant-hunting exploits of Dog Detective. Wall-to-wall agrarian angst was more the order of the day for Leonard Kingston's 'Joe and the Sheep Rustlers' (1973), featuring Struan Rodger as a young farmhand on the trail of *ovis aries*-nicking local bad guys in a world of coded messages and luminescent paint trails. The first *Look and Read* serial to be broadcast in colour, with theme music from Paddy Kingsland and Joe himself presenting the teaching segments from a cowshed full of conveniently learning-friendly farm implements as well as his self-made 'Picture Stretcher' and 'Type Lighter', it cemented the *Look and Read* format as somewhere between sophisticated, intelligent drama and an interactive puzzle that children could play along with without ever realising that they were learning about compound adjectives by stealth – although the show was soon joined by someone who was only too happy to emphasise the joys of the formal study of language.

Opening with a suitably ominous electronic thunderclap-punctuated theme from Roger Limb and time-lapse footage of deserts blooming, 'Cloud Burst' (1974) concerned the nightmarish tale of Renu Setnu as Ram Pandit, inventor of a 'Rain Gun' which could potentially end global famine but which other parties – including his 'Gas Gun'-wielding twin brother Ravi – inevitably want for less benevolent purposes, with only Nigel Rathbone and Tina Heath as teenagers Tim and Jenny to help him stay one step ahead. Closer to a Cold War thriller than a schools' television play, the disconcerting contrast between the clean and clinical and the shabby and neglected – Richard Carpenter's script specified that Pandit's laboratory should have an untidy feel with bodged repair work, at least partly to distract from the computers looking outdated in any future repeat runs – it certainly gave any children watching a good deal of pause for thought, and it's doubtful that any of them spotted the deliberately low-tech twist at the climax coming.

In a neat metatextual move, Richard Carpenter presented the teaching segments as the writer in his 'office', but he wasn't alone. Keen to give the human presenters something to interact with, incoming producer Sue Weeks hit upon the idea of Mr Watchword, a floating letter-festooned orange puppet voiced by Charles Collingwood and ostensibly resembling an electronic typewriter print head. Wordy, as he insisted on being addressed by his fellow 'Word-Watchers', would generally emerge from something word-related lying around the set and regale viewers with smug interjections that mainly served to proclaim how much better he was at spotting linguistic patterns and conventions than you. Wordy was loved and loathed in equal measure, and more often than not both simultaneously.

Presumably in no way related to Wordy's winning demeanour, Richard Carpenter remained strictly off-screen for 'The King's Dragon' (1977), presented instead by Kenneth Watson as *Hastings Times* editor Jack Dunbar, struggling to paste up a story about a local archaeological mystery in the face of continual interruptions from the hovering pedant. With an artefact-purloining gang communicating via personal ads and crossword clues, Frankie Jordan as intrepid investigative journalist Ann Mills and Sean Flanagan as history-fixated schoolboy are hot on their heels in a whirl of superstition and museum security, but inevitably there's a surprise in store for everyone and the errant King's Dragon is not entirely what it seems. With the emphasis on anachronistic intrigue everywhere from Roger Limb's theme music to the extensive location filming at Hastings Castle and

St Clements Caves, viewers were encouraged to put together their own newspaper front-page story about an exhibit in their own local museum or library, and we can only guess at how teachers must have felt about the paste-and-spatula mayhem that awaited them.

Leonard Kingston's 'Sky Hunter' (1978) boasted a brilliantly sinister turn from Geoffrey Bayldon as the head of a birdnapping ring, who went to often frightening lengths to prevent Donald Waugh, Luke Batchelor and Jayne Tottman as peregrine falcon-bothering teen enthusiasts Trevor, Butch and Jackie from exposing their activities. Perhaps to offset Roger Limb's haunting theme and visuals, which would not have looked out of place in an episode of *The Professionals*, Michael Maynard presented the teaching segments from the gaudy giant book-festooned 'Wordy's Word Lab'.

Astronaut Phil Cheney arrived at Space Station WORDLAB-1 for a retelling of 'The Boy from Space' (1980); although the original serial had been broadcast in black and white, the actual film segments had been made in colour and were reused – with new brief links by the older reminiscing Dan and Helen – for this new version. The original edits were tightened up, Paddy Kingsland added fresh music and effects and, perhaps most significantly, Derek Griffiths, a regular vocal contributor to the animated inserts since the early seventies, performed a new theme song; an icily celestial rumination on whether out there in space we shall find friends or a place where the universe ends, swooping off into the twinkling void on the repeated line 'space goes on forever'. Everyone working on the new version was apparently specifically requested to lighten the tone slightly from the frequently harsh and nightmarish original, but judging from how many schoolchildren still continued to be terrified by the 'Thin Man', it's debatable how far they manged to accomplish this.

Andrew Davies came on board as a writer for 'Dark Towers' (1981), an unusually comic if still appropriately dark tale in which Juliet Waley and Gary Russell, as Tracy and Edward, teamed up with the resident phantoms of a strange old house to prevent a group of thieves posing as antiques experts from making off with its fixtures and furnishings. Derek Griffiths and Roger Limb invited all and sundry to come and see the dust and cobwebs everywhere and footsteps on the winding stairs – if they dared – with Denise Coffey's librarian on hand to help Wordy get in the way.

Christopher Russell's 'Fair Ground!' (1983) – where fortunes can be lost and found as you whirl around – saw Paul Russell as Ozzie concluding that fair was most definitely not fair at the fairground as he investigated an outbreak of ride sabotage, with Wayne Laryea purportedly illustrating the accompanying booklet in his studio, also home to a mouse that proved pleasingly aggravating to Wordy.

Julia Millbank portrayed white-streaked naturalist Debbie in Andrew Davies' 'Badger Girl' (1984), battling to foil a pony-smuggling plot with theme song encouragement to leave the town behind along with the traffic and the street, and Margo Gunn's National Trust custodian relating the teaching sections with reference to Debbie's scrapbook. Leon Armstrong's Spuggy had to choose between running hard and flying past as he eschewed his family's love of a good sprint in favour of pigeon fancying in Christopher Russell's 'Geordie Racer' (1988), with Wordy joining local radio DJ Peter Rowell in his studio for some decidedly non-pop-picking word-watching.

The most outlandish production yet, Russell's 'Through the Dragon's Eye' (1989) cast Marlaine Gordon, Nicola Stewart and Simon Fenton, as Amanda, Jenny and Scott, into an elaborate role-playing, game-inspired fantasy landscape as they sought to

THAT'S NOT A CHILDREN'S PROGRAMME

help Gorwen the Dragon prevent the magical kingdom of Pelamar from slowly vanishing thanks to the machinations of Charn the Evil One. As their bid to reconstruct energy source the Veetacore hinged directly on their ability to read and interpret on behalf of other characters, separate teaching segments were not considered necessary and, possibly to nobody's major dismay, Wordy was left on the substitute bench this time around; in a further sign of the times, the serial also tied in with an accompanying BBC Micro game.

To balance the books slightly after this big-budget excursion, 'Sky Hunter II' (1992) saw the original serial updated with a dramatic new theme song and new links from Wordy and the now grown-up Trevor, Butch and Jackie on an RSPB bus. It was Sue Weeks' last *Look and Read* production and the last appearance by Wordy, who bid viewers a possibly not entirely unwelcome goodbye at the conclusion. When *Look and Read* next returned, ecological parable 'Earth Warp' (1993) came accompanied by the very first stirrings of interactive material hosted in the exciting new interactive world of the World Wide Web, which if nothing else was a long way from Bob and Carol reading price labels with a magnifying glass.

The world had changed, technology had changed and education itself was changing, and *Look and Read* – fittingly for a show that was always trying to emphasise the difference between vowels and adjectives through dialogue about walkie-talkies and radar signals – was only too happy to change with them. There was a time, though, when whether you were watching in school or at home – where, shorn of its proper classroom context, it could seem even weirder still – *Look and Read* never failed to deliver thrills, action, mild scares and interactive excitement on a scale you just didn't get elsewhere, and in a programme that wasn't meant for you, to boot.

12

The Pre-News Slot

'When Custard Stole the Show'

So, you've had your fun for the day — or not, if you'd just witnessed an especially hard-hitting episode of *Grange Hill* — and it's time for important stories about Princess Anne, Zimbabwe Rhodesia and high court challenges to Tiny Rowland's latest business takeover bid for boring men in ties to read out for the benefit of your boring old parents. Fortunately, there's still five minutes to go before The News, and there's just enough time to squeeze in one last wry, whimsical and frequently decidedly odd animation — and what's more, the unexpected additional audience of grown-ups who had tuned in just that bit too early to see whatever for the late-afternoon headlines found that they weren't exactly averse to them either.

With the news serving up a daily diet of unrest, discord and causes for concern at the best of times, a quick off-the-wall animation was a useful buffer against the harsh realities of harsh reality that children were often best being kept away from, especially without a John Craven on hand to break the breaking headlines to them in a more suitable manner. More importantly, they were also a buffer against 'buffers', with oblique and sometimes just plain direct humour at the expense of those droning men making decisions nobody seemed that much in favour of, which would have done Monty Python,

Mike Yarwood or *Private Eye* proud. Having a bit of silliness at their expense ahead of what they probably considered their starring moment, often with undertones that may not have been explicitly political but certainly suggested that Evil Edna and Custard had no time for any of that nonsense, was as big a two fingers to the establishment as any waved by any passing punk rocker.

Even before Dougal and Zebedee did their best to beat the Prime Minister in a popularity contest, Hergé's intrepid boy detective dashed into the slot with Snowy in hot pursuit in *The Adventures of Tintin* (BBC, 1962–64). Originally shown in France between 1957 and 1964, the Peter Hawkins-led dubs of adapted serialised cliff-hanging comic strip adventures like *Red Rackham's Treasure* and *The Crab with the Golden Claws* were still being shown – with the famous bellowed exhortation to watch the following instalment immediately imitated by anyone within earshot – over twenty years later.

Captain Haddock and company were soon joined in the timeslot by 1966's *La Maison de Toutou* – better known as *Hector's House* (BBC, 1968–70) – where Hector the Dog's houseproud attempts at garden maintenance were frequently undermined by unsolicited contributions from his helpful but naive neighbours Kiki the Frog and Zsazsa the Cat, invariably leading the lugubrious hound to directly address the camera proclaiming himself to be 'a great big [insert theme of story] old Hector'. A 1968 adaptation of Jean de Brunhoff's classic children's stories about an elephant born to be king – also a great favourite on *Jackanory* at the time – gained an Eric Thompson narration for *Babar* (BBC, 1969), and with his simultaneous narration on *The Magic Roundabout* also part of the equation, you could be forgiven for thinking that France was exerting an undue if welcome influence over this most innocuous of timeslots, especially once they were joined by *Barbapapa* (BBC, 1970) and his family of amorphous shape-shifting problem-solving blobs. Doubtless all of those humourless men on The News would have had something to say about that.

There were plenty of homegrown contributions, however, notably Smallfilms with *Clangers* and later the colour remake of *Ivor the Engine*, the many productions of Ivor Wood and FilmFair, and a certain other remake from children's television's distant yet recent past. John Ryan had originally created *Captain Pugwash* (BBC, 1957–66, 1974–75) and his bumbling horde of underachieving piratical rogues – who never really managed to display very much in the way of rogueishness – for a strip in *Eagle* comic, before turning their seafaring blundering war of treasure-mislaying attrition with Cutthroat Jake into a series of accordion-accompanied television adventures, using an innovative animation style where cut-out characters and scenery were moved around in real time courtesy of paper levers and tabs.

The Captain's original adventures had proved a huge cross-platform phenomenon and had varied across a number of days and timeslots, but when Master Mate and Tom the Cabin Boy set sail in *The Black Pig* again in colour in the mid-seventies, they were firmly anchored in the pre-news slot – and not just because Willy forgot to haul the anchor – where the Captain's way with an alliterative exclamation of alarm ('Suffering Seagulls!') won over a whole new generation of fans. On a similarly historical trajectory, John Ryan also created *The Adventures of Sir Prancelot* (BBC1, 1972), a serialised mini-crusade by a Crusades-bound knight who probably would have helped everyone more if he'd just stayed at home, plagued by the schemes of Count Otto the Blot and the recommendations of his bank manager, and joined against his wishes on his journey by his family and a lute-wielding minstrel, who 'played' the surprisingly rocking electric sitar theme music under the closing credits.

Hilary Hayton – who designed the original Play School house – created *Crystal Tipps and Alistair* (BBC, 1972–74), a psychedelically hued voluminously haired girl and her cumbersome dog who enjoyed abstract silent garden-centric adventures with their appropriately named friends Butterfly and Birdie, set to a chunky Farfisa organ soundtrack, while Mick the Marmaliser and Nigel Ponsonby-Smallpiece got up to all manner of 'By Jove!'-occasioning puppet mischief in *Ken Dodd and the Diddy Men* (BBC, 1969).

Meanwhile, pioneering independent animator Bob Godfrey – who had caused a sensation with his advertiser-baiting satirical 1961 short *The Do-It-Yourself Animation Kit*, and a very different kind of sensation with some deliberately unerotic sex comedy shorts in the early seventies – quietly dominated the slot without anyone really noticing; well, apart from parents complaining that their children's eyesight was being ruined. Using marker pens and an intentionally loose style, he had hit on a technique that made the cartoon images continually appear to be 'bouncing' and which ideally suited the cast of Richard Briers-voiced eccentrics that populated his shows. In a manner entirely befitting of the chaotic rasping theme music, over-enthusiastic floppy green dog *Roobarb* (BBC, 1974) continually tried his hand at ill-advised lifestyle pursuits which were perpetually undermined by the sarcastic disdain of prank-prone neighbouring pink cat Custard, and a source of continual amusement to the tittering birds permanently parked in adjoining trees.

Sou'wester-sporting *Noah and Nelly in SkylArk* (BBC, 1976) travelled around in their all-terrain flying submarine/boat full of plurally named two-headed animals helping out the eccentric inhabitants of far-off lands, usually courtesy of Nelly's installable multifunctional knitting habit. Laissez-faire food-fixated daydreamer *Henry's Cat* (BBC, 1983–93) and his friends Chris Rabbit and Pansy

Pig invariably found that their well-intentioned attempts at making their own entertainment got on the wrong side of Farmer Giles and Constable Bulldog, not to mention their woolly arch enemy Rum Baa Baa; Henry himself was nowhere to be seen, only ever glimpsed in response to a letter to *Points of View* asking what he looked like. Unusually for a show in this timeslot, some of which struggled to come up with one that was any degree above cursory, *Henry's Cat* managed to accumulate three tunes; two separate chirpy electronic instrumentals punctuated by synthesised miaows, and a song confirming that he knows everything about nothing, and not too much about that.

Willo the Wisp (BBC1, 1981) began as an animated mascot for British Gas before being joined by fairy Mavis Cruet, Arthur the caterpillar, Carwash the cat, indefinable impractically limbed dog thing the Moog, transmutated former prince the Beast, mushroom-rocketing interplanetary explorers the Astrognats and fiendish talking television Evil Edna for a series of ludicrous vignettes in Doyley Wood, for which he also gained an uncanny resemblance to narrator Kenneth Williams, to the extent of looking more like him than the genuine article.

On a more angular tangent, father-and-son animation team and *Vision On* alumni Mirek and Peter Lang came up with the Beethoven-scored *Ludwig* (BBC, 1977), an oval crystalline multi gadget-facilitated violin-playing robot helping out woodland wildlife to the benign amusement of Jon Glover's binocular-toting birdwatcher. With only moderately less surrealism, Czechoslovakian twosome *Bob a Bobek* – internationally known as Rodney Bewes-voiced Bob and Bobby, *The Top Hat Rabbits* (BBC, 1983) – took on a procession of odd jobs that they were singularly unsuited for, accompanied by a single phrase electric piano melody that played incessantly throughout.

These shorts didn't just represent a time when animation was becoming more do-it-yourself and open to amusing experimentation from enterprising independents, though; they also, by virtue of their fondness for off-the-wall humour, gave the faintest echo of that column or cartoon in the newspaper that your dad guffawed at and you couldn't understand why but wanted to – and sometimes this was literally the case. Lionel Jeffries lent his voice to the *Daily Mail*'s fine-living philosophical hound *Fred Bassett* (BBC, 1977), and a distinguished voice cast – Peter Hawkins as Marlon and B.H., Sheila Steafel as Maisie and Baby Grumpling, Judy Bennett as Wellington and Leonard Rossiter as Boot – filled out the squelchy synth-introduced moneymaking philosophical drollery of the *Daily Mirror*'s *The Perishers* (BBC, 1979). Ultimately, though, even Boot's all-knowing rockpool-dwelling crustacean associates couldn't outthink the self-importance of The News, and once the blathering men in ties demanded that their failure to give direct answers to direct questions warranted a more prestigious timeslot and the BBC launched *The Six O'Clock News* in 1984, the associated schedule rejigging meant that was pretty much that.

The obvious solution was to move the next generation of what would have been pre-news cartoons to the start of the children's schedules, and plenty of new favourites found their way there too, notably an impressive trilogy of sort-of linked catchily theme-tuned shows from newspaper cartoonist Peter Maddocks. *The Family-Ness* (BBC, 1984) posited that there wasn't just one Loch Ness Monster but a whole family, including Eyewit-Ness, Forgetful-Ness and Lovely-Ness, summoned by savvy local youngsters Angus and Elspeth McTout on their 'thistle whistles' to run rings around the tourism industry. Serenaded by a procession of plane-spotters before colliding with the control tower, *Jimbo and the Jet Set* (BBC, 1986) followed a jumbo jet who was accidentally constructed using incorrect smaller dimensions and was forever causing exasperation to ground control staff with his associated aviatory ineptitude, while *Penny Crayon* (BBC, 1989) owned a set of wax sticks that could make whatever she drew into a solid three-dimensional object, usually involving moderately more ambition than the theme song's boast that she could create plates of chips and fishes. Terry Wogan wearily related the exploits of *Stoppit and Tidyup* (BBC, 1988), a pair of furry gonks created to promote the Keep Britain Tidy campaign, who constantly found themselves at odds with the likes of Go and Play, Clean Your Teeth and The Big Bad I SAID NO. The major problem they faced, however, was competition.

With a prestigious and notably revenue-generating ad break to separate *On Safari* from the *ITN News at 5.40*, ITV had never really bothered signing off their children's programmes with a cartoon, and since the 'Watch It!' strand was formalised in 1980 they'd been deploying one at the start of the slot instead. Orange blob man haunted by the tin can-themed formalities of modern admin and his own collapsing car *Aubrey* (ITV, 1980); Peter Ustinov-voiced and Douglas Adams and John Lloyd-penned inventor *Doctor Snuggles* (ITV, 1979) and his notably more intellectual animal friends; David McKee's Una Stubbs-narrated girl and bear duo *Victor and Maria* (ITV, 1981); *Towser* (ITV, 1984) and his Roy Kinnear-related tussles with the Terrible Thing and Goblin Gobble; Hilary Hayton's stylish silent feline *Doris* (ITV, 1983–85); *James the Cat* (ITV, 1984) and his theme song that was even more indolent than he was; and a famously spooky felt puppet-animated adaptation of Tove Jansson's *The Moomins* (ITV, 1983–85) with a suitably haunting ambient electronic theme, and especially the Willie Rushton-voiced Berk and Boni struggling to meet the culinary demands of The Thing Upstairs from beneath the *Trap Door* (ITV, 1986), had all already proved hugely popular on a scale that the BBC struggled to replicate.

Eventually – starting with Floella Benjamin's collection of silly stories and party games *Lay On Five* (BBC, 1985–86) – the BBC diversified into live-action, educational and even quiz-based programmes, and the brief but glorious tradition of sending up The News, or at the very least disrupting its gravitas with a crystalline alien probe thing helping a small bird batter a damaged bicycle horn back into shape, was quietly forgotten about. There may well be those, of course, who might suggest that certain latter-day politicians itching for a good send-up have increasingly come to resemble characters from some long-forgotten pre-news animation. I couldn't possibly comment on this, though you can be fairly certain that Evil Edna would.

'"It's nearly time for the news," said Florence'

As much as some may have railed against their garlic, their public displays of affection and their inconveniently fully functional and reliable cars, European tastes had a bigger influence on British life from the sixties onwards than anyone who didn't like the taste of that 'foreign muck' would ever have cared to admit. Rail, road, sea and air links were getting quicker and closer – especially with talk about a great big new supersonic jet with a weirdly dipped nose cone literally in the air – and as the less linguini-averse traversed further afield, so the excitingly new and modern lifestyle and entertainment options began to make their way back with them, and British consumers were only too keen to avail themselves of continental alternatives.

THE PRE-NEWS SLOT

Mods zipped about from Yardbirds gig to Graham Bond Organisation gig on Italian scooters, connoisseurs began to slurringly sing the praises of German beers, those who had stayed sober the night before discovered the wellbeing benefits of Swiss muesli, and the latest hot fashions direct from the Milan catwalks — or at least a licensed copy of them — were suddenly something you could actually wear yourself. In 1965's *The Ipcress File*, there's even a scene where Michael Caine's Harry Palmer argues with his secret service superior in a supermarket over whether those fancy French mushrooms are really worth the price he's paying for them when you can get a bigger can of literally homegrown produce for a shilling or so less. Let's just say that it's not Colonel Ross' lifestyle that the audience comes to envy.

If you fancied a quick trip to experience some of it for yourself, there was a series of BBC foreign language instruction shows to help you pick up useful phrases for the hypermarket, including West German couple Heidi and Dieter's tentative romance in *Komm Mit!* (BBC, 1964), the coffee-adjacent dating mishaps of *Parliamo Italiano* (BBC, 1963), the ups and downs of life in an agency full of eccentric models in *Bonjour Françoise!* (BBC, 1965), and the codename-strewn sinister Alpine intrigue of *Suivez la Piste!* (BBC, 1966). It's not clear how much use many of the phrases from the latter would have been to anyone who didn't have 'Black Sun' on their trail.

Of course, no matter how much of a gourmet Harry Palmer may have been, the decidedly non-sophisticated British palate wasn't quite ready for any of this in its full-strength undiluted form just yet, and anything mass marketed often had to assume a not entirely metaphorical watered-down Anglicised form. Françoise Hardy and Vicky Leandros were obliged to 'Sing in English', your espresso may well have possibly been in the same room as some caffeine at some point but there was no guarantee of that, and even Heidi and Dieter and company had to have an over-explaining voiceover for the benefit of anyone who couldn't quite work out what was going on from the on-screen action and the captions. There was one European television show, however, that got its own entirely rebuilt narration for British audiences, and few would dispute that – for once – they got the better end of the deal.

Advertising executive Serge Danot had created five-minute animation *Le Manège Enchanté* for French television station RTF in 1963, working throughout the year with a team including a young British artist named Ivor Wood on an initial set of episodes in a makeshift studio in a derelict Parisian house, which was so desperately underequipped that the studio lights kept blowing the fuses. Enjoying short and simple adventures around a roundabout in a white garden decorated by stylised trees and flowers, Pollux the dog and his friends Ambroise the snail, Flappy the rabbit, Azalee the cow, Père Pivoine the roundabout operator, human girl Margote and a magical jack-in-the-box named Zébulon were first seen on French television on 5 October 1964. *Le Manège Enchanté* was instantly popular and new episodes continued to be made through to 1971, inspiring a slew of toys, games, storybooks and records, but even this was nothing compared with what would happen almost by chance when the show caught the eye of the BBC's Head of Family Programmes Doreen Stephens at a European television trade fair early in 1965.

Attracted by the visuals and convinced that the show was ideal for a weekday pre-news slot at the end of the children's schedules, Doreen was less sure about the actual content of the episodes. As the original soundtracks were cluttered and noisy and the storylines simplistic to the point of being negligible – not to mention the associated cost – direct translation did not seem to be a viable option. Instead, *Play School* presenter Eric Thompson was drafted in with a brief to rewrite the scripts and the characters as he saw fit; also unenamoured by the original soundtracks, he opted to simply watch each episode at home with the sound turned down and make up his own interpretations of what was happening on screen.

Pollux became curmudgeonly Dougal, Père Pivoine the bewildered Mr Rusty, Margote the quietly underwhelmed Florence, Ambroise the irritatingly positive Brian, Azalee became – supposedly inspired by his wife and fellow *Play School* presenter Phyllida Law – the chaotically theatrical Ermintrude, Flappy the laconic beatnik Dylan, doubtless named in honour of a certain harmonica-toting troubadour, and Zébulon the mysterious sage Zebedee. The scripts became freewheeling musings on aspects of the modern age, packed with topical gags about The Rolling Stones and 'I'm Backing Britain' and frequently with cultural and social references that the younger viewers might not have recognised but would still have understood, and *The Magic Roundabout* (BBC, 1965–77) made its debut on BBC1 on 18 October 1965. To say it became a success would be pretty much equivalent to what you might have got if you asked Dylan to describe its astonishing, overwhelming and unprecedented level of popularity.

Although it was almost certainly the charming, attractive and quasi-psychedelic look of its inhabitants that initially drew children into the Magic Garden – and almost equally certainly what initially inspired an avalanche of tie-in merchandise – it was Eric Thompson's dry narration and quirky scripts that really made *The Magic Roundabout* into the phenomenon it instantly became. His decidedly off-the-wall approximation of what was actually unfolding on screen was infused with dry wit and frequently subversive topical gags that slowly but surely hooked any news-anticipating parents accidentally catching a couple of minutes of it too. Much of this was down to the repositioning of Dougal as a dour and pessimistic snob with ideas above his overly hairy sugarcube-scoffing station, frequently clashing with the impenetrably cheerful Brian, the clumsily high-spirited Ermintrude and the frustratingly laid-back Dylan as they interfered with his ambitions towards cultural and intellectual self-advancement. Florence and Zebedee, meanwhile, acted as the adults in the room and Mr Rusty was never entirely sure whose side he was on, while the lesser-sighted likes of Florence's friends Paul, Basil and Rosalie, flower-chomping gardener Mr McHenry and Penelope the spider just regarded the unravelling nonsense as best they could.

A great believer in crediting children with intelligence, who more than once told an interviewer that he wrote his scripts for 'people' of all ages, Eric Thompson took great delight in personally refuting any and every objection from parents and educational experts alike; he reputedly once replied to a letter from a mother who complained that he used too many long words with a response using the longest words he could find in the dictionary, and on another occasion sent a strongly worded rejoinder to another who held him accountable for her children taking to calling each other 'molluscs'.

They were in the minority, however, as *The Magic Roundabout* was loved by pretty much everyone else – including Serge Danot, or at least once he had got over his concern that 'Dougal' was a punning slight on the name of French President and former hero of the Resistance Charles de Gaulle. Infrequent attempts to move it to an earlier timeslot were invariably met with a flood of letters demanding that it was restored to one where adults could see it too, and when *Blue Peter* ran a *Magic Roundabout*-themed competition it generated more than 100,000 entries.

THE PRE-NEWS SLOT

That said, that very first run of thirty-nine episodes was subtly but notably different to what most viewers would probably now recognise as *The Magic Roundabout*. As well as a slower version of the famously manic and naggingly insistent runaway organ theme music, it also has a running storyline; the very first instalment opens with Mr Rusty more or less on his own for an entire episode, lamenting the fact that nobody visits his roundabout any more, until Zebedee suddenly arrives in the post, promising to help him bring a bit of magic back to the miniature funfair. The remaining characters and the four children – who have their own running storyline about building a house in the Magic Garden – are slowly introduced over the following weeks, just in time to celebrate Roundabout Christmas on 22 December 1965. Following that, each new episode essentially became a free-for-all where saying anything could happen would be doing an understated disservice to Eric Thompson's apparently limitless imagination.

From Brian and Dylan forming a band – sounding uncannily like the recently controversially gone 'electric' Bob Dylan – who preferred to play with their sheet music upside down, to uppity flowers demanding to be treated with the due deference conferred by their self-designated social status, to the resident unpredictable and uncontrollable train announcing its intention to compete in the Olympics with no particular individual sport in mind, *The Magic Roundabout* could and did go anywhere with often not even the mildest concession to conventional logic, all of it dressed up in offbeat gags and humorous cultural references.

From books and story records to puppets and kaleidoscopes to pillowcases and board games to biscuits and plastic giveaway cereal toys – and from an ingenious playset allowing you to operate card representations of Mr Henry and company in a mock-television set through to a range of die-cast Corgi models, including a full-size Magic Garden playset with a moving roundabout and train – the cast of *The Magic Roundabout* was staring back at you every time you set foot in a shop. This did, however, have one ironic unintended effect – mindful of this proven commercial track record, Serge Danot's next series *Les Poucetofs* was as good as priced out of the UK broadcast market, eventually disappearing into contractual headaches following a bidding war between ITV companies, and was never seen over here in the UK.

In 1972, the characters made the leap to the big screen for *Pollux et le Chat Bleu – Dougal and the Blue Cat –* which cast them in a much darker tale about a feline interloper named Buxton who aligns himself with Fenella Fielding's mysterious 'Blue Voice' in a plot to seize control of the Magic Garden and refashion it in his own hue, with only Dougal able to see through his faux-innocent charisma, although his concerns are initially written off by the others as mere jealousy. Drenched in political subtext that pretty much wears its actual colours on its sleeve, and featuring some genuinely terrifying moments where even Buxton appears frightened, Eric Thompson's translation of *Dougal and the Blue Cat* noticeably attempted to play down the more extreme elements and lighten them with jokes. Almost certainly not what parents might have been expecting when they took their children to see their pre-news favourites on the big screen, it met with a decidedly muted reception at the time but has since become a cult favourite – albeit generally with adults who were traumatised by it as children.

Back in the happier surroundings of the front room, the BBC began showing *The Magic Roundabout* in colour in 1970, and it continued as a near-constant in the pre-news slot through to 1978, with repeats in other timeslots – notably across the school holiday mornings – continuing up to 1985. In 1991, Channel 4 purchased the rights to a batch of episodes of *The Magic Roundabout*, including some previously untranslated ones, to show as part of their new breakfast programme *The Channel 4 Daily*. Nigel Planer was brought in to provide the new scripts, and although he did a more than creditable job, somehow managing to capture the essence of Eric Thompson's version while still adding his own distinctive 'voice', it was inevitably never quite afforded the same degree of adulation.

The originals may be rarely seen now, largely on account of rights complications, but Eric Thompson and *The Magic Roundabout* are pretty much indivisible, tellingly underlined by the fact that a big-budget 2005 big-screen revival aimed at an international market stayed true to the spirit and setting of *The Magic Roundabout*, rather than *Le Manège Enchanté*; while the adoption of a traditional linear plot rather than random whimsical oddness didn't sit well with many, great care was still taken to avoid updating the setting and the characters themselves any more than was necessary.

This wasn't *The Magic Roundabout*'s only lasting legacy. Ivor Wood, who had originally suggested having a hair-covered shaggy dog puppet, largely on the basis that the lack of visible feet would save on animation time, returned to the UK in 1967, where his track record caught the attention of eccentric American producer Graham Clutterbuck and his London-based production company FilmFair. Ivor and FilmFair first worked together on *The Herbs* (BBC, 1968), a stop-motion presentation of *Paddington* creator Michael Bond's short stories about a bunch of anthropomorphised herbaceous plants who live in a well-tended walled garden, for the 'Watch with Mother' slot. Although the setting was slightly familiar, *The Herbs* more looked back to the eccentricities of modern British history than a magical pop-art white void vista, with the quaint string and woodwind accompaniment and Gordon Rollings' well-mannered narration lending it the feel of an Edwardian storybook gone wildly out of control.

Politely introducing himself as very friendly and with a tail for doing jobs of every kind, Parsley the Lion – who despite being mute was still able to break the fourth wall and communicate with both Gordon and the viewers – did his best to marshal the mayhem invariably caused by his harder-of-thinking neighbours, chaotically dashing Dill the Dog, pompous Sage the Owl, officious Constable Knapweed, rustic Bayleaf the Gardener, fire-breathing Tarragon the Dragon, academically inclined Mr and Mrs Onion and their family of chives, snake-charming Pashana Bedhi, and the garden's nominal custodians, the huntin' shootin' and fishin' Sir Basil and Lady Rosemary. Usually this involved such minor yet apparently vitally important incidents as Sage's nest blowing down and the disappearance of a bumper crop of strawberries, although a lightning-festooned encounter with Belladonna the Witch proved a little much for the BBC, who only showed it a handful of times. Packed with similarly distinctive wit that appealed as much to parents as children – while leafing through potential suitors for Aunt Mint, Bayleaf dismisses Birdbush as 'too common' – *The Herbs* later returned in the pre-news form of *The Adventures of Parsley* (BBC, 1970), introduced by Parsley's emulation of the MGM Lion and continuing their wonky philosophical musings in a shorter form.

Wood, Bond and FilmFair collaborated again for the pre-news slot with *Paddington* (BBC, 1976–80), a series of shorts inspired by the original books with narration from Michael Hordern and an unusual animation technique wherein the three-dimensional floppy-hatted well-meaning but mishap-prone stop-motion bear interacted with the people and places of a flatter cardboard cut-out world. The

THE PRE-NEWS SLOT

definitive adaptation for an entire generation, it bowed out with a series of longer specials and Paddington's unique performance of 'Singin' in the Rain'.

A Bernard Cribbins-narrated series based on Elizabeth Beresford's creations *The Wombles* (BBC, 1973–75) was, if anything, even more successful – not least on account of the fact that the catchy theme song by Mike Batt not only became a hit in its own right but also led to a string of top twenty smashes for Orinoco and company, who, courtesy of *Top of the Pops* performances by top session musicians in Womble costumes, went on to become the top-selling singles act of 1974. The fact that it was so imaginatively realised, with many a youngster seething with envy at Tobermory getting to have a car door as his workshop door, was not exactly a hindrance either.

Subsequently, Ivor Wood formed Woodland Animations and turned John Cunliffe's idea for a series about a postman and his black-and-white cat into *Postman Pat* (BBC, 1981), which followed Pat and Jess up hill and down dale as they made their rounds in Greendale, a village apparently entirely inhabited by folk in permanent need of a hand with odd jobs. A runaway success in the newly launched 'See-Saw' slot, *Postman Pat* went on to inspire many further series as well as a quiz show spin-off, a movie, books, adverts and a life-size Greendale at Longleat Safari Park, and Ken Barrie's sprightly theme song reflecting on Pat's happiness with his lot in life and the enticing suggestion that 'maybe, you can never be sure – there'll be knock, ring, letters through your door' skirted the top forty on more than one occasion. Woodland went on to furnish the 'See-Saw' slot with the anarchic go-getting grandchild-surprising exploits of *Gran* (BBC, 1983), the hectic manufacturing schedule of Spottiswood & Co and their 3D printer-anticipating wonder machine *Bertha* (BBC, 1985) and the slightly more unconventional saga of marooned clown

Charlie Chalk (BBC, 1988), trapped on Merrytwit island with a bunch of workshy eccentrics propping up a would-be capitalist paradise.

The Magic Roundabout showed, in its own wilfully eccentric way, that you just can't predict what will make a good children's programme. It was made on a shoestring, and redubbed in an even more cost-conscious manner, but it still somehow generated a not especially small fortune from merchandising revenue. It was the work of many individuals, but at the same time the work of one. It was very resolutely for children but still appealed to everyone. Focus groups and algorithms are all very well and good, but – much like you couldn't stop anyone from listening to Brazilian Octopus and Jacques Dutronc while drinking a macchiato underneath a poster for *Buenos días, condesita* way back when – you ultimately can't predict what the audience will and will not like and when; and so many people of so many different ages loved and still love a show that routinely ended with Zebedee wearily announcing that it was 'time for bed'. Maybe it *is* time for bed. But you could always try asking to 'stay up' for Kenny Everett . . .

Acknowledgements

When you're dealing with a subject as vast as this, there's always a risk that your acknowledgements could end up a bit like that credit for the musicians with seven Mr Benns playing a big, long flute. I'll try and keep it shorter than CP & Qwikstitch seemed to go on for though. I'm especially grateful to everyone who — to my astonishment — also believed that there was mileage in a book that had more to say about Marmalade Atkins than *Doctor Who*, particularly Simon Spanton, who had the idea in the first place, and Campbell Brown, Thomas Ross and Emma Hargrave, who patiently helped me to wrangle it into a publishable state.

For encouragement and advice way above and beyond the call of duty, I am deeply indebted to Stephen O'Brien, Garreth Hirons, Vikki Gregorich, Chris Farrell, Emma Burnell, Andy Miller and Paul Abbott. You all deserve a place on the *Swap Shop* Top Ten Board. *Crackerjack* — CRACKERJACK! — pencils must also go to Kevin Aitchison, Bob Stanley, Jim Sangster, Andy Durrant, Jim and Clare McGibbon, John Connors, Gill Kiernan, Will Maclean, Estelle Hargraves, Stewart Lee, Sam Trafford, Jim North, Suzy Hesselberg, Kate Haldane, Grace Dent, Stuart Maconie, Samira Ahmed, Mitch Benn, Minnie Driver, Marcus Hearn, Peter Ware, Steve 'The Other One' O'Brien, Jason Hazeley, Helen Gardner, Shanine Salmon, Mark Griffiths, Toby Hadoke, Jac Rayner, Louis Barfe, Hanna Flint, Allison Wharam, Kate Goldberg, Jonathan Sloman, Justin Lewis, Tom Williamson, Mic Wright, Richard Herring, Rae Earl,

THE GOLDEN AGE OF CHILDREN'S TV

Paul Putner, Andy Lewis, Jill Nolan, everyone at Times Radio and *Good Morning Scotland*, Andrew Pixley, Steve Rogers and everyone at the much-missed Network, George Grimwood, Joel Morris, Dave Bryant, Suzy Norman, Martin Ruddock, Tyler Adams and Chris Shaw, as well as a couple of people I really wish could have been able to see their names here: Paul Condon, John Trainer, Jo Cox, Kris Ealey, Anita Swan and especially Elizabeth Knowles. Yes, Liz, someone really did let me write a book about Captain Zep – Space Detective.

Knock Your Block Off Pop-Up Digital Watches to all my fellow contributors to the original and best nostalgia website TV Cream: Phil Norman, Steve Berry, Steve Williams, Graham Kibble-White, Jack Kibble-White, Jill Pythian, Ian Jones, Chris Hughes, Chris Diamond, Matthew Rudd, Ian Tomkinson and Simon Tyers. Due to the gestalt writing style we have always deployed, it's entirely possible that some of your jokes and observations may have been assimilated into mine, so you really do deserve as much credit as I can possibly convey here. Similarly, I Saw The Mersey Pirate badges to all of the guests on my nostalgia podcast *Looks Unfamiliar* and in particular Phil Catterall, Joanne Sheppard, Gary Bainbridge, Gabby Hutchinson Crouch, Mark Thompson, Lisa Parker, Andrew Trowbridge, Una McCormack, Jonny Morris, Bob Fischer, Georgy Jamieson, Melanie Williams, Anna Cale, Deborah Tracey, Bibi Lynch, Rose Ruane, Lydia Mizon, Gillian Kirby, Nina Buckley, Ricardo Autobahn, Meryl O'Rourke, Katy Brent, Genevieve Jenner, Al Kennedy, Hilary Machell, Lucy Pope, Adam S. Leslie, Suzy Robinson, Juliet Brando, Sophie Davies, Jane Hill, Richard Littler, David Smith, Carrie Dunn and Catrin Lowe.

Book Tower Recommended Read stickers for *The Art of Smallfilms* by Jonny Trunk, *Ben Baker's Festive Double Issue* by Ben Baker,

ACKNOWLEDGEMENTS

Beware of the Bull: The Enigmatic Genius of Jake Thackray by Paul Thompson and John Watterson, *Broken Greek* by Pete Paphides, *The Encyclopedia of Classic Saturday Night Telly* by Jack Kibble-White and Steve Williams, *Filmed In Supermarionation* by Stephen La Rivière, *From Fringe to Flying Circus* by Roger Wilmut, *The Great British Tuck Shop* by Steve Berry and Phil Norman, *The Hill and Beyond* by Mark J. Docherty and Alistair McGown, *A History of Television in 100 Programmes* by Phil Norman, *Into The Box of Delights* by Anna Home, *Morning Glory* by Ian Jones, *Psychedelia and Other Colours* by Rob Chapman, *Scarred For Life* by Stephen Brotherstone and Dave Lawrence and *Where Did it All Go Right?* by Andrew Collins. Also, a *Blue Peter* badge is on its way to Peter Thomas for some useful early feedback, to Danny Kodicek for some key clarifications, and to Clive Banks for allowing me to use some crucial details from his Oliver Postgate interview.

Finally – while side-eyeing a certain cat who grew so disgruntled at the *Camberwick Green* residents popping in and out of the Music Box that she hit the screen with such force that the television had to be replaced – thank you to anyone involved in the creation of all of these sometimes enjoyable, sometimes not, but never less than retrospectively fascinating shows. Yes, even Wordy. Though he can still keep that 'word-watching' business very much to himself.